FOREWORD

Spanning the entire industrial core of the United States and providing a marine avenue to the sea, the Great Lakes form the basis of a unique transportation system. Economically and culturally the lakes have played a major role in the growth and development of commerce in this nation. Fifty years ago the Great Lakes fleet pioneered automated bulk cargo handling with the first self-unloading ships. In 1959, the completion of the St. Lawrence Seaway signalled a major increase in Great Lakes shipping with upwards of 15 million tons per year moving directly overseas from Great Lakes ports. In the past five years the successful application of ice control techniques have extended the Great Lakes shipping season from just over eight months to a full 12 months.

Even though this strategically located and dynamic system has sometimes led the way in technological innovation, other technological changes, such as containerization and larger ocean vessels, are conspiring to reduce the volume of ocean shipping to Great Lakes ports. Despite these and other trends, which could adversely affect the Great Lakes-St. Lawrence Seaway Transportation System, the system, nevertheless, remains a vital link in the industry-resource complex upon which the United States depends.

The authors of this book have carefully and objectively examined the varied factors which are affecting this unique transportation system. They have offered a series of recommendations, uncolored by emotional or political leanings, and these form the basis for a sound program under which the vital Great Lakes-St. Lawrence Seaway Transportation System can continue to develop.

December 1, 1975

Robert A. Ragotzkie, Director
University of Wisconsin
Sea Grant College Program

iii

THE GREAT LAKES TRANSPORTATION SYSTEM

by

ERIC SCHENKER
Director, Urban Research Center
Professor of Economics
Senior Scientist, Center for Great Lakes Studies

HAROLD M. MAYER
Professor of Geography
Associate Director, Center for Great Lakes Studies

HARRY C. BROCKEL
Lecturer, Center for Great Lakes Studies

With the Collaboration of

Margaret S. Balfe
Thomas M. Corsi
Ronald L. Heilmann
Wayne R. Wendling

Project Assistants

UNIVERSITY OF WISCONSIN SEA GRANT COLLEGE PROGRAM

Technical Report #230
January 1976

ACKNOWLEDGMENTS

This research was supported by the University of Wisconsin Sea Grant College Program, which is a part of the National Sea Grant Program, maintained by the National Oceanic and Atmospheric Administration of the U.S. Department of Commerce.

Many people have contributed in a variety of ways to this study. Those singled out below for special recognition by no means exhaust the list of those to whom our gratitude is extended.

During the course of this study, the special expertise of many was called upon. Dr. Frederick J. Wegmann, while at the University of Wisconsin-Milwaukee and later at the University of Tennessee, provided most of the documentation for Chapter 8. His work is acknowledged on page VIII-1. Mr. James Johnson was our research assistant throughout this project. Assistance in programming was provided ably by the Social Science Research Facility of the College of Letters and Science, University of Wisconsin-Milwaukee. Ms. Sandra Schroeder reviewed an early draft and provided enlightening editorial comments.

Special thanks are due to Ms. Christine Lamke and Ms. Joyce O'Keane who displayed uncommon patience and cooperation in editing and typing this manuscript.

To all others who have contributed, our thanks. Of course, responsibility for whatever errors remain herein must be counted as part of our original contribution.

CONTENTS

LIST OF FIGURES

Chapter 1

Chapter 5

Chapter 6

LIST OF TABLES

Chapter 2

Chapter 3

Chapter 4

Chapter 5

Chapter 7

Chapter 8

I.

Introduction

Introduction

Significant changes are now under way that affect
shipping on the Great Lakes. These changes involve internal
Great Lakes shipping, including both domestic and international U.S.-Canadian trade, and external shipping between
the Great Lakes, lower St. Lawrence River ports, and overseas.
The purpose of this study is to review some of these recent
changes, changes which are in progress and prospective
changes in Great Lakes shipping that are relevant to policy
decisions, both public and private.

The Great Lakes together constitute the largest body of
navigable fresh water in the world. With a relatively small
drainage basin of 295,000 square miles, the Lakes themselves
have a surface area of just under 100,000 square miles
(Figure 1.1). Elevations above sea level range from an average
of 248 feet for Lake Ontario to 602 feet for Lake Superior
(Figure 1.2). From the head of the Lakes at Duluth and
Chicago, distances to the head of tidewater at Montreal are
1,337 and 1,244 statute miles, respectively, while Montreal
is 800 or 1,000 miles from the Atlantic Ocean south or north
of Newfoundland, respectively. While a significant proportion
of the Great Lakes, as well as the Great Lakes-St. Lawrence
r 'oute, involves open-water navigation, the connecting channels
between the Lakes, and much of the St. Lawrence River,
especially above Montreal, involve transit through confined
channels. These place serious limitations upon the dimensions--
especially the drafts--of vessels. Also, the seasonality
of the inter-lake and St. Lawrence operations imposes further
handicaps. Among the most significant current and prospective
developments are the attempts, at least partially, to overcome
these limitations.

History of the Seaway System

The St. Lawrence route between the Great Lakes and overseas was not created anew with the opening of the present
St. Lawrence Seaway in 1959. Small Canadian canals had cir-
cumvented the rapids of the St. Lawrence, and the predecessor
of the Welland Canal had connected Lakes Erie and Ontario
since shortly after the War of 1812, when Canada developed
a route competitive with the Erie Canal which crossed
New·York State between the Great Lakes and tidewater. As
early as the mid-1850's, wheat was shipped from the Upper
Lakes to Europe. A series of consecutive enlargements of
the route culminated, in the early years of the present
century, in a number of canals along the present Seaway
route. In 1932 the Welland Ship Canal, with eight locks,
opened up Lake Ontario to the large "upper laker" bulk
carriers. Subsequently partially rebuilt, that canal
constitutes part of the present Seaway. In 1933 the first
regularly scheduled cargo liner service, utilizing small

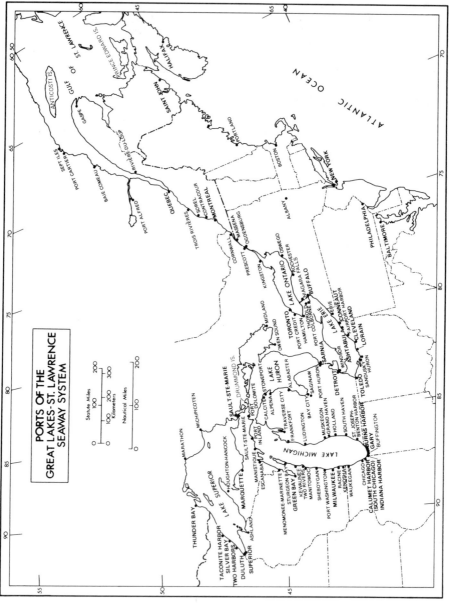

Figure 1.1

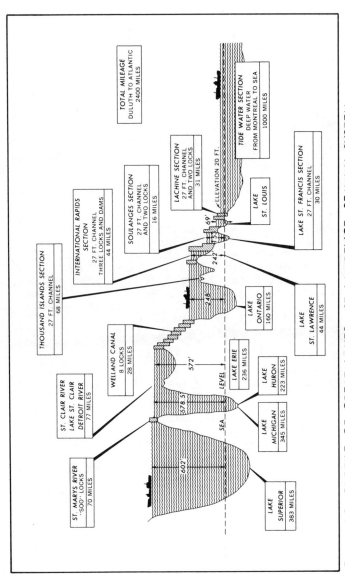

Figure 1.2 PROFILE OF GREAT LAKES – ST. LAWRENCE SEAWAY SYSTEM

SOURCE: International Great Lakes Levels Board, Regulation of Great Lakes Water Levels, Appendix E., Commercial Navigation. Report to the International Joint Commission, 1973, p. E-7.

vessels, connected the Great Lakes with Europe. Such services, except for interruption during World War II, have been continuous, and after the opening of the present enlarged Seaway, larger vessels have been used for such liner services, in addition to numerous bulk-carrying tramp vessels. The depths to which the channels were dredged and the dimensions of the locks along the route, however, were much more influenced by the anticipated transits by lake-type bulk vessels than by the characteristics of salt water ships. The standard Seaway depth is 27 feet, and most of the major Great Lakes harbors have been dredged to the same depth, normally permitting access and transit by vessels of up to 25.75 feet draft. The results of these decisions, made several decades ago, is that a rapidly decreasing proportion of the world's oceangoing vessels can utilize the Great Lakes-St. Lawrence route, and the economies of scale currently realized on most of the principal ocean routes cannot be realized to the same extent for Great Lakes-overseas movements.

Until 1959, there were 22 small locks in the six canals bypassing the rapids of the St. Lawrence River in the 110 miles above Montreal. Lake vessels transiting to and from the Lower St. Lawrence were designed to fit these locks. They were limited to a length of 259 feet, a beam of 43.5 feet, and a draft of 14.25 feet. With those dimensions, they could carry up to 3,000 tons of cargo. Over 200 such "canallers" were in operation through the St. Lawrence system during the period between World War II and the opening of the enlarged Seaway in 1959. Virtually all under Canadian registry, they included both "package" freighters and bulk carriers. The early pre-Seaway general cargo liners, which pioneered the Great Lakes-overseas direct trades between 1933 and 1959, were limited to the same dimensions, but because of their necessarily finer lines as seagoing ships, such "salties" could not move more than 1,600 tons on canal draft. They usually topped off with an additional thousand tons in the Lower St. Lawrence for the ocean voyage. Whether lakers or "salties," the vessels moved slowly through the canals and channels paralleling the St. Lawrence above Montreal. They commonly took three days between Lake Ontario and tidewater.

After five years of construction between 1954 and 1959, the Seaway was opened. The St. Lawrence portion involved the building of two dams: (1) a diversion dam at Iroquois, and (2) the Moses-Saunders Dam, with two million kilowatts of electric-generating capacity between Massena, New York and Cornwall, Ontario. Without the power, the Seaway as a navigation project would probably have been economically and politically unfeasible because the entire construction cost of facilities jointly used for navigation and power are charged against the power, rather than navigation. The costs and benefits originally were assigned for navigation on the basis of 29 percent to the United States and the remainder to Canada; later this ratio was changed slightly. Toll revenues are similarly assigned to the two nations. Of the seven locks between Lake Ontario and tidewater, two are within and were constructed by the United States, in addition to the ten-mile Wiley-Dondero Canal.

Although most of the pre-opening traffic estimates for the Seaway were initially optimistic, during the early 1970's the traffic reached the volume projected for that period. However, during 1974 there was a substantial decline in traffic. As anticipated, throughout the entire 16 years of its operation the Seaway has been predominantly an artery for bulk traffic rather than for general cargo. These bulk cargoes are carried in lake-type vessels, slightly modified for Seaway operation. Many of them were specifically built to the maximum dimensions of the Welland and Seaway locks: 730 feet long, 75 feet beam, and a maximum draft of 25.75 feet. With these dimensions they can normally carry up to about 28,000 tons of cargo. Because of higher costs of the U.S.-flag operation, the overwhelming proportion of such "maximum lakers" is under Canadian registry, although recent additions to the American-flag fleet are modifying that circumstance to an increasing extent.

A relatively recent development of great significance is the completion of the Poe Lock at the Sault Ste. Marie locks, which opened in 1970. In contrast to the other and parallel locks which limit the dimensions of the vessels operating between Lake Superior and the other Lakes to Seaway size, the Poe Lock admits vessels of up to 1,000 feet length and 105 feet beam; such lakers can carry over 57,500 tons at normal lake draft, or more than twice as much as any prior lakers. Almost immediately, vessels of these dimensions were under construction. U.S. Steel's Roger Blough, built at Lorain, Ohio, was the first of the craft exceeding the earlier dimensions, although not of maximum possible length, and Bethlehem Steel's Stewart J. Cort, assembled at Erie, Pennsylvania, became the first of the lakers at the new maximum size. Subsequently, other vessels of similar size were ordered, and some of the older vessels were enlarged. A new generation of lake ships is well under way. For the first time since 1932, however, a portion of the Great Lakes fleet is once again unable to operate east of Lake Erie because the vessels exceed the dimensions of the locks in the Welland Ship Canal as well as in the Seaway proper.

Except for the unusual circumstances of 1974, when strikes partially crippled the movements, a collision blocked the Welland Canal during the peak of the season and the business recession reduced industrial activity, it now appears that the St. Lawrence Seaway System will be limited, not by its ability to attract bulk cargoes, but rather by its physical capacity to handle the movements. In the early 1970's, the Lake Ontario-Montreal section handled nearly 60 million tons of cargo per year, very close to the early estimates of its capacity. Fortunately, the efficiency of the waterway route has been substantially improved by the trend toward larger vessels, handling more tonnage per transit; the "maximum laker" has superseded the very few surviving pre-Seaway small "canallers." Also, additional annual capacity has been provided by the successive lengthening of the navigation season, both with earlier openings and later closings, as discussed in Chapter IV.

Major Commodity Flows

Along the shores of Lakes Ontario, Erie and Michigan, and in the nearby hinterlands of these lakes, is the world's largest concentration of basic iron and steel production. Innumerable associated metal fabricating, machinery and other establishments utilize the output of the iron and steel plants. Geographers have long recognized the Lower Lakes area as the "core region" of the United States and Canada. Great Lakes transportation is the vital link connecting this area with the sources of raw materials: ore, limestone and coal. Major changes have taken place in recent years, and are continuing, with respect to the direction and character of movement of these materials, and, in the cases of ore and coal, of the characteristics of the materials them-selves. The characteristics of the vessels and of the port terminals reflect these changes.

For example, direct shipments of iron ore from the ranges around Lake Superior, the principal source for over a century, began in 1855 with the opening of the first canal circumventing the rapids of the St. Marys River and connecting Lake Superior with the Lower Lakes. The subsequent series of enlargements of locks at Sault Ste. Marie has been accompanied by increments of larger ship sizes. With the opening of the present Welland Canal in 1932, with locks identical in dimensions to what was then the largest of the Saulte Ste. Marie locks and the later locks of the St. Lawrence Seaway proper, the "maximum lakers" gained access, first to Lake Ontario, and later to the Lower St. Lawrence. But with the opening of the Seaway the ores of the Quebec-Labrador area have become competitive with those of Lake Superior at the Canadian plants of Lake Ontario and in the Cleveland-Youngstown-Pittsburgh area. Through the Lake Ontario-Montreal section of the Seaway proper, the predominant cargoes consisted of upbound movements of iron ore, principally from the Quebec-Labrador area, and grains downbound. The complementary nature of the eastbound grain and the westbound ore move-ments is a fortunate circumstance. Many of the lakers carry grain from both Canadian and United States lakehead ports to the Lower St. Lawrence for transfer there to larger oceangoing vessels. The proportion of laker to "salty" vessels engaged in Seaway grain movement is in major part a function of the worldwide demand for tramp bottoms; when the demand is high for oceangoing, dry-cargo ships, as during the American actions in Southeast Asia, a higher proportion of the outbound grain is transshipped in the Lower St. Lawrence, and fewer "salties" are loaded at the Lake ports.

The grain movement in the Great Lakes has fluctuated from year to year, but the development of larger canals and locks along the entire Great Lakes-St. Lawrence System has shifted the movements substantially. Buffalo was, until 1932, the easterly head of lake grain movement, except for the small "canallers" previously mentioned. With the opening of Lake Ontario to the large upper lakers in that year, Buffalo declined as a major flour milling center, as did Baltimore, the closest rail-connected United States saltwater port, as an exporter of grain. Grain was transferred from lake to canal vessels at Prescott, Ontario and Ogdensburg, New York, which between 1933 and 1959 constituted the lower head of navigation for the lake vessels, and at other ports of the Upper St. Lawrence and Lake Ontario. In such instances, another transfer of export grain took place between "canallers" and oceangoing ships at Montreal or other Lower St. Lawrence ports.

Coal, like grain, constitutes a complementary movement to iron ore. Lower Lake ports, particularly those along the south shore of Lake Erie, and to some extent South Chicago, handled return cargoes of coal. Coal, moved through Lake Erie ports, originates in the Appalachian region, while the coal, moved through South Chicago, originates in central and southern Illinois and western Kentucky. Coal moved to the thermal electric utilities of the Upper Lakes, including those serving such industrial cities as Detroit, Chicago and Milwaukee. While these complementary ore and coal movements are still important, low sulphur coal is producing a rapidly expanding traffic which is the reverse of the previous lake coal movement: namely, a downbound movement of western low sulphur coal from Lake Superior for receipt at Lower Lake ports and the Detroit area. In several instances, long-term investments have been committed to assure that downbound lake coal movements will increase, but competition of through unit-train movement may be, in the long run, a constraint. This change in coal movement patterns is a direct result of the current energy crisis and is discussed in detail in Chapter V.

Great Lakes-overseas direct trades, have also changed in character, as well as volume, in the past several years. In spite of the long-term growth of Great Lakes-overseas traffic since the opening of the enlarged St. Lawrence Seaway in 1959, traffic that is internal to the Great Lakes still accounts for the overwhelming volume of tonnage moving on the Lakes. Direct overseas traffic moving to and from Great Lakes ports accounts annually for less than 7.5 per cent of the total. After an initial experimental period, the volume of general cargo carried by scheduled liner services peaked several years ago at about five million tons per year, with about 60 regular liner services. Since then tonnage has been declining, precipitiously in 1973 and even more so in 1974. Preliminary figures for 1975 indicate some recovery has been experienced. Paralleling the decline in tonnage, the number of cargo liner services between the Great Lakes and overseas has declined to about a dozen. No U.S.-flag vessels have offered such services since the early years following the Seaway opening. However, Lykes has begun to offer such service during the 1975 season, and other lines have expressed an interest. Currently a high proportion of the service is by vessels of eastern European nations: the Soviet Union, Poland and Yugoslavia.

Although there is virtually no general cargo moving internally within the Lakes, a small but significant volume of relatively valuable general cargo moves between the Lakes and overseas. As a result, the ratio of value to total tonnage is higher for overseas movements than it is for internal traffic. Because of this greater value public port agencies and the general public have recently directed some attention toward the decline in this traffic and alternative means to alleviate the situation.

Since the opening of the Seaway, radical changes in the technology of both inland and ocean transportation have had an almost catastrophic effect upon the Great Lakes-overseas general cargo trades. In the early years, and still to a dominant extent, these movements involved break-of-bulk at the Great Lakes ports. Within the Lakes, turnaround time of breakbulk liners is slow, and the port operations are labor intensive. As elsewhere throughout the world, "load centers" developed, involving concentrations of cargoes at fewer but larger and more efficient ports. Then in the late 1960's, as containerization became dominant on the world's major ocean routes, intermodal transportation rapidly replaced breakbulk movements on many such routes. The effect of this major innovation on Great Lakes shipping is detailed in Chapter III.

As is evident from the preceding discussion, the evolving life of the Great Lakes-St. Lawrence Seaway System has included changes affecting both internal and overseas shipping as well as bulk commodities and general cargo. Discussion of current and prospective changes as they affect the future of Great Lakes shipping constitute the balance of this study.

II.

Technological Change,

Labor Relations and Great Lakes-

St. Lawrence Seaway Transportation

Introduction

The Great Lakes and the St. Lawrence Seaway have a
number of special geographic and physical conditions which
give rise to distinctive technological and labor requirements. The physical constraints of the Seaway, the
connecting channels between the Lakes and the Great Lakes
harbors have combined to make necessary unique types of
vessels and port terminal development. The System consists
of a series of end-to-end links. Because interruption of
traffic through any one of the links would disrupt the
entire System, stable labor-management relations are
critical.

Worldwide developments in the handling of cargoes--
both general cargo and bulk commodities--on land, on water
and at the ports, continue to influence significantly the
nature, volumes, routes and methods of handling Great Lakes
waterborne commerce. The balance of this chapter considers
the effects of specific categories of technological change
and concludes with a discussion of the special role of
labor.

Size of Vessels

As discussed in the introductory chapter, the Great
Lakes-St. Lawrence Seaway System imposes physical limitations upon the dimensions of the vessels entering or leaving
the Lakes, as well as upon those operating within the Lakes.
The lock systems in the St. Lawrence Seaway, the Welland
Canal and at Sault Ste. Marie, as well as channel depths in
the major Great Lakes harbors, impose such dimensional
restrictions. Maximum allowable vessel draft is normally
25.75 feet. All of the locks except the newest one at
Sault Ste. Marie limit the length of vessels to 730 feet,
with beam limited to 75 feet. The Poe Lock at Sault Ste.
Marie allows vessels to transit with a 1,000 foot length and
105 foot beam.

Within these dimensions, there are significant differences between the carrying capacities of Lake vessels and of
ocean-going ships that are able to transit the Great Lakes-
St. Lawrence Seaway System. Capacity is determined by the
"block coefficient," or the amount of streamlining of the
immersed portion of the hull, which is due, in turn, to
differing wave characteristics within the Great Lakes and on
the oceans. A typical "laker" is flat-bottomed, with blunt
bow and stern; its high "block coefficient" enables it to
carry more cargo than could an ocean-going ship of similar
basic dimensions.

13

TABLE 2.1

CHARACTERISTICS OF MAJOR GREAT LAKES VESSEL TYPES

Vessel Types	Length (ft)	Beam (ft)	Draft (ft)*	Cargo Tonnage	Employment
Pre-Seaway "Canaller" (Lake service)	258	43.5	14.00	3,000	Great Lakes-St. Lawrence[1] Pre-Seaway Canal System
Pre-Seaway "Canaller" (Lake-Overseas Service)	258	43.5	14.00	1,600[2]	Great Lakes-Overseas Direct via Pre-Seaway Canal System
Cuyahoga River Laker	630	68.0	25.75	18,000	Great Lakes, St. Lawrence[3]
"Maximum Laker" (pre-1970; post-1959)	730	75.0	25.75	28,000	Great Lakes, St. Lawrence west of Sept. Isles, Quebec
"Maximum Laker" (post-1970)	1,000	105.0	25.75	57,500	Great Lakes, west of Welland Ship Canal
Typical Great Lakes-Overseas General Cargo Liner	500	75.0	24.0	9,000	Great Lakes-Overseas Direct
Typical Lake-Ocean Bulk Carrier	600	75.0	25.75	25,000	Irregular Great Lakes-Ocean Service

NOTE: * Maximum draft normally allowed for transit of lock system.

[1] Obsolete since opening of enlarged Seaway System in 1959.

[2] On Seaway draft; additional 1,000 tons on 18 foot draft east of Montreal.

[3] Dimensions limited by Cuyahoga River at Cleveland, Ohio.

Table 2.1 shows the dimensions of the largest vessels of each type. It is especially noteworthy that, in the past, each time that a new and larger standard has been adopted for the locks and connecting channels of the Great Lakes-St. Lawrence System, vessels of the maximum size permitted by the new standard have immediately been constructed. Thus, there is a cluster of vessels at each maximum size.

A special case is the Cuyahoga River at Cleveland, Ohio, where several large iron and steel plants, located up-river, are reached only through the relatively shallow channel, with numerous sharp bends that limit the length and draft of vessels operating on that river. To meet this need, a number of recently-constructed laker vessels are of "Cuyahoga River" dimensions.

Ocean-going vessels that operate to, from and within the Great Lakes-St. Lawrence Seaway System vary much more widely in dimensions and other characteristics than do the lakers. The basic fact is that ocean-going vessels generally are much larger now than when the System was designed, and a declining proportion of the world's merchant vessels can transit the Seaway. Until recently, general cargo liners of moderate size were being built for the System, but with the decline in general cargo movement through the Seaway and the limited prospects for the future of such traffic, that type of vessel is declining in significance. Many of the ships that formerly served the trade are now being employed on marginal trade routes elsewhere, where the competition of containerized traffic is less serious than it is in the Great Lakes Region. Nevertheless, "handy size" breakbulk general cargo liners continue to enter the Great Lakes in limited numbers. Among such ships, the principal size limitation is the ship's draft.

Ocean-going bulk carriers are of major importance in the movement of traffic through the St. Lawrence Seaway System, since most of the Great Lakes-overseas direct movements are of bulk commodities. Here, too, the physical limitations of the System are serious. Most of the more efficient and larger bulk carriers that constitute the world's merchant fleet are too large for this service.[1] As noted in Table 2.1, ocean-going bulk carriers transiting the Seaway to and from the Great Lakes ports generally have somewhat smaller cargo capacities than do "lakers" of similar basic dimensions.

In anticipation of the Seaway, and in the years immediately following its opening, a number of vessels of "hermaphrodite" type were constructed. These combine cargo features of the Lake vessels with bow and stern characteristics that make them useful in ocean service. Such vessels can operate internally within the Great Lakes-St. Lawrence System for a large part of each year and in worldwide bulk cargo service on the oceans while the Lakes are closed. In size, such vessels are somewhat smaller than the "maximum lakers."

15

New Types of Vessels

The evolution of vessel design on the Great Lakes and in the Great Lakes-St. Lawrence Seaway System is subject to the influences of both worldwide trends in Marine architecture and developments peculiar to the Great Lakes-St. Lawrence System itself.

As pointed out above, the trend toward increased economies of scale with larger vessels is worldwide, but it is somewhat offset by the development of specialized vessel types, including those specific to the Great Lakes-St. Lawrence System. The physical constraints of the System and the consequent inability of the large, efficient ocean-going vessels to utilize the System have produced a dichotomy in vessel types. For example, the modern containership, that has captured the preponderant traffic on many of the world's ocean trade routes, is too large to transit the St. Lawrence System.[2] On the other hand, there are many "feeder" full and partial container vessels serving various parts of the world that pick up and deliver containers to and from load center ports which are served by the larger vessels. One operator, a British company, time-charters a small fleet of such feeder vessels and operates a regular, scheduled container service between Chicago, other Lake ports, and overseas. It transfers the containers between the feeder vessels and larger ocean-going containerships at Montreal.[3] Turnaround time at the Lake ports is substantially reduced for both vessels and cargoes in comparison with conventional breakbulk methods, but the overall transit time is slower than by movement overland through coastal ports, where fast, frequent containership services are available. Many of the "handy size" breakbulk vessels employed in scheduled liner service between the Great Lakes and overseas carry limited numbers of containers.

Another technological development in ocean transportation that has a potential effect upon the Great Lakes-St. Lawrence System and upon the Lake ports is the "kangaroo" ship, or barge-carrying vessel.[4] These vessels are of the Seabee or LASH ("lighter-aboard-ship") type, depending upon whether the barges are loaded and discharged to and from the mother ship by elevator at the stern (the former) or by cranes mounted on the deck of the vessel (the latter). Barge-carrying vessels are in operation on most of the major transoceanic routes. Offering non-break-of-bulk service between inland ports on opposite sides of the ocean, the barges have operated from New Orleans and other Gulf of Mexico ports as far inland as Chicago via the Illinois-Mississippi waterway and, at the other end, as far up the Rhine as Basle, Switzerland. Present Seabee and LASH barges can be, and are, handled in conventional river tows on the Mississippi system. A type of barge can be developed that would be capable of short, open-water transits, as on the Great Lakes. Thus, the advantages of the scale economy of the large ocean-going vessel could be combined with the flexibility of a smaller craft to serve Great Lakes ports, with New Orleans and other Gulf ports, on the one hand, or Montreal and other eastern Canadian ports, on the other hand, serving as load centers. An alternative could be the use of the New York State Barge Canal that connects the Great Lakes with the Port of New York.

Specialized Equipment Aboard Vessels

The unique conditions of the Great Lakes and the St. Lawrence Seaway dictate the need for certain specialized equipment aboard vessels that is uncommon, or at least not ubiquitous, aboard vessels elsewhere. In the case of ocean-going ships within the Great Lakes-St. Lawrence System, some of the specialized equipment is mandatory. For example, all must have stern anchors and constant-tension winches to secure the mooring lines within the locks, as the water-levels are adjusted. Many vessels have special fenders that can be lowered to prevent damage to the ship sides against the lock walls. Because dispatching in the Seaway is in the English language, vessels are required to have aboard personnel who can communicate in English. This stipulation has caused some interruptions to service because of the objections of French-Canadian personnel.

Celestial navigation is not generally used within the Great Lakes-St. Lawrence System, so that the electronic devices, such as the Loran, Decca and Omega position-fixing systems, increasingly used at sea are not needed for internal use. On the other hand, specialized radio equipment is used for the communication channels within the System. Determination of position within the Lakes is by dead-reckoning and landmarks, with electronic triangulation. Positioning is much more critical in the confined waterway System than at sea.

Vessels operating on the Great Lakes and in the St. Lawrence Seaway spend a high proportion of their voyage time enroute in confined channels and in entering, standing in and leaving locks. For this reason, speed is not so important as maneuverability and the efficiency of pilotage, navigation and dispatching. Port turnaround time is relatively more important than top speed in open water. Thus, for many vessels, high-speed propulsion is not significant as contrasted with maneuverability. Modern vessels, both for Lake and for ocean services, are increasingly equipped with bridge or pilot-house control of engines, and many have twin or multiple rudders. Also, vessels are built with, or retrofitted with, bow thrusters that permit turning in short radius and reduce or eliminate the use of tugs in docking and undocking.

Cargo handling within the Great Lakes varies with the commodity. General cargo in the direct Lake-ocean trades is generally breakbulk, and it utilizes mobile equipment on the wharves and the ship's tackle to move the goods between hold and shore. There are currently no specialized container cranes at Great Lakes ports, although Duluth is installing one, and Chicago is considering such installation.

Handling of bulk cargoes is highly specialized and largely automated. Developed many decades ago, conveyors, gravity spouts, and other continuous-flow devices enabled Lake ports to establish many world records for speed of cargo handling, and the methods have subsequently been widely adopted elsewhere. The Hulett ore unloader, for example, is a complicated but efficient device that was developed for rapid turnaround at lower Lake ports.

The bulk-carrying Lake vessel is now undergoing a rapid evolution, in addition to its increased size. Iron ore, the principal bulk cargo, formerly consisted primarily of hematite, which is heavy and high in water content, making it unwieldy in freezing weather. The typical ore carrier was--and many still are--of "straight-decker" type, with no equipment on board for either loading or discharging cargo and completely dependent upon elaborate shore-based facilities.[5] Meanwhile, substantial numbers of Lake vessels of the "self unloader" type were built. Such vessels are provided with hopper holds, continuous belt conveyors and a rotatable above-deck structure that carries a conveyor, enabling continuous discharge of bulk cargoes independent of shore-based equipment. Such vessels were designed especially for the coal and limestone trades. With the advent of iron concentrate, particularly taconite, which is now responsible for about 90 per cent of the total ore movement on the Lakes, the weight and water content of the ore no longer precluded the use of self-unloading vessels. Consequently, all of the Lake bulk vessels recently or currently under construction are of the self-unloader type.[6] This development allows greater flexibility and speed in unloading at ports; also, the equipment is not subject to interruption by cold weather since dehydrated taconite pellets do not freeze.

Many of the older Lake bulk vessels have recently been, or are being, retrofitted with self-unloading equipment. At the same time, some of them are being "jumboized": cut in two and provided with a new mid-section. Typically such vessels were of the pre-1970 "maximum laker" size, but with the advent of the new Poe Lock, they are being lengthened at the expense, however, of being operable eastward of Lake Erie. All lakers exceeding 730 feet in length and 75 feet beam are operated under United States registry, because Canadian vessels generally must operate through the Welland Ship Canal and the St. Lawrence Seaway, while many United States vessels are designed specifically for interlake trade above the Welland Canal.

Because of the proximity of the Appalachian coal fields and the complementarity of the coal and iron ore movements, until recently the Great Lakes represented the last stand of

the large coal-fired ship. In spite of the increasing cost
and limited availability of petroleum, all of the new
"laker" vessels utilize petroleum, either as oil-burning
steamships or as diesel-powered motorships. In large part,
because of environmental objections to coal, older vessels,
where practicable, have been and are being re-engined or
re-boilered for petroleum. Diesel-engined motorships
within the Lakes are increasingly common because the elimination of boilers not only increases cargo capacity but also
excludes the need for boiler water. Diesel engines have
greater availability and flexibility than steam engines, but
the initial capital cost is higher. Gas turbine power is
also being introduced into the Great Lakes.

Cargo Handling Technology and Port Development

Paralleling the technological changes in vessels is a
series of technological changes in cargo handling at the
ports and in the hinterland areas that the ports serve.
Great Lakes ports, like ports elsewhere, are evolving to
handle the cargoes that are now and prospectively available.

The objective of port installations is to secure the
fastest possible turnaround of both vessels and cargoes at
the lowest possible cost. In the Great Lakes-St. Lawrence
System, turnaround time constitutes a higher proportion of
the total round-trip time for a vessel than is general on
ocean trade routes because distances between ports on the
Lakes are relatively short. Consequently, the efficiency of
the entire System is in some ways more heavily dependent upon
terminal efficiency than in the case of most ocean ports.

As indicated above, the Great Lakes Region has long
been recognized for the efficiency of its bulk cargo transfer
methods that have constituted, in many ways, the prototype
for bulk cargo handling in other parts of the world.
Continuous flow methods are constantly being improved. The
newer bulk cargo terminals, including those now under construction, embody long experience. Both shoreside installations and self-unloading equipment aboard vessels are more
efficient now than in the past.

As elsewhere, bulk-carrying vessels, both lakers and
oceangoing ships within the Lakes, tend to call at fewer
ports than formerly. This is a reflection of the higher
vessel capital and operating costs that call for higher-
volume cargo transfer and place a premium upon ports and
terminals that can generate sufficient and regular traffic
to justify large capital investments.

Most of the bulk commodities handled in both internal
Great Lakes movement and in Great Lakes-overseas vessels are
transferred at private terminals. Iron ore, coal, limestone,
grain, petroleum, cement and other bulk commodities normally
move in shipload volume and are handled at terminals

specifically designed for such movements. Many such
terminals are in proximity to the industries that they serve
directly and constitute waterfront portions of the adjacent
industrial plants. Some of the bulk terminals, especially
those handling coal and ore, are owned and operated by the
railroads that haul the commodities to and from the
respective port hinterlands. Others, especially grain
elevators at some ports, are owned and operated by coopera-
tives. At Great Lakes ports, as elsewhere in the United
States, the responsibility for providing and maintaining the
main channels is a federal one administered by the U.S. Army
Corps of Engineers, but depth alongside the terminals and the
building, maintenance and operation of the terminals themselves are either private or the responsibility of a public
non-federal agency. In any event, efficiency is the objective, and that means not only sufficient depth alongside for
the largest vessel expected to use the terminal but also
efficient mechanical equipment, labor force and hinterland
access.

General cargo, too, which in the Great Lakes is almost
entirely intercontinental, requires efficient turnaround.
In such traffic, the handling at Great Lakes ports is most
commonly by breakbulk methods, although some unitization,
such as the use of pallets, is common. These methods,
however, are losing ground world-wide in competition with
containerization. The Great Lakes ports, as discussed in the
next chapter, are suffering from their inability to generate
sufficient cargo to justify investment in expensive and
sophisticated terminals for the specialized handling of
containers. Furthermore, the land requirements for modern
back-up of general cargo terminals, including access rail
and highway routes, marshalling and sorting yards and other
facilities, are substantial. A modern container berth,
typical of the ocean ports, requires from 30 to 40 acres of
back-up land.

Thus, both bulk terminals--whether public or private--
as well as general cargo terminals, demand larger land areas
than formerly. The finger piers, characteristic of the older
installations at Great Lakes ports as elsewhere, were
designed to maximize the number of vessels that could be
berthed and were located near the densely-developed central
city areas that generated the industrial and commercial
traffic. With fewer but larger vessels, larger and more
efficient port terminal facilities, and the need for larger
volumes of cargo "throughput" at such facilities, the finger
piers became obsolete. In many metropolitan areas of the
Great Lakes, the newer terminals and port installations are
no longer located up narrow, winding rivers or near the cores
of the cities. They are increasingly located at or beyond
the urban periphery, where abundant land is available at
relatively low cost and where, subject only to environmental
constraints, industrial and port areas can easily be extended,
in some instances, by land-fill into the Lakes. At such

locations, the back-up landward facilities, including access routes and staging areas, can more easily be developed. At the same time, these changing technological requirements for waterborne commerce make available substantial areas of former port land and waterfront areas near the central parts of cities for redevelopment and renewal, serving non-transportation purposes. Among such recent and prospective developments are the waterfront civic center in Detroit, the Illinois Center in downtown Chicago and the reuse of Navy Pier for recreational purposes, the extensive area fronting on Toronto Harbor, the new city park at the entrance to the harbor of Duluth, and the North Harbor tract in Milwaukee.

An important impact of changing technology in ports' cargo handling is that upon the labor force, both on the vessels and ashore.[7] Manpower aboard vessels is significant to ports in that the crews require services that are provided ashore: outfitting of vessels, chandlering, entertainment during shore leave, repair of vessels, and shoreside paperwork, including financial services, purchasing and, in the case of international traffic, customs services and associated public functions. With fewer and larger vessels, both in internal and external Great Lakes trade, the personnel aboard ships within the Great Lakes is substantially less than formerly despite the increased volumes of cargoes. The indirect employment created by the multiplier effect of ships' personnel is, then, much less than even a few years ago.

Bulk cargoes require relatively little labor in direct handling; consequently, the direct as well as the indirect employment effects of the cargo handling are relatively minor, insofar as the ports themselves are concerned. On the other hand, the availability, or potential availability, of bulk commodities can, and often does, constitute a major attraction to bulk-producing and bulk-consuming industries to locate within or near a port. The iron and steel industry of the Great Lakes Region, as indicated in another chapter, is virtually completely dependent upon Great Lakes transportation of ore, limestone and, to some extent, coal and steel products. The automobile and other steel-consuming industries represent, in part, the multiplier effect of the availability of Great Lakes transportation to their principal supplier industries. In other words, improving the competitive efficiency of Great Lakes transportation can enhance the economic base of the port regions, and, ultimately, of the entire Great Lakes Region. The basic industries which directly utilize Great Lakes transportation benefit from the availability of large waterfront sites. Some of them, in fact, have developed their own private harbors: Taconite Harbor and Silver Bay on Lake Superior; Port Inland, Port Washington, Oak Creek, Buffington and Gary on Lake Michigan; Rogers City on Lake Huron. Others occupy large portions of the shorelines of public harbors, without which they would have located elsewhere, perhaps outside the Great Lakes Region.

Technology and Competing Routes and Modes

Transportation to, from and within the Great Lakes by water carriers is affected not only by the available volumes and types of cargoes but also by the proportion of the available traffic that is actually carried on the Lakes.

Intercontinental traffic to and from the Great Lakes Region need not transit the St. Lawrence Seaway. Indeed, the Seaway has captured only a small share of the potentially available traffic between the Great Lakes hinterland region and overseas. There are several reasons, both technological and non-technological, for this failure. The technological constraints upon maximization of traffic involve, among other things, consideration of the technological developments on competing routes and modes of transportation.

In addition to the St. Lawrence Seaway route, and the older but now largely obsolete New York State Barge Canal, the Great Lakes are connected with salt water by another major route: The Illinois Lakes-to-Gulf Waterway, which is part of the Mississippi River System, the dominant inland waterway route of North America. The Mississippi System, operated almost entirely with barges and towboats, has witnessed a rapid long-term increase.[8] Aided by massive federal funding of a minimum nine-foot channel throughout a system of more than 12,000 miles of inland waterways, the Mississippi River barge system (including major tributaries such as the Ohio, Illinois and, more recently, the Arkansas waterways) now handles substantially more tonnage of bulk commodities than do the Great Lakes. In 1972, 158.5 billion ton-miles of freight were handled on the Mississippi River System, while the corresponding figure for the Great Lakes System was 108.9 billion ton-miles.[9] Its technology is highly developed: a series of multiple purpose dams and locks on the upper rivers create still-water pools with minimum channel depth of nine feet; large-scale revetments and new channels circumvent many of the meanders of the lower rivers; huge levee and revetment projects stabilize the channels insofar as possible; powerful diesel towboats generate up to 10,000 horsepower and are capable of moving groups of barges (tows) of up to 60,000 tons against the river currents; modern electronic devices aid navigation; standardized barge dimensions permit interchangeability; and sophisticated bulkloading and discharging facilities are alongshore.

The development of barge-carrying ships--the LASH and Seabee vessels--gives Chicago as well as nearby ports on the Lake Michigan shore, from Burns Harbor, Indiana, on the east to Milwaukee and Green Bay on the north, the opportunity to develop direct overseas services via the two competitive routes, one to the Atlantic and the other to the Gulf. Both can optionally involve transfer at deepwater ports near the sea or direct barge service without break-of-bulk, the barges being carried across the oceans by LASH or Seabee ships. Until now, these "kangaroo" services primarily had

22

facilitated turnaround time for the large vessels, and the barges normally did not venture far inland, although some have reached Chicago, St. Louis and other upriver ports from New Orleans. The other alternative, using LASH and Seabee barges through the Great Lakes-St. Lawrence route to the lower St. Lawrence, has not yet been developed, but a study of its potential is underway.

In addition to the technological developments in inland waterway barge transportation and the related localization of many heavy industrial establishments along the waterway system, the series of rate relationships that were established by the parallel and complementary overland carriers are important considerations for Great Lakes shipping. Railroads paralleling the waterway system lowered rates in order to minimize diversion of traffic. In many instances, combination rail-barge rates were established at levels considerably under the all-rail rates for the same movements. While federal regulations generally inhibit control of barge operations by railroads, even that constraint is now less rigid than formerly. A number of combination unit-train-barge routes, with combination rates, have been established.

The result has been a curtailing of the hinterlands both for domestic and for overseas traffic.[10] On the west, the Upper Mississippi barge rate structure constricts the hinterland of such ports as Duluth-Superior, Milwaukee and Chicago with respect to Minnesota, the Dakotas, Montana, Iowa and even western Wisconsin. To the south, the Ohio River and its tributaries limit the hinterlands of the ports on Lakes Erie and Michigan. In both instances, low-cost barge movements and rail rates adjusted to barge competition favor the Gulf of Mexico ports, such as New Orleans and Houston. Barge traffic, such as export grain, moves from as far north as Peoria, Illinois, through New Orleans and Houston, rather than through Chicago, even though the Gulf ports are several times more distant. Similarly, traffic from the Ohio River region commonly moves through Gulf rather than Great Lakes ports.

Technological developments in railroading have also affected the potential bulk and general cargo traffic of Great Lakes ports. In spite of recent public attention to the physical and economic deterioration of the railroads, particularly in the Great Lakes Region, the long-term trend has been toward increased efficiency in railroad freight transportation. Technological developments include heavier roadbeds, improved signalling and communications systems, computerized record-keeping and control of movements, centralized traffic control by electronic methods, electronic classification yards, more powerful locomotives, larger and more specialized freight cars, and unit-trains.[11] Rate-making innovations, in spite of official constraints upon freedom of experimentation, have responded to many of these technical developments. The development of the unit-train concept for movement of coal and other bulk commodities has stimulated lower-cost railroad transportation.[12] This economy has been, in part, at the expense of Lake traffic since the regulatory agencies have been slow to permit low unit-train rates on the rail portions of combined rail-Lake movements but have been more than willing to permit all-rail, unit-train rates that bypass the Lake ports and carriers, as discussed in Chapter V.

In merchandise and high-class freight movements, the railroads have also competed effectively with the Lake and Seaway vessels. Internal general cargo ("package freight") movements on the Great Lakes between United States ports terminated with World War II with the advent of intercity trucking and the improvements in rail service. More recently, the domestic "package freight" movements between Canadian ports are similarly threatened.

Direct Great Lakes-overseas movements of general cargo have declined in the past few years, in large part because of the technological improvements and consequent competitive rates of the overland carriers—both railroad and highway—between the Great Lakes Region and coastal ports. The advent of piggyback—Trailer on Flat Car (TOFC)—by rail, following authorization by the Interstate Commerce Commission of joint and combination rates between rail and highway carriers in the early 1950's and, a few years later, the development of intermodal containerization—Container on Flat Car (COFC)—stimulated the growth of general cargo movements between the Great Lakes Region and the larger coastal ports in combination with containerships and roll-on/roll-off (ro/ro) vessels, with through and joint rail-water rates.

Similarly, the rapid development of intercity trucking and the expansion of the federal interstate system and other major highways diverted much of the potential general cargo traffic from the Great Lakes-St. Lawrence Seaway route. Large common and contract truckers, some of them nationwide and international, together with the growing number of private truckers on the new highways, have tended to favor coastal ports at the expense of the Great Lakes ports. The "double bottom," or semitrailer and trailer combination, the removal of some restrictive weight and dimensional limits on trucks by individual states, and the general maturity of the intercity trucking industry have combined to produce formidable competition with the Seaway route for international merchandise movements. Movement by rail or truck to and from coastal ports is generally much faster, and commonly more dependable, than through the Seaway; it is non-seasonal and much more flexible. As a result, the major coastal ports have made inroad into what otherwise would have been the dominant hinterlands of the large Great Lakes ports, especially Cleveland, Toledo, Detroit, Milwaukee and Chicago.

The Role of Labor*

The Great Lakes-St. Lawrence Seaway System has proved to be extremely susceptible to shutdowns. Because of the several bottlenecks created by the physical structure of the System, collapse of labor-management relations could lead to the closing of the entire System or of major portions of it. Efficiency and reliability of labor play a crucial role in expediting cargo movement so that the maximum number of round trips can be completed during each shipping season. This applies to both internal and Great Lakes overseas operations. Pilots must be available immediately in all designated waters; lock operators must be manning their positions; vessel crews must be under contract; and shoreside labor must be available at the ports.

Because of their special relevance to operation of salt-water vessels within the System, the problems of shoreside labor and of pilotage are singled out for discussion.

1. Longshore Labor

Since containers have not been utilized to a great extent on the Great Lakes, most general cargo moves in the conventional breakbulk manner. Loading and discharging of breakbulk cargo are labor-intensive. In order to minimize time in port and to increase the number of "payloads" per vessel, longshore labor must be efficient and efficiently utilized.

Because multiple port calls on the Great Lakes are usually necessary to meet a vessel's load factor, time in each port must be minimized. Delays caused by work stoppages or scheduling errors can add several days to transit time, reduce revenues, increase costs, and discourage use of the Seaway System.

Labor has been severely and adversely affected by the decline in general cargo moving through the Great Lakes. In Milwaukee, for example, registered employees, members of the International Longshoremen's Association (ILA), declined from 800 in 1971 to approximately 290 in 1975. This declining general cargo traffic has altered bargaining strategy between the ILA and the stevedores. Previously, the parties to the negotiations had maintained an adversary relationship. Bargaining agreements were reached on a port by port basis,

---

*Much of the information in this section was obtained through conversations with Mr. Patrick Sullivan of Great Lakes District of International Longshoremen's Association, Mr. Douglas Kubic of Local 815, Milwaukee, International Longshoremen's Association, and Mr. George R. Skuggen, Director of the Great Lakes Pilotage Staff.

tending to produce an unstable environment as disagreements over local issues in one port could spread and cause sympathy work stoppages in other ports.

The fundamental change has been the abandonment of this adversary relationship. For the first time, beginning with the 1975 season, one master agreement covering a three-year period and all United States ILA represented Great Lakes ports, has been reached by the ILA and the Great Lakes Association of Stevedores. Its specific objective is to provide stability in Great Lakes ports so that shippers of general cargo will be encouraged to use them.

The agreement contains a special clause pertaining to container movement. Previously, any container load, unless under a manufacturer's label, that was consolidated within a fifty-mile radius of a Great Lakes port had to pay a special penalty unless the container was stripped and restuffed by ILA labor. This requirement was lifted in the December 1974 agreement to encourage shipment of containerized general cargo through the Great Lakes ports.

Although the ILA is the major representative of long-shore labor in Great Lakes ports, other unions also represent shoreside labor: the Teamsters, District 50-United Mine Workers, Operating Engineers, United Steel Workers, and the Brotherhood of Railway and Steamship Clerks. Jurisdictional disputes have existed, but positive progress is being made to eliminate them.

Employment has dropped considerably both in terms of the number of workers and the number of hours worked. In previous years, much of the labor was casual; longshoremen held second jobs or worked on the wharves on weekends or evenings. Attrition has trimmed the roster of workers. Yet many of those who remain are underemployed. According to Patrick J. Sullivan, extension of the shipping season and removal of penalty fees on container cargo assembled within a fifty-mile radius should more fully employ the remaining longshore labor.

2. Pilotage

Pilotage is indispensable to transit of the Seaway System. Registered vessels of the United States, Canada and other foreign countries are required to have either a registered United States or Canadian pilot on board in their service when operating in designated waters of the Seaway System.[13] United States and Canadian enrolled (domestic) vessels are not required to do so when all deck officers have First Class Pilot Licenses.[14] Designated waters include: District 1, the St. Lawrence River from St. Regis to Lake Ontario; District 2, the Welland Ship Canal and western Lake Erie from Sandusky through the connecting channels to Lake Huron; and District 3, the St. Marys River and the Sault Ste. Marie Locks.[15]

Registered pilots are not required for registered vessels navigating in undesignated waters if a regular crew member is a "B" Certified Officer. "B" certification requires that the Master of the vessel possess an unlimited Master's license, have knowledge of the Great Lakes rules of the road, be fluent in the English language, possess a radio-telephone license and have made within the past year two round trips over the waters to be traversed.[16] If a registered vessel is not "B" certified, it must wait up to six hours for a pilot before transitting undesignated waters. If no pilot is available within that time, the vessel may receive a waiver of the pilot requirement. Only rarely is a waiver granted for transit through designated waters.[17]

Two organizational situations involving Great Lakes pilotage could create unstable conditions. One is the difference in employment status between Canadian pilots and United States pilots. The other is the existence of separate pilotage districts and pilot associations on the Great Lakes.

Registered Great Lakes Canadian pilots are subsidized employees of the Canadian government and have all the rights of Canadian public employees, including the right to strike. Registered United States Great Lakes pilots are entre-preneurs, not government employees. Though they are regulated by the United States government, they receive no financial support from it. In some districts, United States and Canadian pilots work together, alternating assignments. The problems of allocating assignments, a source of instability, become exacerbated when income sources or seasonal earnings differ. With a continued decline in over-seas trade and the subsidization of Canadian pilots, allocations of assignments could cause serious disputes, resulting in service interruptions.

Great Lakes pilotage is broken into three districts, each one serviced by a voluntary association of the United States Great Lakes pilots. The St. Lawrence Seaway Pilots Association serves District 1, the Lakes Pilots Association, Inc., serves District 2, and Upper Great Lakes Pilots, Inc., serves District 3. The Canadian pilot force consists of two organizations. Those pilots registered for District 1 belong to the Corporation of Upper St. Lawrence Pilots. In Districts 2 and 3, the registered Canadian pilots are organized into the Corporation of Professional Great Lakes Pilots.[19]

In addition, registered Great Lakes pilots in Districts 2 and 3 have organized bargaining locals of the International Longshoremen's Association (ILA).[20] Organization of the United States pilots is somewhat of an anomaly because pilots have not been considered employees. Rather, they are

self-employed, according to the U.S. Internal Revenue
Service and the courts.

Fragmentation of this sort increases the number of vital
negotiations. Four different associations involved in three
crucial areas of designated waters could through work actions
close down the Seaway System to overseas trade.

Footnotes

[1]"Merchant Vessel Size in United States Offshore Trades by the Year 2000," The American Association of Port Authorities Committee on Ship Channels and Harbors (Washington: June, 1969), 54 pp.; Douglas K. Fleming, "The Independent Transport Carrier in Ocean Tramp Trades," Economic Geography, Vol. 44, No. 1 (January, 1968), pp. 21-36.

[2]"U.K. and U.S. Container Ships Compared: Service Experience with Two Classes of Giant Vessels," Fairplay International Shipping Weekly, Vol. 254, No. 4,776 (March 6, 1975), pp. 7-9; Eric Rath, Container Systems (New York: John Wiley & Sons, 1973), 581 pp.; Patrick Finlay, ed., Jane's Freight Containers (New York: McGraw-Hill Book Co., annual); Eric Schenker, "The Effects of Containerization on Great Lakes Ports" (Milwaukee: Center for Great Lakes Studies, The University of Wisconsin-Milwaukee, February, 1968; revised May, 1973).

[3]Manalytics, Inc., "Great Lakes/St. Lawrence Feeder Systems: A Feasibility Study," prepared for the St. Lawrence Seaway Development Corporation (Springfield, Va.: National Technical Information Service, 1972), 71 pp. & appendices.

[4]Harold M. Mayer, "Some Geographic Aspects of Technological Change in Maritime Transportation," Economic Geography, Vol. 49, No. 2 (April, 1973), pp. 145-155; Wallace T. Sansome, "The Evolution and Economics of Barge Carrying Ships," Proceedings, Twelfth Annual Meeting, Transportation Research Forum, Vol. 12, No. 1 (1971), pp. 209-216; "Design Features of the Seabee Barge Carrier," Fairplay International Shipping Weekly, Vol. 250, No. 4,622 (March 23, 1972), pp. 49 ff.; "Barges Aboard Ship--Principles and Practices," Fairplay International Shipping Weekly, Vol. 252, No. 4,753 (September 26, 1974), pp. 29-30.

[5]E. B. Williams, "The Great Lakes Iron Ore Carrier," Inland Seas, Vol. 18, No. 3 (Fall, 1962), pp. 172-189.

[6]Lake Carriers' Association, Annual Report 1974 (Cleveland, 1975), pp. 26-30.

[7]Harry Bridges, Thomas W. Gleason, and Joseph P. Goldberg, "Labor Utilization and its Effects on U.S. Port Planning and Development," in Eric Schenker and Harry C. Brockel, eds., Port Planning and Development as Related to Problems of U.S. Ports and the U.S. Coastal Environment (Cambridge, Md.: Cornell Maritime Press, Inc., 1974), pp. 59-81.

[8]U.S., Department of the Army, Corps of Engineers, Waterborne Commerce of the United States, Part 2, Waterways and Harbors, Gulf Coast, Mississippi River System (New Orleans, La.: District Engineer, U.S. Army Engineer District), annual.

[9]U.S., Bureau of the Census, Statistical Abstract of the United States 1974 (Washington, D.C.: U.S. Government Printing Office, 1974), p. 585.

[10]U.S., Department of the Army, Corps of Engineers, "Grain Traffic Analysis to Accompany Great Lakes Harbors Study" (Chicago: U.S. Army Engineer Division, North Central, June, 1965), map, p. 21.

[11]Edward Miller, "Economies of Scale in Railroading," Proceedings, Fourteenth Annual Meeting, Transportation Research Forum, Cleveland, Ohio, Oct. 15-17, 1973 (Chicago, 1973), pp. 683-701; Improving Railroad Productivity: Final Report of the Task Force on Railroad Productivity (Washington, D.C.: The National Commission on Productivity and the Council of Economic Advisors, November, 1973), 327 pp.

[12]John T. Starr, Jr., The Evolution of Unit Train Operations in the United States (Chicago: Department of Geography, The University of Chicago, 1975), Research Paper No. 158.

[13]National Oceanic and Atmospheric Administration, U.S. Department of Commerce, Great Lakes Pilot 1973 (Washington, D.C.: U.S. Government Printing Office, 1973), p. 50.

[14]U.S., Department of Transportation, Great Lakes Pilotage Review (Draft Status Report, May, 1973), p. VI-1.

[15]National Oceanic and Atmospheric Administration, Great Lakes Pilot 1973, p. 50.

[16]Great Lakes Pilotage Administration, U.S. Department of Commerce, "Great Lakes Pilotage" (Washington, D.C.: U.S. Government Printing Office, 1966).

[17]U.S., Department of Transportation, Great Lakes Pilotage Review, p. II-10.

[18]Ibid., p. II-36.

[19]Ibid., p. II-43.

[20]Ibid., p. II-60.

Bibliography

"Barges Aboard Ship--Principles and Practices," Fairplay
    International Shipping Weekly, Vol. 252, No. 4,753
    (September 26, 1974), pp. 29-30.

Bridges, Harry; Gleason, Thomas W.; and Goldberg, Joseph P.
    "Labor Utilization and Its Effect on U.S. Port Planning
    and Development." In Eric Schenker and Harry C. Brockel,
    eds., Port Planning and Development as Related to
    Problems of U.S. Ports and the U.S. Coastal Environment.
    Cambridge, Maryland: Cornell Maritime Press, Inc.,
    1974, pp. 59-81.

"Design Features of the Seabee Barge Carrier," Fairplay
    International Shipping Weekly, Vol. 250, No. 4,622
    (March 23, 1972), pp. 49, 51, 55.

Easton, James. Transportation of Freight in the Year 2000
    with Particular Reference to the Great Lakes Area.
    Detroit: The Developing Detroit Area Research Project,
    Detroit Edison Company, 1970.

Fleming, Douglas K. "The Independent Transport Carrier in
    Ocean Tramp Trades," Economic Geography, Vol. 44, No. 1
    (January, 1968), pp. 21-36.

Finlay, Patrick, ed. Jane's Freight Containers. New York:
    McGraw-Hill, annual.

Gilmore, James. "The St. Lawrence River Canals Vessel,"
    The Society of Naval Architects and Marine Engineers
    (May 3-4, 1956).

Greenwood's Lake Boats. Cleveland: Freshwater Press, Inc.,
    annual.

Howe, Charles W., et al. Inland Waterway Transportation,
    Studies in Public and Private Management and Investment
    Decisions. Baltimore: The Johns Hopkins Press, for
    Resources for the Future, Inc., 1969.

Hull, William J., and Hull, Robert W. The Origin and
    Development of the Waterways Policy of the United
    States. Washington, D.C.: National Waterways Confer-
    ence, Inc., 1967.

Improving Railroad Productivity: Final Report of the Task
    Force on Railroad Productivity. Washington, D.C.:
    The National Commission on Productivity and the Council
    of Economic Advisors, 1973.

Lake Carriers' Association. Annual Report 1974. Cleveland,
    1975, pp. 26-30.

Manalytics, Inc. "Great Lakes/St. Lawrence Seaway Development Corporation." Springfield, Va.: National
Technical Information Service, 1972.

Mayer, Harold M. "The Great Lakes: The Tie that Binds,"
American Institute of Architects Journal (June, 1969),
pp. 50-58.

_____. "Some Geographic Aspects of Technological Change
in Maritime Transportation," Economic Geography,
Vol. 49, No. 2 (April, 1973), pp. 145-155.

"Merchant Vessel Size in United States Offshore Trades by
the Year 2000." Washington, D.C.: The American
Association of Port Authorities Committee on Ship
Channels and Harbors (June, 1969).

Miller, Edward. "Economies of Scale in Railroading."
Proceedings, Fourteenth Annual Meeting, Transportation
Research Forum, Cleveland, Ohio, October 15-17, 1973.
Chicago, 1973, pp. 683-701.

Rath, Eric. Container Systems. New York: John Wiley &
Sons, 1973.

Sansone, Wallace T. "The Evolution and Economics of Barge
Carrying Ships." Proceedings, Twelfth Annual Meeting,
Transportation Research Forum, Vol. 12, No. 1. Chicago:
Transportation Research Forum, 1971, pp. 209-216.

Schenker, Eric. The Effects of Containerization on Great
Lakes Ports. Milwaukee: Center for Great Lakes
Studies, The University of Wisconsin-Milwaukee,
February, 1968; revised May, 1973.

"St. Lawrence-Great Lakes Water Route: Diagrams and
Statistical Charts." Ottawa: St. Lawrence Seaway
Authority, 1971.

Starr, John T., Jr. The Evolution of Unit Train Operations
in the United States. Chicago: Department of
Geography, The University of Chicago, Research Paper
No. 158, 1975.

"U.K. and U.S. Container Ships Compared: Service Experience
with Two Classes of Giant Vessels," Fairplay International Shipping Weekly, Vol. 254, No. 4,776 (March 6,
1975), pp. 7-9.

U.S. Department of the Army, Corps of Engineers. Waterborne
Commerce of the United States, Part 2, Waterways and
Harbors, Gulf Coast, Mississippi River System. New
Orleans, La.: District Engineer, U.S. Army Engineer
District, annual.

U.S. Department of the Army, Corps of Engineers. "Grain
Traffic Analysis to Accompany Great Lakes Harbors Study."
Chicago: U.S. Army Engineer Division, North Central,
June, 1965, map, p. 21.

U.S. Department of Commerce, Bureau of the Census.
Statistical Abstract of the United States, 1974.
Washington, D.C.: U.S. Government Printing Office, 1974.

U.S. Department of Commerce, Great Lakes Pilotage Administration. Great Lakes Pilotage. Washington, D.C.: U.S.
Government Printing Office, 1966.

U.S. Department of Commerce, National Oceanic and Atmospheric
Administration. Great Lakes Pilot 1973. Washington,
D.C.: U.S. Government Printing Office, 1973.

U.S. Department of Transportation. Great Lakes Pilotage
Review. Draft Staff Report, May, 1972.

Williams, E. B. "The Great Lakes Iron Ore Carrier," Inland
Seas, Vol. 18, No. 3 (Fall, 1962), pp. 172-189.

III.

Containerization and the

Great Lakes Transportation System

Introduction

The most significant recent technological development in general cargo transportation is the widespread adoption of containerization and the concomitant spread of intermodal through movements.

In the mid-1970's, the concept of containerization can no longer be considered revolutionary. Though there was limited consolidation of breakbulk cargo into containers before World War II, the major increase in containerization of cargo dates to the mid-1960's. This form of packaging has not only allowed economic gains but also influenced trade patterns and port competition.

The development and proliferation of container service have afforded general cargo shippers the opportunity to capitalize more fully on the inherent advantages of the various transportation modes. Although some variations in container size exist, the container has provided a standardized packaging form for many types of general cargo. The standardized container form has allowed four transportation modes--truck, rail, water and air--to develop container transport equipment, and has also fostered the development of transshipment centers.

The shipper who uses containers is able to choose the transportation mode or combination of modes that will be most efficient. Intermodal handling of containers depends on adequate intermodal coordination. Examples of intermodal transportation fostered by containerization include: (1) the land bridge, in which goods are shipped across the continental United States or Canada by railroad or truck, rather than through the Panama Canal; (2) the servicing of the Port of Portland, Oregon, through the Port of Seattle, Washington, by using motor carriers between Seattle and Portland; and (3) the movement of container traffic from Sacramento, California to the ports of Oakland and San Francisco by feeder barges.

The following are some of the major attractions of containerized transport:

1. Door-to-Door Distribution

A significant advantage of containerization is the ability to move goods door-to-door in the same container. With door-to-door distribution, goods are "stuffed" into a container at the point of origin, and are not unloaded or otherwise disturbed until the container reaches its destination. Benefits, in the form of possible cost savings, resulting from the door-to-door distribution are: (a) limited handling and reduced packaging; (b) reduced theft, pilferage and damage; and (c) increased safety.

37

(a)   Limited Handling and Reduced Packaging

Consolidation of several small packages into
one container reduces the number of times the
packages are handled and, hence, also reduces the
labor costs associated with their movement.

Packaging requirements are reduced considerably
by the container, for it is a package itself capable
of protecting the contents from water, weather, break-
age and contamination. Goods formerly protected by
expensive crates now can be packaged in cardboard
boxes or paper bags and remain quite secure in
containers. In addition, if the container is initially packed securely, no extra precautions need
be taken for the differing levels of stress upon
packaging posed by the several transportation modes.

(b)   Theft, Pilferage and Damage

Theft, pilferage and damage are substantially
reduced by container transport, for the container is
sealed at the origin of the shipment and is not
opened until it reaches its destination, unless subject
to restuffing rules. Opportunity for theft is
reduced because of both the container's seal and the
container's unascertainable contents as well as the
shorter transit time permitted by effective intermodal coordination. Damage enroute and at the
terminal is less likely as long as special adjustments, such as ventilating or refrigerating, are made
for cargoes sensitive to atmospheric conditions.
Also, reduction in damage to cargo has a feedback
effect upon insurance rates, which tend to be lower
for containerized cargo.

(c)   Safety

Containerization of cargo and the mechanizing
of the transshipment process reduce the onerous work
for the laborers involved and the opportunity for
injury to the workers. With this higher degree of
safety for the work force, workmen's compensation
premiums could be reduced and compliance with the
OSHA standards made less costly.

2.   Unitization

Containers provide the potential for unitization, that
is, the consolidation of several small packages or articles
into one large package. Unitization offers several advantages:
reduced handling and related labor costs in the movement of
goods. In addition, initial unitization allows further
unitization into larger shipments and the use of more specialized facilities such as roll-on/roll-off (ro/ro) and

LASH. Finally, unitization provides greater flexibility in the movement of goods since the shipper can make use of any or all modes that move containers.

3. Reduced Transit Times

The use of containers may reduce transit times in two ways. Containerization reduces the time spent in port for the loading and discharging of vessels. Twenty men can load and discharge 6,000 tons of containerized cargo in a ten-hour shift. If the cargo is palletized, 50 men are needed to load and discharge 1,800 tons in an eight-hour shift. When the cargo is breakbulk, 90 men are needed to load and discharge 1,200 tons in an eight-hour shift.[1] Thus, the turnaround time of vessels in port can be reduced by containerization. For if effective intermodal coordination exists, containers can be moved by the most efficient inland mode.

Insurance premiums may drop as transit times are improved because each consignment will be subject to risk for a shorter period. Moreover, a given level of demand for containers and transportation equipment can be served by a smaller inventory level as it can be more efficiently dispatched with the advent of reduced transit times.

Containerization Within the United States

A. Present and Future Extent of Containerization

Statistics detailing the extent of containerization within the United States are limited. One study indicates that most of the ports covered experienced strong growth in containerization between 1972 and 1973 and also predicts strong future growth.[2] Tables 3.1, 3.2 and 3.3 list container ports and data from that study.

Containerized packaging and transit have traditionally been considered suitable for only a selected portion of general cargo. "Ten years ago, the list of containerizable commodities comprised hardly more than 50 per cent of general liner cargo."[3] Many now believe that almost all general cargo and certain bulk cargo shipments can be containerized. In 1971, 37.7 per cent of all liner cargo carried between the United States, Europe, the Far East and the Caribbean was containerized. By 1972, the figure had risen to 44.1 per cent.[4] It has been estimated that 23.4 per cent of the general cargo moving through Great Lakes ports may be suitable for containerization.[5]

Tables 3.4 and 3.5 provide a breakdown of imported and exported commodities which have moved largely in containers. Some caution should be exercised in interpreting these data, as they were based upon a sample biased in favor of larger shipments.[6] Since containers tend to handle smaller shipments,

39

TABLE 3.1 --LISTING OF CONTAINER PORTS — UNITED STATES
Based on Number of Loaded Sea Vans(20-foot equivalents)

Port	Estimated 1974	Per cent Increase 73-74	Actual 1973	Per cent Increase 72-73	Actua 1972
Anchorage	71,287	7.0	66,629	3.6	64,30(
Baltimore	264,000	9.1	242,000	14.7	211,00(
Boston	80,814	17.7	68,675	27.4	53,88(
Charleston	63,340	18.4	53,510	17.6	45,50(
Chicago	11,300	(5.0)	11,904	(5.4)	12,57'
Cleveland	6,700	55.3	4,315	39.2	3,10(
Galveston	35,000	66.7	21,000	40.0	15,00(
Hampton Roads	317,256	30.0	244,043	31.5	185,52(
Honolulu	180,000	.6	178,932	(4.9)	188,15!
Houston	186,716	20.0	155,596	81.1	85,90:
Jacksonville	97,727	13.6	86,000	-	*
Long Beach	426,217	8.6	**392,314	87.1	209,65(
Longview	*	-	6,400	11.9	5,72:
Los Angeles	208,496	23.4	168,961	89.4	89,19(
Miami	40,000	2.2	39,150	206.3	12,78:
Milwaukee	2,421	.5	2,312	35.0	1,71:
New Orleans	97,000	42.4	68,107	50.5	45,26:
New York	1,130,000	25.6	899,398	54.3	582,73)
Oakland	*	-	436,590	24.9	349,65:
Philadelphia	124,445	24.5	100,000	64.5	60,778
Portland	48,800	13.8	42,895	-	*
Sacramento	1,400	0.0	1,400	-	*
San Diego	4,800	9.7	4,367	193.5	1,49)
San Francisco	56,000	-	*	-	*
San Juan	*	-	621,000	15.0	540,00C
Savannah	45,818	57.2	29,145	9.3	26,673
Seattle	**430,000	14.1	**377,000	97.9	190,486
Stockton	9,599	13.4	8,463	41.6	5,975
Tacoma	19,600	27.3	15,400	-	*
Wilmington	21,000	61.5	13,000	261.1	3,600

* - Figures Not Available
** - Updated Figure
SOURCE: Flexi-Van Corporation, "The State of Containers, Part I; Containerized Movements Through World Ports," Intermodal World (San Francisco and New York: July 1974).

TABLE 3.2

Listing of Container Ports - Canada
Based on Number of Loaded Sea Vans
(20-Foot Equivalents)

Port	Estimated 1974	Per cent Increase 73-74	Actual 1973	Per cent Increase 72-73	Actual 1972
alifax	**155,000	33.2	116,405	18.4	98,326
ontreal	129,568	10.0	117,789	31.7	89,455
uebec	75,000	18.0	63,519	16.7	54,427
aint John	39,000	11.0	35,134	32.7	26,475
oronto	** 12,651	26.1	** 10,051	35.3	**15,496
ancouver	79,000	.6	74,753	14.3	65,381

- Updated Figure

Source: Flexi-Van Corp., "The State of Containers, Part I:
Containerized Movements Through World Ports,"
Intermodal World (San Francisco and New York; July
1974.

41

TABLE 3.3 - 1973 RANKING OF CONTAINER PORTS
Based on Number of <u>Loaded</u> Sea Vans(20-foot equivalents)

-- Port and Number of Vans Handled --

Rank	UNITED STATES		Rank	CANADA	
1	New York	899,398	1	Montreal	117,7
2	San Juan	621,000	2	Halifax	116,4
3	Oakland	436,590	3	Vancouver	74,7
4	Long Beach	**392,314	4	Quebec	63,5
5	Seattle	**377,000	5	Saint John	35,1
6	Hampton Roads	244,043	6	Toronto	**10,0
7	Baltimore	242,000			
8	Honolulu	178,932	Rank	WORLD	
9	Los Angeles	168,961	1	Rotterdam	587,0
10	Houston	155,596	2	Bremen/ Bremerhaven	394,6
11	Philadelphia	100,000			
12	Jacksonville	86,000	3	Helsingborg	337,0
13	Boston	68,675	4	Yokohama	301,0
14	New Orleans	68,107	5	London	281,0
15	Anchorage	66,629	6	Belfast	251,0
16	Charleston	53,510	7	Hamburg	247,4
17	Portland, Ore.	42,895	8	Melbourne	237,0
18	Miami	39,150	9	Liverpool	218,5
19	Savannah	29,145	10	Antwerp	217,4
20	Galveston	21,000	11	Southampton	214,3
21	Tacoma	15,400	12	Hong Kong	213,7
22	Wilmington, N.C.	13,000	13	Le Havre	188,3
23	Chicago	11,904	14	Larne	187,5
24	Stockton	8,463	15	Felixstowe	169,1
25	Mobile	7,606	16	Gothenburg	157,2
26	Longview	6,400	17	Keelung	150,2
27	San Diego	4,376	18	Sydney	142,7
28	Cleveland	4,315	19	Tokyo	130,5
29	Milwaukee	** 3,083	20	Dublin	122,0
30	Sacramento	1,400			

** - Updated Figure

<u>NOTE</u>: No data are available on the 1973 container traffic for San Francisco.
However, an estimate for 1974 sets this year's movement at 56,000 vans.
<u>SOURCE</u>: Flexi-Van Corp., "The State of Containers, Part I: Containerized Movement Through World Ports," Intermodal World (San Francisco and New York: July 1974); Compiled by Port of Seattle, Planning and Research Department.

TABLE 3.4 - VESSEL EXPORTS — CONTAINERIZED CARGO, INTERNATIONAL AND DOMESTIC
SHIPMENTS: 1970. Product categories with 100 million pounds or
more containerized, listed in descending order.

| Commodity Description | Total Vessel Exports (million pounds) | containerized | |
		Weight (million pounds)	% of Total
1. Chemical elements and compounds.	15,858	884	5.6
2. Fruits and vegetables.	2,298	656	28.5
3. Feeding-stuff for animals, excluding unmilled cereals	11,571	566	4.9
4. Machinery, other than electric	3,079	504	16.4
5. Synthetic resins, regenerated cellulose and plastic materials.	1,632	448	27.5
6. Wood and cork manufactures, n.e.c.	7,515	417	5.5
7. Transport equipment.	1,462	320	21.9
8. Hides, skins and furskins — undressed, raw or cured	741	296	39.9
9. Fertilizers and minerals — crude, excluding coal, petroleum and precious stones	8,742	282	3.2
10. Pulps and waste paper	6,011	248	4.1
11. Nonmetallic mineral manufacturers, n.e.c.	998	244	24.4
12. Paper, paperboard and manufacturers thereof	4,906	216	4.4
13. Textile yarn, fabrics, made-up articles and related products	448	216	48.2
14. Textile fibers (not manufactured into yarn, thread or fabrics) and their waste	536	192	35.8
15. Cereals and cereal preparations; and preparations of flour, starch or malt extract	3,971	189	4.8
16. Petroleum and petroleum products	17,734	187	1.1
17. Metalliferous ores and metal scrap	18,282	184	1.0
18. Nonferrous metals	1,558	182	11.7
19. Iron and steel	13,639	168	1.2
20. Tobacco and tobacco manufacturers.	702	160	22.8
21. Chemical products and materials, n.e.c. .	2,254	160	7.2
22. Animal oils and fats, n.e.c.	2,202	152	6.9
23. Electrical machinery, apparatus and appliances	586	144	24.6
24. Manufacturers of metal, n.e.c.	664	128	19.3
25. Wood, lumber and cork	24,043	104	0.4
TOTALS	151,432	7,247	4.8

Source: U.S. Department of Commerce, Bureau of the Census, Domestic and
International Transportation of U.S. Foreign Trade: 1970 (Washington
D.C.: U.S. Government Printing Office, 1972), p. 55.   Calculations by
Brasch & Walter, Intermodal Container Transportation & Development,
p. 1.11

TABLE 3.5

Vessel Imports—Containerized Cargo, International and Domestic
Shipments: 1970 Product categories with 100 million pounds
or more containerized, listed in descending order.

	Commodity description	total (million pounds)	Containerized (million pounds)	% of total
1.	Beverage	1,632	984	60.3
2.	Machinery, other than electric . . .	1,989	682	34.3
3.	Wood, lumber, and cork	5,629	630	11.2
4.	Miscellaneous manufactured articles, n.e.c.	1,381	577	41.8
5.	Transport equipment	3,713	511	13.8
6.	Iron and steel	23,501	504	2.1
7.	Nonmetallic mineral manufactures, n.e.c.	5,053	475	9.4
8.	Electrical machinery, apparatus, and appliances	1,217	402	33.0
9.	Coffee, cocoa, tea, spices, and manufactures thereof	3,819	383	10.0
10.	Chemical elements and compounds . . .	9,312	334	3.6
11.	Fruits and vegetables	2,031	328	16.1
12.	Manufactures of metal, n.e.c.	2,369	306	12.9
13.	Meat and meat preparations	1,644	246	15.0
14.	Textile yarn, fabrics, made-up articles and related products . . .	1,852	210	11.3
15.	Petroleum and petroleum products . .	3,020	180	6.0
16.	Fish and fish preparations	1,266	174	13.7
17.	Fertilizers and minerals—crude, excluding coal, petroleum, and precious stones	12,334	156	1.3
18.	Furniture	300	126	42.0
19.	Sugar, sugar preparations, and honey	3,747	105	2.8
20.	Clothing and accessories; elastic or rubberized knit fabric; knit house furnishings and articles; and articles made of fur	474	102	21.5
	Totals	86,263	7,415	8.6

Source: U.S. Department of Commerce, Bureau of the Census,
Domestic and International Transportation of U.S. Foreign
Trade: 1970, (Washington, D.C.: U.S. Government
Printing Office, 1972), p. 56. Calculations by Brasch
& Walter, Intermodal Container Transportation & Development,
p. 1.12.

the possible unreliability of these figures must be considered. As indicated in Tables 3.4 and 3.5, only 25 of the export commodities and 20 of the import commodities had more than 100 million pounds containerized, or only 4.8 per cent and 8.6 per cent respectively, of the total tonnage for each type. If these figures are reliable, 30 export commodities and 35 import commodities within the broad category of general liner cargo had not been containerized to any degree for internal shipment in 1970.

Forecasts of container traffic predict that it will continue to grow for the next few years. Two studies predict that total containerizable volume should increase through 1983.[7] According to one of the studies, containerizable cargo (in 1968) represented about 83 per cent of liner cargo volume. The proportion of liner cargo that is containerizable should remain constant at about 83 per cent through 1983, according to the study. But with the expected increase in liner cargo volume from 53.6 million tons in 1973 to 61.7 million tons in 1983, container traffic should increase as well, even if the containerized traffic does not approach the anticipated percentages.

The study further indicates that the proportion of containerizable cargo carried by container ships will range from 80 per cent for general cargo that is handled through the North Atlantic ports down to 20 per cent for that handled through the Gulf/Atlantic region.

Another study predicts an increase through 1980 for containerizable commodity flows (destined for or originating in practically all overseas areas), both for imports and exports, through all five coastal seaboard regions (North Atlantic, South Atlantic, Gulf, Pacific, and Great Lakes).

That study forecasts that, for the entire United States, imports of containerizable commodities should increase from 1.4 million T.E.U. (Twenty-foot Equivalent Units) to 1.7 million T.E.U. from 1968 to 1975, an increase of 26 per cent. From 1975 to 1980, the increase for imports is expected to be from 1.7 million T.E.U. to 2.1 million T.E.U., an increase of 23 per cent.

For the movement of exports of containerizable commodities, the study predicts an increase of 27 per cent between 1968 and 1975 and an increase of 20 per cent from 1975 to 1980. Increases of this magnitude would produce a flow of about 1.5 million T.E.U. by 1980.

B.   The Movement to Load Centers

The major characteristics of containerization can be summarized under three headings: (1) faster turnaround times; (2) improved inland distribution; and (3) high fixed costs.[8]

Each of these has contributed to the development of load centers: ports or other transshipment points at which traffic is consolidated for most efficient movement through highly capital intensive methods.

Decreases in vessel turnaround time--the time spent in moving into and out of port and loading or unloading cargo--result in an increased number of trips per vessel. Thus, the same amount of traffic can be carried by fewer ships and the required amount of ocean-going capital may be correspondingly reduced. To accomplish such decreased port times, the port itself must become more capital and land intensive. Expensive cranes are required to lift the containers on and off ships, and additional capital equipment is necessary to move and stack the containers.

Since container ships remain in port for minimal amounts of time, extensive open spaces for the storage, sorting and marshalling of containers must be available. These storage spaces require maintenance in order to support heavy loads and, in some cases, additional features such as electric hookups for refrigerated containers. With the reduced need for manpower, the investment in port facilities becomes highly fixed. Use of this capacity most efficiently requires huge flows of traffic and minimal idle time for the equipment.

Because a single container can be readily adapted for carriage by a variety of inland modes or combinations of modes,

> ...inland distribution is faster, more
> efficient, and ...cheaper. For short-sea
> trade, where inland costs are relatively
> more important, these factors encourage the
> substitution of land for sea miles. In
> both short and deep-sea trade, inland costs
> are reduced to such an extent that economic
> operation is possible through a small number
> of ports, thus creating the high-density
> flows between ports necessary to achieve
> adequate utilization of the specialized
> capital equipment involved.[9]

These characteristics of containerization tend to concentrate traffic, especially traffic destined for a relatively long voyage, in very few ports. As a result of these pressures, load centers, ports having great capacity, are now developing. Because of their efficiencies, these load centers can attract traffic from ever wider hinterlands and from less competitive ports on the same and other coasts.

To concentrate cargoes and thus to justify the provision of high-capacity load centers, the mini-bridge has developed, so that traffic to and from hinterlands is transported overland--or in a few instances by coastal feeder vessel services--

to the load centers, in spite of the fact that other ports
may be closer. Some mini-bridge movements may be transcontinental, with traffic between the Pacific Coast area
and Europe handled through Gulf or Atlantic Coast ports.
Transpacific traffic originating in the Atlantic coastal
area or the Gulf is transshipped at Pacific Coast ports
rather than (in either instance) moved by all-water routes
through the Panama Canal. The ultimate is the land bridge
(between transatlantic and transpacific vessels), or the
transcontinental movement of cargoes which neither originate
nor terminate in North America, but which are transported
by overland carriers across the continent.

Some of the most important trade routes are increasingly
being served by only a limited number of ports. Philadelphia,
Pennsylvania, on the Atlantic Coast and Portland, Oregon,
on the Pacific Coast have experienced diversion of a substantial proportion of their general cargo traffic with the
advent of containerization, because their location is un-
favorable for rapid turnaround. Their misfortune is in being
located in the shadow of larger nearby ports which can attract
the preponderant volumes of traffic: New York and Baltimore,
Maryland, in the case of Philadelphia; and Seattle, Washington, in the case of Portland. Smaller ports such as
Sacramento, California, have container services by all-water
routes in which feeder vessels transport the containers to
the load centers.[10]

With this trend unlikely to be reversed, the economic
pressures toward regional or even coastal container centers
grow inexorable. The economic feasibility of mini-bridge and
land bridge movements will sharpen competition between coasts
of the United States more than between ports or even regions
on a given coast.

The Role of the Great Lakes in Containerization

In order to understand the present and prospective roles
of containerization on the Great Lakes and the St. Lawrence
Seaway, it is necessary to examine the nature and volume of
traffic, especially general cargo traffic, on the waterway
system.

A. Levels of Overseas Traffic

As Tables 3.6 and 3.7 show, the tonnage of general cargo
moving directly between the Great Lakes and overseas points
through the St. Lawrence Seaway has fluctuated considerably
from year to year, with 1971 being the peak year. General
cargo tonnage decreased slightly in 1972, but a rise in bulk
tonnage made that year the highest in total direct overseas
tonnage. In general, overseas trade in these years has been
dominated by bulk movements, which in 1973 accounted for more
than twice the tonnage of general cargo.

47

TABLE 3.6

OVERSEAS CARGO, MONTREAL-LAKE ONTARIO SECTION, ST. LAWRENCE SEAWAY, 1968 - 1974

(Thousands of Short Tons)

Year	INBOUND (Upstream)			OUTBOUND (Downstream)			Grand Total		
	Bulk	General	Total*	Bulk	General	Total*	Bulk	General	Total*

COMBINED U.S. - CANADIAN

Year	Bulk	General	Total*	Bulk	General	Total*	Bulk	General	Total*
1968	1,353	6,613	7,966	6,225	1,048	7,273	7,578	7,661	15,239
1969	1,517	5,073	6,591	6,373	1,760	8,133	7,890	6,833	14,724
1970	1,295	4,716	6,011	6,729	1,567	8,296	8,024	6,283	14,304
1971	1,073	7,278	8,350	9,885	1,026	10,911	10,958	8,304	19,262
1972	1,694	6,690	8,384	11,072	982	12,054	12,766	7,672	20,438
1973	1,662	4,879	6,541	10,576	788	11,365	12,238	5,667	17,906
1974	1,623	3,639	5,262	5,583	779	6,362	7,206	4,417	11,623

CANADIAN

Year	Bulk	General	Total*	Bulk	General	Total*	Bulk	General	Total*
1968	869	684	1,553	870	324	1,194	1,739	1,008	2,747
1969	989	819	1,809	911	288	1,199	1,901	1,107	3,008
1970	978	483	1,461	1,313	377	1,689	2,291	860	3,150
1971	678	737	1,415	1,843	199	2,042	2,520	936	3,456
1972	1,159	961	2,120	2,033	364	2,397	3,193	1,324	4,517
1973	965	551	1,517	1,297	225	1,523	2,263	774	3,040
1974	449	460	909	1,436	171	1,606	1,885	631	2,515

U.S.

Year	Bulk	General	Total*	Bulk	General	Total*	Bulk	General	Total*
1968	484	5,929	6,413	5,355	724	6,079	5,839	6,653	12,492
1969	528	4,254	4,782	5,462	1,472	6,933	5,990	5,726	11,716
1970	317	4,233	4,550	5,416	1,190	6,606	5,733	5,423	11,156
1971	395	6,541	6,936	8,043	827	8,870	8,438	7,368	15,805
1972	535	5,729	6,264	9,039	618	9,657	9,574	6,347	15,921
1973	696	4,328	5,024	9,279	563	9,842	9,975	4,890	14,866
1974	1,174	3,179	4,353	4,147	608	4,756	5,321	3,787	9,109

* - Totals may not add due to rounding.

Source: St. Lawrence Seaway Authority and the St. Lawrence Seaway Development Corporation

TABLE 3.7

OVERSEAS CARGO, MONTREAL-LAKE ONTARIO SECTION,
ST. LAWRENCE SEAWAY, 1968 - 1974

(Percentages)

| | INBOUND (Upstream) | | OUTBOUND (Downstream) | | Grand Total | |
Year	Bulk	General	Bulk	General	Bulk	General
		COMBINED U.S. - CANADIAN				
1968	17	83	86	14	50	50
1969	23	77	78	22	54	46
1970	22	78	81	19	56	44
1971	13	87	91	9	57	43
1972	20	80	92	8	62	38
1973	25	75	93	7	68	32
1974	31	69	88	12	62	38
		CANADIAN				
1968	56	44	73	27	63	37
1969	55	45	76	24	63	37
1970	67	33	78	22	73	27
1971	48	52	90	10	73	27
1972	55	45	85	15	71	29
1973	64	36	85	15	74	26
1974	49	51	89	11	75	25
		U.S.				
1968	8	92	88	12	47	53
1969	11	89	79	21	47	53
1970	7	93	82	18	51	49
1971	6	94	91	9	53	47
1972	9	91	94	6	60	40
1973	14	86	94	6	67	33
1974	27	73	87	13	58	42

Source: Information presented in Table 3.6 converted to
percentages.

Outbound movements--exports from Canada and the United States--have exceeded inbound movements in most years. This imbalance is even more obvious when the division between bulk and general cargo movements for each year is examined. Inbound overseas traffic is dominated by general cargo, a high proportion of which consists of iron and steel products.

In 1971, 87 per cent of total inbound overseas traffic was classified as general cargo. Conversely, outbound traffic between the United States and Canada and overseas points is overwhelmingly bulk in nature. Though bulk traffic made up the largest percentage, 93 per cent, of total outbound overseas traffic in 1973, in no year between 1967 and 1974 has the proportion fallen below 80 per cent.

The pattern is different for United States traffic as contrasted with Canadian traffic. For Canada, total overseas Seaway traffic in both directions grew steadily until 1972, after which it steadily decreased.

While Canadian outbound traffic is consistently dominated by bulk movements, general cargo does not always dominate inbound. Nevertheless, general cargo movements inbound constitute a significantly greater percentage of total movements in that direction than in the case of outbound movements.

For the United States, the inbound traffic is heavily dominated by general cargo in substantial part consisting of iron and steel products. The outbound traffic is made up almost entirely of bulk movements. United States overseas traffic through the Seaway is less balanced directionally than is the Canadian traffic. However, even inbound overseas Seaway general cargo traffic to the United States has been decreasing.

United States and Canadian foreign trade through the Seaway is divided into broad commodity categories--Agricultural Products, Animal Products, Mine Products, Forest Products, and Manufactures and Miscellaneous--in Table 3.8. A sixth category, Package Freight, is insignificant in overseas traffic and does not appear on the table.

The commodities table gives insight into the characteristics of the foreign trade traffic through the Seaway between 1968 and 1974. That imports to the United States and Canada are heavily dominated by Manufactures and Miscellaneous is not surprising since this category includes iron and steel. Chapter VI of this report indicates that iron and steel products comprise a large percentage of United States imports through the Great Lakes-St. Lawrence Seaway System and are the most dominant of all commodities moved on that system.

50

TABLE 3.8

OVERSEAS TRAFFIC, MONTREAL-LAKE ONTARIO SECTION,
ST. LAWRENCE SEAWAY, 1968 - 1974

(thousands of short tons)

Year	From Overseas To			To Overseas From		
	Canada	U.S.	Total*	Canada	U.S.	Total*
AGRICULTURAL PRODUCTS						
1968	32	38	70	758	4,473	5,231
1969	23	32	55	492	3,567	4,059
1970	17	12	30	828	3,734	4,562
1971	19	40	59	1,557	6,896	8,454
1972	28	39	66	1,660	7,835	9,495
1973	35	18	53	1,075	7,812	8,887
1974	11	2	13	1,241	3,447	4,689
ANIMAL PRODUCTS						
1968	8	8	17	32	314	346
1969	8	4	12	27	309	336
1970	5	5	10	21	336	357
1971	7	30	38	23	368	391
1972	5	8	12	29	287	316
1973	3	6	9	9	269	278
1974	2	3	5	16	234	250
MINE PRODUCTS						
1968	204	224	429	16	66	82
1969	281	245	526	106	122	228
1970	250	196	446	88	229	316
1971	263	215	478	89	263	352
1972	328	206	534	89	165	254
1973	264	287	551	34	99	133
1974	145	8 67	1,012	120	270	390
FOREST PRODUCTS						
1968	35	44	79	8	33	42
1969	43	60	103	9	38	47
1970	21	60	82	11	37	48
1971	41	85	126	10	38	48
1972	63	79	142	17	40	57
1973	33	25	58	21	43	64
1974	21	22	44	20	36	56

TABLE 3.8 (Continued)

OVERSEAS TRAFFIC, MONTREAL-LAKE ONTARIO SECTION
ST. LAWRENCE SEAWAY, 1968 - 1974

(thousands of short tons)

Year	From Overseas To			To Overseas From		
	Canada	U.S.	Total*	Canada	U.S.	Total*
MANUFACTURES AND MISCELLANEOUS						
1968	1,274	6,098	7,372	380	1,192	1,572
1969	1,455	4,441	5,896	565	2,897	3,462
1970	1,167	4,276	5,443	742	2,270	3,012
1971	1,085	6,565	7,650	363	1,304	1,667
1972	1,694	5,932	7,629	602	1,330	1,932
1973	1,182	4,678	5,860	383	1,620	2,003
1974	730	3,458	4,188	210	768	978
MANUFACTURES AND MISCELLANEOUS LESS IRON AND STEEL**						
1968	1,047	985	2,032	287	683	970
1969	1,181	1,036	2,217	298	910	1,208
1970	1,039	830	1,869	315	800	1,115
1971	741	1,068	1,809	291	853	1,144
1972	1,210	1,090	2,300	389	736	1,125
1973	879	983	1,862	200	524	724
1974	445	608	1,053	138	265	403

* - Totals may not add due to rounding.

** - The specific items deleted are pig iron; iron and steel bars,
     rods or slabs; iron and steel nails or wire; manufactured iron
     and steel; and scrap iron and steel.

Source: St. Lawrence Seaway Authority and the St. Lawrence
         Seaway Development Corporation. Traffic Report of
         the St. Lawrence Seaway. Annual Report. 1968-1974.

The dominance of iron and steel can be easily inferred from the final section of Table 3.8. Almost every year shows this traffic as significant in both directions, though the impact is strongest in overseas shipments to the United States. By comparison, the traffic in other commodities seems insignificant.

Since container cargo consists primarily of general cargo items, Table 3.9 summarizes the past trends in total general cargo levels and compares them to the same figures from which iron and steel have been excluded. Chapter VII of this study contains projections that have been made for future levels of general cargo, and it presents four new projections based on differing assumptions. Of the four projections made for general cargo, only the one which weighs the immediate past most heavily shows decreasing levels of total general cargo through 1985. Since the projections indicate increasing tonnage of iron and steel in all cases, this loss must be attributed to decreasing tonnages of other general cargo commodities. These projections and their methodologies are shown in Table 3.10. The differences in these projections emphasize the sensitivity of projections to the underlying assumptions and methods. Nevertheless, the relatively low level of even the highest projections for general cargo indicates a weak probability for large volume container movements on the Lakes.

B. Physical, Economic, and Institutional Limitations to Overseas Container Traffic on the Great Lakes-St. Lawrence Seaway System

The Great Lakes-St. Lawrence Seaway System is handicapped as a competitor for overseas movements of containerized general cargo. Some impediments are economic in nature, several are related to the physical characteristics of the system, and others involve institutional constraints.

The benefits of containerizing cargo are largely due to economies of scale. The ability to move efficiently large amounts of cargo in a single unit decreases the costs per ton. Unfortunately, the physical limitations of the Seaway System substantially eliminate the realization of these economies in the movement of overseas containerized general cargo through the System.

1. Physical Limitations

Vessels entering the Great Lakes through the St. Lawrence Seaway are limited in size to the dimensions permitted by the locks of the Seaway. The maximum dimensions of vessels is 730 foot length, 75 foot beam and 25.75 foot draft. The larger container vessels, then, are effectively locked out of the Great Lakes.

53

TABLE 3.9

GENERAL CARGO, MONTREAL-LAKE ONTARIO SECTION,
ST. LAWRENCE SEAWAY, 1968 - 1974

(Thousands of short tons)

Year	Total*	Iron and Steel**	Total Less Iron and Steel
1968	8,003	5,475	2,528
1969	7,055	4,471	2,583
1970	6,547	4,337	2,110
1971	8,582	6,196	2,386
1972	7,846	5,734	2,112
1973	5,825	4,358	1,468
1974	4,522	3,604	918

* - Totals may not add due to rounding.

** - The specific commodities included here are Iron and Steel bars,
rod, and slabs; Iron and Steel nails and wire; and Manufactured
Iron and Steel.

Source: Port of Montreal Authority, Highlights of the Economic
Impact of the Port of Montreal, (Montreal: Port of
Montreal Authority, 1974).

TABLE 3.10

PROJECTIONS OF DIRECT OVERSEAS GENERAL CARGO TRAFFIC ON
THE ST. LAWRENCE SEAWAY, 1975-1985

(Thousands of Short Tons)

	1975	1980	1985
General Cargo			
1. Unweighted trend	8,222	10,087	11,951
Weight of immediate past:			
2. Slightly Stronger:	6,928	7,784	8,641
3. Strong:	6,972	7,783	8,593
4. Very Strong:	5,783	5,396	5,009
General Cargo/ Iron and Steel			
1. Unweighted trend	6,174	8,012	9,851
Weight of immediate past:			
2. Slightly Stronger:	4,986	5,838	6,690
3. Strong:	5,440	6,520	7,601
4. Very Strong:	4,736	5,100	5,465
General Cargo/ Without Iron and Steel			
1. Unweighted trend	2,047	2,073	2,100
Weight of immediate past:			
2. Slightly Stronger:	1,942	1,946	1,951
3. Strong:	1,532	1,262	992
4. Very Strong:	1,047	296	0

NOTE: Projection #1 was formulated using regression analysis
of the historical tonnage.

Projections #2, 3 and 4 were formulated using an ex-
ponentially weighted average trend of historical tonnage.

#2 - responds slowly and smoothly to variation in
historical tonnage. It assumes that variations
are primarily random.

#3 - responds more rapidly and less smoothly than #2.
It assumes that tonnage variation represents less
random action and more shifts in demand than #2.

#4 - responds more rapidly and less smoothly than #3.
It assumes less random action and more demand shifts
than #3.

Source: Chapter VII of this report.

The seasonality of the Seaway system is a physical limitation on its traffic capacity. A board of government and quasi-government agencies, the Winter Navigation Board, has undertaken a study on the feasibility of a year-round shipping season on the Great Lakes-St. Lawrence Seaway System. Though the study demonstrates that such a season on the Lakes proper is probably practicable, the maximum season for the Seaway seems to be limited to 11 months because of the need for annual maintenance of the locks.[11] This is discussed further in Chapter IV.

Even if efficient container vessels were able to transit the Seaway on a year-round basis, the time needed to pass through the waterway and to gather sufficient cargo to justify the voyage would probably make such movement uneconomical. Overseas general cargo traffic on the Seaway has declined precipitously since 1972, but with a slight revival in 1975.

The number of twenty-foot equivalent container units (T.E.U.) handled by various Lake and Seaway ports is shown in Table 3.11. In contrast to the large numbers of containers handled by some East, West and Gulf ports, most Lake ports handled very few, if any, containers. By comparison, Montreal, not usually considered to be a Lake port, handled 89.5 thousand T.E.U.s in 1972 and 117 thousand in 1973. The port of New York, which competes with the Seaway for traffic of the Great Lakes region, moved 582.7 thousand T.E.U.s in 1972 and 899.4 thousand in 1973.

2. Economic Limitations

Given the relatively small amount of general cargo traffic moving through the Lake ports, it remains questionable whether these ports can better their competitive position relative to the coastal ports for this traffic. To do so would imply promoting some type of advantage. The relative fuel economy of water carriage is advantageous, but it is questionable whether it is sufficiently so to outweigh the much greater voyage time through the Seaway.[12] Unless services which move containerized general cargo overseas through the Seaway can develop other attractions, shippers in the Great Lakes region will continue to be drawn to coastal ports.

3. Institutional Limitations

Among the institutional constraints upon the System in terms of the overseas traffic of the United States, and especially for general cargo, which is particularly susceptible to containerization, have been (1) lack of subsidies for U.S.-flag shipping on this route in competition with alternative routes, and (2) cargo preference and flag discrimination laws of the United States.

Under the Merchant Marine Act of 1936, construction differential subsidies (CDS) and operating differential sub-

TABLE 3.11

NUMBER OF CONTAINERS SHIPPED THROUGH
GREAT LAKES - ST. LAWRENCE SEAWAY PORTS

1972 - 1973

(Twenty-foot Equivalent Units)

	1972	1973
Chicago	12,577	11,904
Cleveland-Cuyahoga County	3,100	4,820
Duluth	N.A.	250
Green Bay	N.A.	100
Milwaukee	1,713	** 3,083
Toledo	764	800
Toronto	15,496	**10,051

** Updated Figures

NOTE: Where Flexi-Van and Container News differed, the
        Container News figure, having a later publication
        date, has been used.

Source: Flexi-Van Corp., "The State of Containers,
         Part I: Containerized Movements Through World
         Ports," Intermodal World (San Francisco and New
         York: July 1974); and "World Container Ports,"
         Container News, December 1974.

sidies (ODS) were provided under certain conditions for
U.S.-flag liner operators on so-called "essential trade
routes," in order partially to overcome the higher costs of
American, as contrasted with foreign, construction and
operation. Several Great Lakes-overseas routes were so
designated. In addition, construction mortgage guarantees
and construction reserve funds were provided by the Act of
1936. Several U.S.-flag operators entered the Great Lakes-
overseas trades with the opening of the Seaway in 1959, but
by 1970 the last of these terminated. The Act of 1970 provided additional incentives for U.S.-flag participation in the
Great Lakes-overseas trades. Among them was the extension
of the construction reserve provisions to the Great Lakes.
Of equal or greater significance was, and is, the cargo
preference legislation which requires that half of the total
movement of certain cargoes, including government and
foreign-aid cargoes under Public Law 480, must be shipped in
U.S.-flag vessels. The paucity of U.S.-flag services between
the Great Lakes and overseas constitutes a severe handicap,
particularly since many of these shipments originate in the
Great Lakes Region. These include not only agricultural
produce but also a wide variety of capital goods, such as
machinery. Much of this cargo is susceptible to containerization.

C. Prospects for Increased Container Traffic

While it is evident that general cargo, including container
traffic, is extremely unlikely to constitute a significant
proportion of the total Seaway traffic, there are some prospects for arresting and reversing the recent decline in such
traffic. Among these prospects are: (1) re-entry of
U.S.-flag vessels into the Great Lakes-overseas general cargo
liner trades, and (2) provision in one or two Great Lakes
ports of specialized container terminal facilities.

After an interval of half a decade, U.S.-flag liner
service between the Great Lakes and overseas resumed on a
small scale with the advent of the Lykes Lines into the Great
Lakes-Mediterranean and Black Sea trade route, with monthly
sailings scheduled during the 1975 season. Under a specific
contract with the Soviet Union, the Lykes vessels are
transporting "heavy lift" capital equipment as their base
cargo. These vessels also offer the opportunity for shipment of a certain amount of general cargo, including containerized cargo on this trade route. Shortly after this service
was announced, Lykes was granted an operating differential
subsidy for it. In mid-1975, it was announced that a
second U.S.-flag cargo liner operator, Farrell Lines, would
enter the Seaway trade route, serving African ports. Also,
early in 1975, a prospective Chicago-based operator announced
tentative plans for the construction of up to three vessels,
approximating the maximum Seaway size limits. These vessels
would emphasize containers but be sufficiently versatile to
handle bulk, breakbulk, roll-on/roll-off and liquid cargoes.

As of late summer 1975, determination of the economic feasibility of such vessels had not been made.

The availability of these new and prospective U.S.-flag services will, it is hoped, reduce the disadvantage of the Great Lakes Region in importing and exporting certain cargoes which heretofore have moved through coastal ports as a combined result of cargo preference laws and the lack of U.S.-flag services.

A recently published inventory of world container ports lists seven Great Lakes ports: Chicago, Cleveland, Duluth, Green Bay, Milwaukee, Toledo and Toronto.[13] As yet, there is no full container terminal on the Great Lakes, though the Seaway Port Authority of Duluth is in the process of constructing one with approximately eight acres of land adjacent to it for the marshalling of containers. The crane will theoretically be capable of handling 25 containers per hour.

Some agencies in Chicago, which has a number of wharves adaptable to containers, attribute the port's decline in overseas trade in part to its lack of a full container terminal. A recent report by the Commission for Economic Development for the State of Illinois concluded that the Chicago Port District is losing business and revenue as Illinois firms choose to ship through out-of-state ports with container facilities.[14]

Both Green Bay and Milwaukee are capable of handling containers and roll-on/roll-off traffic, although they do not have specialized facilities for either. Milwaukee has considered the construction of a major container terminal, the land for which is owned by the Harbor Commission for the City of Milwaukee, but its actual construction seems highly doubtful. A consultant has evaluated present facilities there as adequate for future needs.[15] This conclusion was also reached by the U.S. Army Corps of Engineers, which recommended that the dredging necessary for this proposed terminal not be done.[16]

Many of the ports on the Great Lakes have mobile equipment which is capable of handling containers, but less efficiently so than specialized container cranes. In addition, Windsor, Ontario, and Detroit, Michigan, plan to move into the container trade by developing facilities for the transshipment of containers from eastern Canada. The containers will be shipped to and from Windsor by Canadian railroad.[17] Car ferries across the Detroit River make the Detroit terminal accessible to the Canadian railroads at Windsor.

The Impact of Container Traffic on the
Great Lakes Economic Region

If establishment of additional overseas container services through the St. Lawrence Seaway proves feasible, it would benefit the Great Lakes Region in two ways: (1) if they were capable of reducing the total costs of shipping containers to and from the region, such services would reduce transportation costs for mid-American foreign commerce and extend its marketing possibilities; and (2) they would generate increased activity at the Lake ports.

Transportation costs will be reduced only if the costs of these services are lower than those of competing modes, or mode mixes, or if the added competition of the Seaway keeps other modes from increasing rates. The costs of transportation include both direct money costs and time or inventory costs. Because of the time involved in calling at several Lake ports and in moving through the Seaway, it is unlikely that either a container feeder service or combination vessels could significantly reduce overseas transit times. Whether or not any reduction in the money costs of moving goods would occur depends partially on institutional factors and on future fuel prices. When the cost of transporting a good drops, the full purchase price at the point of final sale may be lower. With a lower price, all other things being equal, more of the product can be expected to be purchased. Likewise, with lower transportation costs, it may be possible to ship a product farther and still maintain a competitive price at destination. In such a case, the range of marketing possibilities open to the producer will be increased, providing that customs duties and other constraints are not increased proportionately.

The second set of benefits would accrue to the ports at which containers were loaded. Such traffic benefits the local community through direct purchases by the ports handling the cargo. These purchases include wages, salaries, supplies and services necessary for the construction and operation of the container facilities. Direct expenditures of the port generate further local income as the individuals and firms which the port employs do their own purchasing. Government income is generated by any taxes paid by the port, including those on wages, salaries and profits as well as indirect business taxes.

The actual value of these impacts will vary among ports, which have different employment requirements, as in minimum work crew size. But there is evidence that the relative impacts of different types of cargo will be similar. The Port of Montreal estimates of per ton impact of different types of cargo are presented in Table 3.12.[18] These estimates are surprisingly similar to those cited by Schenker et al., "$5.00 and $24.00 per ton as an average-direct income per ton

TABLE 3.12

IMPACT PER TON OF CARGO THROUGH THE PORT OF MONTREAL

Category	Direct	Indirect	Total
General Cargo, Non-Containerized	$29.50	$15.22	$44.72
General Cargo, Containerized	$13.83	$ 7.13	$20.96
Dry Bulk	$ 3.40	$ 1.40	$ 5.20
Liquid Bulk	$ 1.42	$ .73	$ 2.15

Source: Port of Montreal Authority, Highlights of the Economic Impact of the Port of Montreal, 1974.

from servicing bulk and general cargo respectively."[19]
A recent study of the Port of Baltimore lends further support
to the observed relationship between cargo types. This
study estimates that the total direct impact of container
cargo is $21.65 per ton as opposed to an estimated impact
for all general cargo of $55.91 per ton and for bulk cargo
of $11.29 per ton.[20]

The difference between the impacts created by containerized and non-containerized general cargo is extremely important for Lake port communities. In weighing the pay-offs of
investment undertaken for the purpose of attracting containerized cargo to a port, the appropriate impact is that associated
with containerized general cargo, not breakbulk cargo, unless
the container services create enough additional traffic to
draw more breakbulk cargo to the port. Differences in impact
may be crucial when, for instance, a given expenditure to
attract dry bulk cargo can be expected to attract five times
the tonnage if directed instead at containerized general
cargo.

Summary and Conclusions

The benefits from the containerization of breakbulk
general cargo are derived from standardization of packaging
and the use of capital intensive technology to handle the
units. Indeed, a large number of containers can be moved
in virtually a fraction of the time required to handle the
same amount of cargo by conventional labor intensive methods.

The volume of container traffic moved directly between
the Great Lakes and overseas through the St. Lawrence Seaway
has been small relative to the movements through coastal
ports. This situation will persist, given the character of
Seaway general cargo traffic and the Seaway's physical
characteristics. Relatively little general cargo moves
through the Seaway to and from overseas ports, and the
direction of this cargo, especially from United States Great
Lakes ports, is virtually one way. In general, the outbound
cargoes through the Seaway are bulk cargoes. This imbalance
implies the unlikelihood of a large number of containers
making a round trip through the Seaway to and from an overseas point, fully loaded. Movements of empty containers
incur costs with no revenues, reducing the economies of
containers.

The physical characteristics of the Seaway dictate
that ocean-going vessels which transit the waterway be
relatively small. These same characteristics make transit
times lengthy. These two constraints as well as the seem-
ingly unavoidable necessity for closing the Seaway for at
least a short time during the winter present an unattractive
economic picture. Though a container service is not ruled
out by these problems, any such service could be seriously
hampered.

Footnotes

[1]K. M. Johnson and H. C. Garnett, The Economics of Container-
zation (London: George Allen & Unwin, Ltd., 1971), p. 71.

[2]Flexi-Van, "The State of Containerization, Part I: Container
ovements Through World Ports," a special report for Intermodal
orld, July, 1974.

[3]Idem. "The State of Containerization, Part II: Containerized
nd Containerizable Cargo," a special report for Intermodal World,
974, p. B-3.

[4]Ibid.

[5]Eric Schenker, The Effects of Containerization on Great Lakes
orts (Milwaukee: The University of Wisconsin-Milwaukee, Center for
reat Lakes Studies, May, 1973), p. 40.

[6]For further information, see Chapter VI of this report.

[7]Litton Systems, Inc., Oceanborne Shipping: Demand and Techno-
ogy Forecasts, June, 1968, pp. 6-19 and 6-21, Tables 6.5 and 6.6;
nd Manalytics, Inc.,Forecast of World Trade in Containerizable
ommodities: 1975 and 1980, June, 1971, pp. 2-5, Tables 1 and 2.

[8]Johnson and Garnett, pp. 49-50.

[9]Ibid.

[10]Panel on Future Port Requirements of the United States, Port
evelopment in the United States (Washington, D.C.: National Academy
f Sciences, August, 1975), p. 2-15.

[11]For a full discussion of the extension of the shipping season,
ee Chapter IV of the report.

[12]The impact of the current energy situation on the Great Lakes-
t. Lawrence Seaway System is treated in Chapter V of this report.

[13]"World Container Ports," Container News (December, 1974). All
urther descriptions of port container facilities not specifically
ootnoted are from this source.

[14] Commission for Economic Development, State of Illinois.

[15] James A. Buckley, Inc., Port of Milwaukee: Evaluation of Potential Container Cargo 1980 and 1990 (Milwaukee: Department of City Development, 1974).

[16] U.S. Army, Board of Engineers for Rivers and Harbors, "Review Report on Milwaukee Harbor, Wisconsin" (Fort Belvoir, Virginia: October 9, 1974).

[17] "Detroit Harbor Terminals Acquired by SEMIT; New Facility Set for Windsor," Traffic World (December 23, 1974).

[18] Port of Montreal Authority, Highlights of the Economic Impact of the Port of Montreal (n.p. [1974]), p. 28.

[19] Eric Schenker, et. al., "An Estimation of the Quantitative Impact of the St. Lawrence Seaway on the Hinterland's Economy," Proceedings of the Thirteenth Conference on Great Lakes Research (Buffalo, New York: 1970).

[20] S. Hille, C. Taff, A. Thieblat, and M. McGee, The Economic Impact of the Port of Baltimore on Maryland: 1973 (College Park, Maryland: Division of Transportation, Business and Public Policy, University of Maryland, April, 1975), pp. 61, 88.

Bibliography

Battelle Memorial Institute. Summary Report: Market Analysis on Container Suitable International Traffic at the Port of Cleveland. Columbus: Battelle Memorial Institute, 1967.

Brasch, John J., and Walter, C. K. Intermodal Container Transportation and Distribution. Lincoln, Nebraska: Omaha-Council Bluffs Metropolitan Area Planning Agency, 1974.

Hille, Stanley J., Taff, Charles A., Thieblat, Armand J., and McGee, Michael P. The Economic Impact of the Port of Baltimore on Maryland: 1973. College Park, Maryland: Division of Transportation, Business and Public Policy, University of Maryland, 1975.

Johnson, K. M., and Garnett, H. C. The Economics of Containerization. London: George Allen & Unwin, Ltd., 1971.

McCaul, J. R., and Associates. Market Environment and Container System Productivity. Lings Point, New York: National Maritime Research Center, 1974.

Panel on Future Port Requirements of the United States. Port Development in the United States. Washington, D.C.: National Academy of Sciences, 1975.

Port of Monroe. Economic Development Study. Monroe, Michigan: Port of Monroe, 1975.

Port of Montreal Authority. Highlights of the Economic Impact of the Port of Montreal. Port of Montreal Authority, 1974.

Port of New York Authority. Container Shipping: Full Ahead. New York: Port of New York Authority, 1967.

Reymond, B. D., and Fessler, E. V. Fourth Coast-Seaway Systems Requirements Analysis, Volume II. Washington, D.C.: Transportation Systems Center, 1972.

Schenker, Eric, et. al. The Effects of Containerization on Great Lakes Ports. Milwaukee, Wisconsin: University of Wisconsin-Milwaukee, Center for Great Lakes Studies, 1968, updated 1973.

_____, "An Estimation of the Quantitative Impact of the St. Lawrence Seaway on the Hinterland's Economy." Proceedings of the Thirteenth Conference of Great Lakes Research, Buffalo, New York: 1970.

U.S. Department of Commerce, Maritime Administration. The Impact of Containerization on the U.S. Economy, Volumes I and II. San Francisco: Matson Research Corporation, 1970.

U.S. Department of Transportation. Great Lakes/St. Lawrence Seaway Feeder Systems: A Feasibility Study. San Francisco: Manalytics, Inc., 1972.

IV.

Great Lakes System

Shipping Season

Introduction

One of the most serious impediments to a realization of the full potential of the Great Lakes-St. Lawrence Seaway System is the seasonality of the System's operation. Being located in relatively northerly latitudes and in the interior of a continent, the Seaway System is subject to severe winter weather conditions. Ice formation and stormy winter weather close inter-lake and Seaway operations each year.

Although the individual lakes do not freeze over, ice usually covers substantial portions of them. Ice near the shores, especially in the northern lakes, affects harbor availability for vessel operation. Ice formations in the connecting channels between the individual lakes and in the St. Lawrence Seaway proper between Lake Ontario and Montreal have necessitated annual closure of operations at those critical points and areas for part of each winter. Recent annual opening and closing dates for various portions of the System are shown in Table 4.1.

During the closed season, shippers resort to alternative routes or modes of transportation or use materials stockpiled over the season of operation to meet winter requirements. Typically these alternatives are more costly and less energy efficient than the use of the Great Lakes-St. Lawrence Seaway System.

Problems of Extending the Seaway Season

As Table 4.1 indicates, not all parts of the Great Lakes-St. Lawrence Seaway System open and close at the same time. (Inter-Lake traffic generally has a slightly longer season than Seaway traffic.) Some of the Lake ports are open for internal Lake traffic year-round, although sometimes needing icebreaker assistance. The configuration, hydrology and meteorology of the Great Lakes System favor some ports and inhibit others.

A. Technical Problems Involved in Extending the Seaway Season

The technical problems of Seaway System extension center around the narrow connecting channels, the locks and the canals of the Lakes and Seaway. The channels most susceptible to winter freeze-over are: the St. Marys River connecting Lakes Superior and Huron; the Straits of Mackinac connecting Lakes Michigan and Huron; and the St. Clair and Detroit Rivers linking Lakes Huron and Erie. Figures 1.1 and 1.2 in Chapter I detail the physical structure of the System.

The locks at Sault Ste. Marie and in the Welland and St. Lawrence canal systems do not provide so difficult a technological problem as do the narrow channels. The locks can be maintained open for operation by certain proved methods such as steam heating. Because the St. Lawrence canal locks

TABLE 4.1

Opening and Closing Dates—Critical Points on the
Great Lakes-St. Lawrence Seaway System: 1958-1975

	St. Lawrence Canals		Welland Ship Canal		Sault Ste. Marie Locks		Strait of Mackinac	
	First passage	Last passage	First passage	Last passage	First passage	Last passage	First passage	Last passage
1958	April 14[1]	Dec. 19[1]	April 1	Dec. 18	April 17	Dec. 14	March 28	Dec. 17
1959	April 25	Dec. 3	April 6	Dec. 15	April 14	Dec. 21	April 4	Dec. 25
1960	April 18	Dec. 3	April 1	Dec. 15	April 7	Dec. 15	April 4	Dec. 18
1961	April 11	Nov. 30	April 1	Dec. 15	April 8	Dec. 17	March 20	Jan. 10, 1962
1962	April 23	Dec. 7	April 1	Dec. 15	April 7	Dec. 19	April 9	Dec. 29
1963	April 15	Dec. 13	April 7	Dec. 18	April 15	Dec. 20	April 15	Dec. 27
1964	April 8	Dec. 7	March 30	Dec. 15	April 1	Dec. 16	March 18	Dec. 22
1965	April 8	Dec. 17	April 1	Dec. 16	April 14	Dec. 18	March 25	Jan. 16, 1966
1966	April 1	Dec. 15	April 4	Dec. 15	April 1	Dec. 20	March 20	Jan. 12, 1967
1967	April 7	Dec. 15	April 1	Dec. 16	April 10	Dec. 30	March 30	Jan. 16, 1968
1968	April 18	Dec. 15	April 1	Dec. 22	April 2	Jan. 4, 1969	March 30	Jan. 4, 1969
1969	April 7	Dec. 15	April 1	Dec. 22	April 4	Jan. 11, 1970	March 21	Jan. 10, 1970
1970	April 4	Dec. 17	April 1	Dec. 30	April 1	Jan. 29, 1971	March 30	Jan. 30, 1971
1971	April 14	Dec. 18	April 1	Dec. 16	April 8	Feb. 1, 1972	March 26	Feb. 1, 1972
1972	April 12	Dec. 23	April 3	Dec. 16	April 10	Feb. 8, 1973	March 28	Feb. 8, 1973
1973	March 28	Dec. 22	March 27	Jan. 4, 1974	March 28	Feb. 7, 1974	March 19	Feb. 21, 1974
1974	March 26	Dec. 17	March 29	Jan. 17, 1975	April 12	*	March 26	*
1975	March 25	--	March 25	--	*	--	*	--

[1] Pre-Seaway Canal System
* No Closing

Sources: For St. Lawrence Canals and Welland Ship Canal 1958-1970: U.S. Army Corps of Engineers Survey Report on Great Lakes and St. Lawrence Seaway Navigation Season Extension, Detroit District, Dec. 1969. Other: Lake Carrier's Association, Annual Report, 1958 through 1974.

are not twinned, however, closing these locks for maintenance and repair limits the maximum possible season for overseas trade to 11 months. Twinning of the Sault Ste. Marie locks allows year-round extension, but incomplete twinning of the Welland Canal locks also limits Lake Ontario to an eleven-month season for inter-Lake traffic.

The greater problem is posed by the ice formation in the narrow connecting channels and in some of the harbors and entrance channels. Icebreakers can maintain open navigation lanes but continual passage through the lanes causes the edges of the tracks to thicken. These edges endanger vessels travelling in rough weather, as friction of the hulls against the edges of the ice can cause hull damage or stalling of vessels in the partially opened track.[1] Navigational aids, such as buoys, must be removed from the channels before ice formation. Without these aids and with the possibility that a strong wind could shift the ice lane, navigation becomes even more treacherous with the possibility of a vessel's running aground.

An air bubbler system has been tested and proved effective in limiting ice formation, therefore maintaining small segments of narrow channels open for navigation. Tested in portions of the St. Marys River and Duluth Harbor, a bubbler system is planned for installation in selected parts of the Detroit and St. Clair Rivers.[2] However, the system has been tested only in the mild winters of recent years. Its effectiveness in more severe winters and in larger channels is not known.

Related to the issue of the ice cover, especially in the connecting channels such as those of the St. Marys River, is the disturbance to the life of nearby communities. Part of the population depends upon ferries during the open season and upon cross-channel movement over the ice during the closed season. When the ice cover is broken to permit winter passage of the large vessels, alternative provisions must be made for cross-channel movement. This problem has not yet been satisfactorily solved.

B. Navigation Season Extension Demonstration Program

For many years, commercial shipping interests and industrial interests in the Great Lakes Region have sought to extend the season of open navigation into winter and to start earlier in spring. There was, however, no systematic approach to the problem.

In 1965, Congress authorized the U.S. Army Corps of Engineers to investigate the feasibility of extending the navigation season.[3] Ice navigation experience and ice modification techniques in other regions of the world, such as the Baltic,[4] were reviewed. It was concluded that winter operation in the Great Lakes-St. Lawrence System was physically possible. Accordingly, in 1970, Congress authorized a Winter

Navigation Program, a series of demonstration projects, the results of which were to be reported to Congress by July 30, 1974.[5] This deadline was later extended to December 31, 1976. A total appropriation of $9.5 million was authorized for the entire demonstration program.[6]

The Program consists of many inter-related component activities. These include gathering, collating, interpreting and transmitting information on ice conditions and effects, testing of winter navigation techniques, studying ice mechanics and engineering, investigating and demonstrating methods of winter navigation in the St. Lawrence Seaway without creating effects intolerable to other interests such as power generation, management of ice in channels, locks and harbors and evaluating the economic and environmental aspects of winter navigation.[7]

The 1974-75 winter saw the partial fruition of shipping season extension as portions of the locks at Sault Ste. Marie remained in operation throughout the entire winter. The success of the ice booms on the eastern segment of the Seaway System had enthusiasts discussing an eleven-month overseas shipping season.[8] Thus, during the winter of 1974-75, the Great Lakes above the Welland Ship Canal (Lakes Superior, Huron, Erie and Michigan) were open for navigation year-round for the first time, as some vessels of U.S. Steel operated throughout the entire winter. But because the winter was unusually mild, it remains to be demonstrated that all-year inter-Lake movements are practicable in more severe winters.

C.   Insurance Problems of Seaway Season Extension

Insurance premiums for Great Lakes vessels have three components: cargo insurance, hull insurance and protection and indemnity insurance. The last two are subject to increases if the vessel is operated beyond the normal navigation season. Premiums can increase as much as two times the daily charge on vessels that operate during the latter half of December and triple the daily charge if the vessel operates during the first week of January. Premiums increase five fold in the month of March, considered to be prior to the normal season opening.[9]

Tied closely to the issue of insurance is the age of the Great Lakes fleet. In 1972, only 46 of the 201 U.S.-flag vessels operating on the Great Lakes had been built after 1948.[10] A large segment of the Great Lakes fleet will not be able to operate during the extended season because in 1948 the ABS (American Bureau of Shipping) rules concerning steel chemistry were upgraded. Ships constructed under the old standards have a low toughness factor and, hence, are more susceptible to cracking in cold weather.[11]

The age of the Great Lakes fleet may not pose the problem that on first glance appears to exist because the fleet is undergoing a changeover to the 1,000 foot vessel with a

capacity of 57,500 tons.[12] Many of the vessels between 600
and 730 feet in length are to be or have recently been
lengthened. Moreover, conversion of the fleet to larger and
longer vessels reduces the number of trips required to fill
raw material needs; consequently, many of the older vessels
will be or have recently been retired. Such conversion will
eliminate the need for pre-1948 vessels. However, insurance
premiums will continue to increase seasonally until vessel
safety records during the extended season alter actuarial
probabilities.

A Great Lakes fleet, composed of larger vessels making
fewer trips, does present one problem for shipping season
extension. Many small vessels making frequent passage help
prevent thick ice cover formation in the navigation lanes.
With fewer trips by large bulk carriers, a thick ice cover
could form between passages and consequently hinder movement.

D. Labor Conditions During the Extended Season

The fact that the Great Lakes, and especially the St.
Lawrence Seaway System between tidewater at Montreal and the
upper end of the lock system at Sault Ste. Marie, are a chain,
any link of which can be interrupted, is especially critical
in relation to the extended season. Collapse of labor-
management relations at any point in the chain can and has
led to the closing of the entire system to overseas trade.

Stable labor-management relations are as important to
shipping season extension as is the engineering task of
maintaining navigation lanes ice-free. Guarantees of a ten
or eleven month shipping season are useless if the threat
exists that labor-management negotiations could collapse and
cause a walkout by or lockout of key personnel. Minimization
of turnaround times and elimination of any possible delays
are crucial in encouraging carriers to deploy their vessels
to the Great Lakes during the extended season. An extended
season would be fruitless with any likelihood that a vessel
may be trapped in the Great Lakes during the months that the
system is closed to overseas shipping.

It is felt by some labor leaders that a ten-month season
would be optimal for overseas trade. Extension to this
length would allow one more European round trip for general
cargo liners and would more efficiently utilize labor and
vessels without subjecting crews, both ship and dock, to
excessive cold and hazardous working conditions.[13]

E. Optimal Duration of Extended Season for Overseas Services

Season extension must be long enough to permit vessels
engaged in overseas trade to complete additional round trips
(pay loads). Proposals to extend the season several additional

weeks are of no use if round trips cannot be completed during the extension by vessels regularly engaged in overseas trade through the Seaway.* '

A general cargo vessel to or from Western Europe usually spends 24 to 30 days for a round trip between the Great Lakes and European ports. Of this time, only eight to ten days are actually spent in transit through the Lakes and Seaway.[14]

The Port of Milwaukee has maintained records of transit times for vessels engaged in overseas trade. During the 1970 shipping season, the average transit time from Milwaukee to the first port of call on Continental Europe was 21.3 days.[15] Transit times have not changed significantly since 1970. Table 4.2 contains a breakdown of average transit times from the Port of Milwaukee to various overseas destinations. Round-trip times were calculated with an assumed turnaround time of two days at each end of the voyage.[16] The two-day assumption may underestimate the turnaround time, given the fact that much of the general cargo shipped through the Great Lakes is breakbulk, not containerized. The calculated number of round trips for each shipping season assumes no time lost for repairs and work stoppages and a vessel speed in January equal to that in July. It was also assumed that a vessel within seven days of completing a round trip when a shipping season ended would alter its schedule at sea to complete the round trip.

Table 4.2 indicates that vessels sailing to six of the ten overseas destinations would have been able to include an additional round trip during a season extended to ten months. An eleven month shipping season would allow an additional round trip to the other four overseas destinations; in three instances, two additional round trips could have been completed.

In evaluating shipping season extension for overseas trade, the crucial question is how many additional round trips can be completed, not the absolute number of trips. The extension must be sufficient to allow a substantial number of vessels to complete additional round trips overseas.

Review of Previous Studies

Several studies of the benefits and costs of extending the open season on the Great Lakes and the St. Lawrence Seaway have been made.

---

*Note that this analysis does not apply to "Tramps," vessels not regularly scheduled but which carry cargo through the Seaway System.

Overseas Destination	Average Transit Time		April 1 – December 15 (259 Days)	April 1 – January 31 (306 Days)		April 1 – February 28 (334 Days)	
	One Way[1]	Round Trip[2]					
Continental Europe	21 Days	46 Days	5 Trips	+ 1	(6 Trips)	+ 1	(7 Trips)
United Kingdom	20 Days	44 Days	6* Trips	+ 1	(7 Trips)	--	(7 Trips)
Scandinavian Area	22 Days	48 Days	5 Trips	+ 1	(6 Trips)	+ 1*	(7* Trips)
Mediterranean Area	26 Days	56 Days	4 Trips	+ 1	(5 Trips)	+ 1	(6 Trips)
Caribbean Area	24 Days	52 Days	5 Trips	+ 1*	(6* Trips)	--	(6 Trips)
East Coast South America	38 Days	80 Days	3 Trips	--	(3 Trips)	+ 1	(4 Trips)
South & East Africa	41 Days	86 Days	3 Trips	--	(3 Trips)	+ 1*	(4 Trips)
Middle East, Arabian Gulf, Indian Ocean	52 Days	108 Days	2 Trips	--	(2 Trips)	+ 1	(3 Trips)
West Africa	29 Days	62 Days	4 Trips	+ 1*	(5 Trips)	--	(5 Trips)
Far East	56 Days	116 Days	2 Trips	--	(2 Trips)	+ 1*	(3 Trips)

Note: [1] Rounded to nearest full day.

[2] Round trip time was calculated as twice the one-way trip time plus two days turnaround time was added at each end of the journey.

*These values are rounded upward because it was felt that the round trip could be completed by making some adjustment on the ocean part of the voyage.

Source: Port of Milwaukee. "Transit Time Study on 228 Voyages From the Port of Milwaukee to the First Port of Call Overseas From April 19 to November 30, 1970" (Milwaukee: 1971) (mimeographed).

A. U.S. Coast Guard Study

One such study by the U.S. Coast Guard in 1968 concluded that it would be relatively inexpensive to extend the season up to two weeks in winter.[17] However, it cited factors requiring investigation.

Ice in the locks in the St. Lawrence Seaway, the Welland Canal locks and also in the channels connecting the five Great Lakes presents the major engineering problem. Also needing study are: (1) the design of an icebreaker barge-and-pusher combination capable of operating in river channels; (2) a means to divert ice from the hydroelectric power plants, while allowing navigation to continue and sufficient water to reach the plant intake; and (3) an aids to navigation system, either using fixed structures or electronic means which are both efficient and inexpensive.[18] According to the report, a major increase in the capacity of the St. Lawrence System depended on enlargement of the physical facilities, rather than on traffic control measures.

B. U.S. Corps of Engineers - 1969 Study

The U.S. Army Corps of Engineers in 1969 concluded that, at that time, no method was available to solve the primary problem of winter navigation on the Great Lakes: wind driven pack ice sometimes accumulated in thirty-foot windrows that would shift and block navigation lanes.[19]

The study further concluded that extensions of the Seaway season would be economically justified, but that conclusion was contingent upon the movement of general cargo in overseas trade through the entire Seaway System.

C. EBS Management Consultants

A 1969 report by EBS Management Consultants on Seaway System extension assumed that the technical problems of maintaining open navigation channels had been solved.[20] Accordingly, it concluded that extension of the shipping season would divert some traffic from the alternative distribution channels which handle this cargo when the System is closed.

Seaway System extension was considered economically viable, at least for an additional four weeks, but with certain possible constraints. Although a strict benefit-cost calculation in terms of cargo movement produced a ratio greater than one, various human factors also needed to be evaluated. Seamen and longshoremen may not wish to work during the extended season; consequently both shipboard and dockside labor productivity might fall considerably. Also mentioned was the probable increased cost of insurance for vessels operating during the extended season.

D. Center for Great Lakes Studies Special Report No. 15

Using a cost-benefit methodology, this study, which was released in 1972, concluded that a four-week extension was the "minimum necessary to generate significant transportation cost savings."[21] Discussion also included indirect or external benefits, such as increased competition between competing modes and more efficient utilization of port and Seaway facilities resulting from longer operation.

Determination of Costs and Benefits

A. Costs

Earlier studies calculated the costs and benefits of extension of the open season on the Great Lakes and the St. Lawrence Seaway for periods of two weeks, four weeks and six weeks. At that time, it was assumed that longer extensions were probably not technologically feasible. Results of the Winter Navigation Demonstration Program and the evidence of the 1974-75 winter season show that under mild winter conditions, a twelve-month shipping season is possible on the four Upper Great Lakes and an eleven-month season is probably feasible for the rest of the System.

Results of the Demonstration Program have considerably altered the cost aspects of such extension. In the previous studies, the Coast Guard's cost estimates generally had been considered the most detailed. However, the Coast Guard relied mainly upon icebreaker capability to keep the navigation lanes and channels open; results of the Demonstration Program indicated that the narrow channels and lanes can be maintained open through less costly methods such as air bubblers, supplemented by icebreakers.[22]

Cost estimates developed by the Bureau of Economic Analysis (BEA) of the U.S. Department of Commerce were based on the assumption that the Demonstration Program would be successful (Table 4.3). The cost estimates have been computed for season extension up to January 31 (six-weeks), February 28 (ten weeks) and year-round. These estimates were made according to October, 1973 prices.

Comparison of the BEA figures with the 1968 estimates developed by the Coast Guard emphasizes the different approaches to season extension. Table 4.4 contains the Coast Guard estimates. In spite of the five-year increase in prices between 1968 and 1973, the BEA estimates are considerably less than the Coast Guard's. Taking the only comparable time period for the extension (six weeks), the capital costs alone estimated at $358 million by the Coast Guard are more than $170 million greater than the total investment costs estimated by BEA.

TABLE 4.3

GREAT LAKES-ST. LAWRENCE SEAWAY SYSTEM TOTAL ANNUAL COSTS
OF NAVIGATION SEASON EXTENSION AT 5-5/8 % INTEREST RATE[1]

IMPROVEMENTS	TO 31 JAN.	TO 28 FEB.	YEAR-ROUND
Air Bubblers	$ 10,900,000	$ 10,900,000	$ 10,900,000
Bubbler-Flushers	180,000	180,000	180,000
Ice Control Devices	18,300,000	24,700,000	24,700,000
Assistance to Ferry Transportation	201,000	201,000	201,000
Powerplant Protection	182,000	182,000	182,000
Lock Modifications	10,100,000	11,600,000	11,600,000
Water Level Gauges & Warning System	144,000	144,000	144,000
Icebreaking Assistance	97,400,000	97,400,000	97,400,000
Additional Search & Rescue Capability	5,850,000	5,850,000	5,850,000
Ice Navigation Center	365,000	365,000	365,000
Aerial Ice Reconnaissance	12,800,000	12,800,000	12,800,000
Mooring Improvements	125,000	125,000	125,000
Oil Pollution Strike Force	4,380,000	4,380,000	4,380,000
Vessel Traffic System	909,000	909,000	909,000
Great Lakes Automated Traffic Information System	287,000	287,000	287,000
Navigation Aids	7,160,000	7,160,000	7,160,000
Precise Navigation System	8,250,000	8,250,000	8,250,000
Shore Structure Protection	467,000	467,000	467,000
TOTAL FIRST COSTS:	$178,000,000	$186,000,000	$186,000,000
Interest During Construction	5,500,000	5,500,000	5,500,000
TOTAL INVESTMENT COSTS:	$184,000,000	$192,000,000	$192,000,000
ANNUAL COSTS:			
Interest	$ 10,400,000	$ 10,800,000	$ 10,800,000
Amortization	718,000	749,000	749,000
Operation & Maintenance	5,710,000	7,090,000	9,060,000
TOTAL ANNUAL COSTS:	$ 16,828,000	$ 18,639,000	$ 20,609,000

NOTE: [1]Costs are for the U.S. portion of the Great Lakes-St. Lawrence Seaway System.

[2]For the year-round estimate, maintenace is required on Welland and St. Lawrence River Locks

Source: Regional Economic Analysis Division, Bureau of Economic Analysis, Social & Economics Statistics Administration, U.S. Department of Commerce, The Economic Effects of an Extension of the Great Lakes-St. Lawrence Shipping Season on General Cargo and Related Industries: A Summary Report, July 1974, Appendix I Section F, page I-F-10.

TABLE 4.4

SUMMARY OF ICEBREAKING COSTS AND CONSOLIDATED ITEMS
FOR SEASON EXPANSION OF PRESENT SYSTEM

(No Discount Rates)

Category	Two Weeks	Four Weeks	Six Weeks
pital	$246,000,000	$299,000,000	$358,000,000
nual	5,165,000	6,967,000	9,785,000
ds to Navigation	12,330,000	20,440,000	24,495,000
e Control Works	-	24,000,000	118,100,000
rt and Harbor Aids to Navigation	1,460,000	1,460,000	1,460,000
TOTAL	$264,955,000	$351,867,000	$511,840,000

urce: U.S. Coast Guard, Report of the Technical Subgroup (Submitted
to the Department of Transportation, St. Lawrence Seaway Task
Force, November 1968), p. 217, 231.

Because the estimates by BEA have been made in light of the Demonstration Program, they will be used as representative. Later in this Chapter, inflationary adjustments in the BEA cost estimates are made. Different assumptions on amortization and the time length of costs and benefits are also employed.

B. Benefits

Benefits from extension of the open season can be divided into two broad categories: primary and secondary.

Primary benefits are produced by cost savings which result from three conditions:

1. Cost savings arise because the shipping season extension allows shippers to send goods by water rather than by rail or motor carrier, whose rates are generally higher than water rates.

2. Cost savings occur because stockpiling is reduced. Thus handling, real estate and capital costs are reduced because season extension allows the needed bulk materials to be shipped year-round.

3. Cost savings arise from more efficient utilization of the fleet. Vessels can be used for longer periods each year with season extension, rather than being redeployed or sitting idle for part of the year.

Secondary benefits accrue to the region as the result of lower transportation costs. It is assumed in these studies that industries sensitive to changes in transportation costs will increase production as the lower transportation costs resulting from shipping season extension will permit expansion of their market area. Secondary benefits include:

1. Direct Benefits: an increase in purchases from those regional firms which supply the transportation cost-sensitive industries.

2. Indirect Benefits: additional purchases made by the supplying firms from other regional firms.

3. Induced Benefits: changes in regional income due to the increased economic activity, initially caused by the increased output of the transportation cost-sensitive industries.

Induced benefits from diverted cargo exist only when
the diversion of cargo from rail and motor carriers does not
reduce employment by those carriers more than it increases
employment in water transportation.

Table 4.5 shows the primary benefits generated by
shipping season extension as calculated by the Bureau of
Economic Analysis (BEA). With 1970 as a starting date, year-
round extension would have produced $68 million worth of
annual benefits by 1975 and $247 million by 2020. Benefits
derived from elimination of the stockpiling of certain bulk
commodities may actually be underestimated. The United States
Steel Corporation estimated that year-round shipping in
1974-75 and related reductions in stockpiling produced savings
in excess of $10 million.[23] For the five-year period ending
in 1975, the BEA estimated that annual cost savings related
to stockpiling for all users would be approximately $19
million.

Although secondary benefits have also been calculated by
BEA, they will not be presented here because of several considerations. The prime generator of secondary benefits is
general cargo. Each ton of general cargo generates between
$24 and $29 of direct income for the region.[24] However, the
quantity of general cargo shipped through the Great Lakes
and the St. Lawrence Seaway is declining. Also, an increasing
proportion is being containerized. The direct income effect
of a ton of containerized cargo has been estimated to be
$14.[25] Consequently, secondary benefits need to be recal-
culated.

Benefit-Cost Calculations for Season Extension

A. Previous Results

Two studies completed within the past four years have
investigated the extension of the Seaway shipping season using
a benefit-cost approach. One of them examined two-, four-
and six-week extensions of the shipping season, employing
interest rates of 5, 7, and 8 per cent, and amortization
periods of ten, fifteen and twenty-five years. This report
concluded:

> The four-week extension is the most consistently
> profitable. The six-week extension period is more
> profitable than the four-week extension, however,
> under the conditions of a twenty-five year capital
> amortization scheme and a 7 or 8 per cent interest
> rate. The two-week extension period's net present
> value shows it to be the least desirable of these
> three extension periods.[26]

As discussed earlier, the Winter Navigation Demonstration
Program has shown that it is technologically possible, under
mild weather conditions, to have a year-round navigation season
on the four Upper Great Lakes and possibly an eleven month

TABLE 4.5

TOTAL BENEFITS FOR GREAT LAKES-ST. LAWRENCE SEAWAY SYSTEM FROM SEASON EXTENSION[1] ($1,000)

YEAR	Total Tons (1,000)	Trans. Savings	Stockpiling Capital Cost	Stockpiling Real Estate	Handling	Vessel Utilization	Total Benefi
TOTAL BENEFITS FOR U.S. GREAT LAKES-ST. LAWRENCE SEAWAY SYSTEM THRU 31 JAN.[1]							
1975	15,564	14,183	13,040	3,297	2,723	7,038	40,28
1985	26,221	42,738	20,071	4,701	4,281	13,413	85,20
2005	37,457	63,218	28,723	6,420	6,199	14,531	119,09
2025	49,174	88,764	37,263	8,062	8,106	8,479	150,67
TOTAL BENEFITS FOR U.S. GREAT LAKES-ST. LAWRENCE SEAWAY SYSTEM THRU 28 FEB.[1]							
1975	22,639	20,630	18,968	4,796	3,961	10,238	58,59
1985	38,139	62,165	29,194	6,838	6,226	19,510	123,93
2005	54,483	91,953	41,779	9,338	9,017	21,136	173,22
2025	71,526	129,111	54,201	11,726	11,790	12,333	219,16
TOTAL BENEFITS FOR U.S. GREAT LAKES-ST. LAWRENCE SEAWAY SYSTEM YEAR-ROUND[2]							
1975	27,003	22,323	22,953	5,767	4,802	12,378	68,22
1985	45,211	66,094	35,342	8,230	7,548	23,610	140,82
2005	64,603	98,204	50,586	11,246	10,932	25,586	196,55
2025	84,796	138,385	65,638	14,129	14,295	14,933	247,38

NOTE: [1] Traffic on total Great Lakes-St. Lawrence Seaway System attributable to U.S. extended season program from 15 December through 31 January and 28 February.

[2] Period during which maintenance is required on Welland Canal and St. Lawrence River Locks.

SOURCE: Regional Economic Analysis Division, Bureau of Economic Analysis, Social & Economics Statistics Administration, U.S. Department of Commerce, The Economic Effects of an Extension of the Great Lakes-St. Lawrence Shipping Season on General Cargo and Related Industries: A Summary Report, July 1974, Appendix I, Section F, page I-F-13.

navigation season for the entire Seaway System. These results render the conclusions of the 1972 study obsolete for two reasons. The season extension periods were too short, and the cost figures (contained in Table 4.4) were those of the Coast Guard. They were much higher than the cost of the programs that proved to be initially successful in the Demonstration Program.

The Bureau of Economic Analysis (BEA), in accordance with the Demonstration Program, conducted a benefit-cost study for season extension to January 31, February 28 and year-round. Costs that were used are those listed in Table 4.3, and the benefits calculated are listed in Table 4.5. Only primary benefits were calculated: those benefits resulting from transportation cost savings, stockpiling savings and savings due to more efficient vessel utilization. Secondary benefits were not included. The benefits and costs were discounted at a 5-5/8 per cent interest rate for 50 years. Employing these assumptions, these benefit-cost ratios were obtained: 5.3 for the January 31 season extension, 6.9 for the February 28 season extension and 7.1 for year-round operation (Table 4.6).

Although at first glance, the results are very impressive, the structure of the benefits must be closely examined. The benefits due to transportation savings, according to the BEA study, range from one-third to over one-half of the benefits, depending on the year and the length of the extension. Transportation savings are obtained primarily from overseas general cargo and grain traffic. General cargo traffic has declined since 1971.

Part of the decline in general cargo tonnage resulted from accidents, strikes on the Seaway and the closing of the Welland Ship Canal for two weeks in 1974. Furthermore, the many bottlenecks experienced in 1974 may have discouraged shippers and operators initially intending to use the Seaway for general cargo. It is primarily the changing nature of transportation technology that has made the Seaway less desirable to shippers of general cargo (see Chapters II and III). Two major factors affecting general cargo movement are containerization and the increased sensitivity to time as well as to price.

Preliminary figures from the Demonstration Program indicate that extension of the season will not necessarily return general cargo to the Seaway. Figures from December 16, 1973 through March 1974 show that 10.6 million tons of cargo originated in the Great Lakes during this period. At most, 4 per cent of the tonnage could be classified as general cargo, and only 2 per cent of all cargo was overseas traffic. Iron ore, coal and stone accounted for 73 per cent of the tonnage moved.[27]

Before the BEA results are widely accepted, further study must be conducted to determine whether general cargo would be shipped during the extended season and whether such

TABLE 4.6

TOTAL AND AVERAGE BENEFITS AND COSTS
FOR SEASON EXTENSION

| | Season Extension to: | | |
	31 January	28 February	Year-Round[1]
TRAFFIC (in 1,000 tons)			
Total Traffic			
1975	15,564	22,639	27,003
2025	49,174	71,526	84,796
BENEFITS (in $1,000)			
Total Benefits			
1975	40,283	58,593	68,223
2025	150,674	219,162	247,381
Average Annual Benefits @ 5-5/8 per cent	89,723	129,051	146,639
COSTS (in $1,000)			
Total Initial Investment	184,000	192,000	192,000
ANNUAL COSTS (@ 5-5/8%)			
Interest & Amortization	11,120	11,500	11,500
Operations & Maintenance	5,710	7,090	9,060
TOTAL	16,800	18,600	20,600
BENEFIT-COST RATIO			
Benefit-Cost Ratio (@5-5/8%)	5.3	6.9	7.1

NOTE: [1]Period during which maintenance is required on Welland
and St. Lawrence River locks.

Source: Regional Economic Analysis Division, Bureau of Economic
Analysis, Social & Economics Statistics Administration,
U.S. Department of Commerce, The Economic Effects of an
Extension of the Great Lakes-St. Lawrence Shipping Season
on General Cargo and Related Industries: A Summary Report,
July 1974, Appendix I, Section F, page I-F-16.

extension would induce shippers to send general cargo via the Seaway System during the rest of the year.

The cost estimating procedure of BEA should also be examined more closely. A time horizon of 50 years and discount rate of 5-5/8 per cent, although required by law, may be too long and too low in view of the rapidly changing technology of the shipping industry and the general economic uncertainty. Shorter amortization periods and higher discount rates would take account of the risk and uncertainty.

B.   Benefit-Cost Calculations

Annual benefits were interpolated from BEA figures for primary benefits (Table 4.5). These benefits were then discounted by two alternative rates of interest, 7 and 8 per cent, in order to obtain the present value (P.V.) of the future stream of benefits. A time horizon of ten years was adopted. The formula is specified as:

$$B = \sum_{i=1}^{n} b_i \bigg/ (1 + r)^i$$

where B = Present Value of future stream of benefits

b = annual benefit

i = time period

r = discount rate

n = time horizon

For a ten-year period, benefits were calculated as $407,392,000 at 7 per cent and $386,947,000 at 8 per cent, based on season extension to January 31. For extension to February 28, the corresponding benefits are $592,573,000 and $562,837,000. Year-round extension produced $680,325,000 of benefits discounted at 7 per cent and $646,307,000 at 8 per cent. Table 4.7 shows the calculated benefits.

Cost calculations were also made using different assumptions. Initially, the BEA cost estimates were maintained, but the initial investment was assumed to be amortized over ten years. The interest rate was maintained at 5-5/8 per cent, but all annual costs were discounted at 7 per cent and 8 per cent. Table 4.8 shows the resulting breakdown.

The present value of the future cost stream was calculated according to the formula:

TABLE 4.7

PRESENT VALUE OF BENEFITS AND COSTS FOR TEN-YEAR TIME SPAN
($1,000)

LENGTH OF SEASON EXTENSION	Discount Rate (Per Cent)	1/10 Amorti Per Year
January 31 Extension		
Present Value of discounted Future Benefits	@ 7	407,392
	@ 8	386,947
Present Value of discounted Future Costs (BEA)	@ 7	252,360
	@ 8	231,540
Present Value of discounted Future Costs (Indexed)	@ 7	308,305
	@ 8	294,542
February 28 Extension		
Present Value of discounted Future Benefits	@ 7	592,573
	@ 8	562,837
Present Value of discounted Future Costs (BEA)	@ 7	260,478
	@ 8	247,852
Present Value of discounted Future Costs (Indexed)	@ 7	330,077
	@ 8	315,342
Year-Round Extension		
Present Value of discounted Future Benefits	@ 7	680,325
	@ 8	646,307
Present Value of discounted Future Costs (BEA)	@ 7	274,312
	@ 8	262,068
Present Value of discounted Future Costs (Indexed)	@ 7	345,526
	@ 8	330,102

TABLE 4.8

ANNUAL COSTS FOR TEN YEARS ACCORDING
TO LENGTH OF SEASON EXTENSION

| | Costs ($1,000) | |
	BEA	BEA Adjusted for Inflation
January 31 Extension		
Total Investment Costs	$184,000	$241,000
Interest	10,400	13,500
Amortization	18,400	24,100
Operation and Maintenance	5,710	6,300
Total Annual Costs	34,510	43,900
February 28 Extension		
Total Investment Costs	192,000	251,000
Interest	10,800	14,100
Amortization	19,200	25,100
Operation and Maintenance	7,090	7,800
Total Annual Costs	37,090	47,000
Year-Round Extension		
Total Investment Costs	192,000	251,000
Interest	10,800	14,100
Amortization	19,200	25,100
Operation and Maintenance	9,060	10,000
Total Annual Costs	39,060	49,200

Source: Regional Economic Analysis Division, Bureau of
Economic Analysis, Social & Economics Statistics
Administration, U.S. Department of Commerce, The
Economic Effects of an Extension of the Great Lakes-
St. Lawrence Shipping Season on General Cargo and
Related Industries: A Summary Report, July 1974,
Appendix I, Section F, page I-F-10; and author's
calculations.

$$C = \sum_{i=1}^{n} c_i \bigg/ (1 + r)^i$$

where C = Present Value of future cost stream

c = total annual costs

i = time period

r = discount rate

n = time horizon

Results of the calculations produced present values of the future costs at $252,360,000 and $231,540,000 for 7 and 8 per cent respectively, for January 31 extension. For February 28 extension, the present value of future costs increased only slightly, to $260,478,000 and $247,852,000, respectively. For year-round extension, the figures were $274,312,000 and $262,068,000. (Table 4.7).

Benefit-cost ratios under the ten-year time horizon and 7 per cent discount rate were 1.6 for January 31 extension, 2.3 for February 28 season extension, and 2.5 for a year-round shipping season. At a discount rate of 8 per cent, the benefit-cost ratio for January 31 extension was 1.7, for February 28, 2.3, and 2.8 for year-round (Table 4.9).

Another series of benefit-cost ratios, incorporating the inflation of late 1973 and 1974, was calculated. Inflation increased the wholesale construction materials index 31.2 points and the unit labor cost index 10.1 points.[28] To reflect this inflation, the BEA investment costs were indexed to the wholesale construction materials index, and operation and maintenance costs to the unit labor index. Benefits were not indexed because it was assumed that the inflation was neutral in that it affected all modes of transportation equally.

Tables 4.7 and 4.9 show the results of adjusting costs on the present values and benefit-cost ratios. The present value of future costs increases significantly, but all ratios are still greater than or equal to one. As is apparent from the summary tables, benefits and costs increase in direct proportion to the length of the navigation season extension, with benefits increasing more rapidly than costs. Benefits and costs are also inversely related to the discount rate that is used, and the benefit-cost ratios increase as the amortization period is lengthened.

TABLE 4.9

BENEFIT-COST RATIOS FOR EXTENSION OF NAVIGATION SEASON

LENGTH OF SEASON EXTENSION	Discount Rate (Per Cent)	1/10 Amortized Per Year
uary 31 Extension		
.V. Benefits/P.V. Costs (BEA)	@ 7	1.6
	@ 8	1.7
.V. Benefits/P.V. Costs (Indexed)	@ 7	1.3
	@ 8	1.3
ruary 28 Extension		
.V. Benefits/P.V. Costs (BEA)	@ 7	2.3
	@ 8	2.3
.V. Benefits/P.V. Costs (Indexed)	@ 7	1 8
	@ 8	1.8
r-Round Extension		
.V. Benefits/P.V. Costs (BEA)	@ 7	2.5
	@ 8	2.5
.V. Benefits/P.V. Costs (Indexed)	@ 7	2.0
	@ 8	2.0

C.   Some Policy Questions

According to the benefit-cost ratios, extension of the
season may be warranted for all three periods that were
considered. Unfortunately, BEA cost estimates are not broken
down by specific task and locality, such as the Welland Ship
Canal or the St. Marys River. Consequently, benefit-cost
ratios can not be calculated for the three distinct regions:
the four Upper Great Lakes, the five Great Lakes and the
St. Lawrence Seaway.

The various projects of the Demonstration Program showed
that navigation lanes on the four Upper Great Lakes could
be maintained operational year round. U.S. Steel was the only
company to cooperate with and to take advantage of this aspect
of the Demonstration Program by operating vessels year-round.
The only concern of the Demonstration Program has been that
of demonstrating the feasibility of year-round navigation,
not determining the number of users and identifying them
individually. However, if it is decided to undertake year-
round extension, an appropriate financing policy, one that
is equitable, efficient and consistent with the goal established, must be determined. If U.S. Steel was the only company
to operate vessels during the Demonstration Program because
it is the only company that would benefit from a year-round
shipping season, policy makers must determine an equitable
and efficient allocation of costs.

Two costs that have not been included in the calculations
are environmental costs and human costs. It is very difficult,
if not impossible, to quantify them. Problems requiring
investigation include the effects of extension on shore
erosion, on local access because of disruption of the ice
cover and on natural ecological cycles. The physical, social
and psychological effects of winter operation upon shipboard
personnel, additional hazards to life and property due to
severe weather conditions and many others also need attention.

The main policy consideration is whether extension of
the open navigation season on the Great Lakes, the St. Lawrence
Seaway or both, would be justified economically or otherwise
and, if so, where and to what extent.

Conclusions

Calculations by the U.S. Department of Commerce,
Bureau of Economic Analysis and those made under the more
restrictive assumptions of this report both result in benefit-
cost ratios greater than one. This agreement indicates that
extension of the shipping season on the Great Lakes and the
Seaway may be economically sound. But before proceeding with
extension Systemwide, several aspects should be carefully
investigated.

Some of them have been discussed earlier in this chapter: the prospective effect of changing technology in transportation, including containerization, upon the amount of general cargo that would move through the system in overseas trade during the extended season; and the potential environmental and human costs associated with such extension. Increased insurance rates for vessels operating during the extended navigation season must be re-examined in view of the findings of the Demonstration Program. The current rates, as high as three times the daily rates for sailings in early January, may no longer be justified. It has also been emphasized that stable labor-management relations throughout the Great Lakes and St. Lawrence Seaway are necessary in order to encourage shippers as well as vessel owners and operators to use the Seaway during the extended season.

Moreover, there are certain shortcomings in the previous cost-benefit studies, including the one described in this chapter. These studies assume that the extension of the open season would occur late in the season. Extending open navigation earlier in the season may also be feasible. Somewhat different techniques, and consequently different costs and benefits, may be involved. These should be investigated.

Benefit-cost studies almost invariably are confined to certain localized aspects. The benefit-cost studies of season extension suffer seriously from these shortcomings. In particular, they fail to consider the effects of extension upon competitive and complementary modes of transportation. For example, significant traffic could be diverted from the railroads serving the Great Lakes Region. Nor are the negative effects of season extension upon other regions that compete with the Great Lakes Region for industrial and commercial activity considered. The economic and other aspects of projects beyond the immediately affected region are not normally considered in benefit-cost studies of individual programs. They have not been studied in this one. Lastly, stimulation of local organized economic activity and a favorable benefit-cost ratio do not necessarily imply that national economic activity will be increased, or that the benefit-cost ratio for the nation will be favorable.

Footnotes

[1] The Great Lakes-St. Lawrence Seaway Winter Navigation Board, First Annual Report (U.S., Department of the Army, 1973), p. 22.

[2] The Great Lakes-St. Lawrence Seaway Winter Navigation Board, Third Annual Report (U.S., Department of the Army, 1975), pp. 80-81.

[3] Public Law 89-298, The Rivers and Harbors Act of 1965.

[4] The Seaway Development Institute, Inc., "Applications of Baltic Ice Information and Ice Control Techniques to the Extension of the Great Lakes-St. Lawrence Seaway Navigation Season," prepared for St. Lawrence Seaway Development Corporation, Contract No. STL-7-247 (neg), March 1971.

[5] Public Law 91-611, Section 107, The Rivers and Harbors Act of 1970.

[6] Public Law 93-25, Section 70, The Water Resources Development Act of 1974.

[7] The Great Lakes-St. Lawrence Seaway Winter Navigation Board, Third Annual Report, 1975, pp. 16-20.

[8] "Seaway Project Results Hailed," Journal of Commerce, March 7, 1975.

[9] U.S. Maritime Administration, U.S., Department of Commerce, The Great Lakes and St. Lawrence Seaway Study of Insurance Rates (Washington: U.S. Government Printing Office, June 1972), pp. 31-35.

[10] Ibid., p. 21.

[11] Ibid., pp. 20-22.

[12] "The New Lakes Fleet," Business Week, May 18, 1974.

[13] Conversations with Mr. Patrick J. Sullivan of the Great Lakes District of the International Longshoremen's Association (ILA), Mr. Douglas Kubic of Local 815, Milwaukee, ILA.

[14] R. D. Reymond and E.V. Fesler, Fourth Seacoast - Seaway System Requirements Analysis, Volume II (Washington: U.S., Department of Transportation, St. Lawrence Seaway Development Corporation, March 1972), p. 6-1.

[15] Port of Milwaukee, "Transit Time Study on 228 Voyages from the Port of Milwaukee to the first Port of Call Overseas from April 19 to November 30, 1970," March 1971, p. 2.

[16] Reymond and Fesler, Fourth Coast, stated that "actual time spent loading and unloading rarely exceeded two days in each port.", p. 6-3.

[17] U.S. Coast Guard, Report of the Technical Subgroup (Submitted to the U.S., Department of Transportation, St. Lawrence Seaway Task Force, November 1968).

[18] Ibid., p. 6.

[19] U.S., Department of the Army, Corps of Engineers, Great Lakes and St. Lawrence Seaway Navigation Season Extension (U.S., Department of the Army, 1969).

[20] EBS Management Consultants, Inc., An Economic Analysis of Improvement Alternatives to the St. Lawrence Seaway System: Final Report (Washington: 1969).

[21] Eric Schenker, et. al., Extending the St. Lawrence Seaway Navigation Season: A Cost-Benefit Approach (Milwaukee: Center for Great Lakes Studies, University of Wisconsin-Milwaukee, 1972), p. 59.

[22] Comparing Tables 4.3 and 4.4 reveals that, for shipping season extension to January 31 (six-weeks), the cost for air bubblers and bubbler-flushers was approximately $11 million and for Ice Breakage Assistance, the cost of $97.4 million, according to the Winter Navigation Board's program, which has been moderately successful. Under the cost estimates of the Coast Guard, the cost for ice breaking alone for a six-week extension would be $358 million.

[23] "Year Round Shipping Advocates Confident," Milwaukee Sentinel, March 14, 1975.

[24] Schenker, Extending the St. Lawrence Seaway Navigation Season, p. 40; and Port of Montreal Authority, Highlights on the Economic Impact of the Port of Montreal, (Montreal: Port of Montreal Authority, 1974), p. 28.

[25] Port of Montreal Authority, Economic Impact of the Port of Montreal, p. 28.

[26] Schenker, Extending the St. Lawrence Seaway Navigation Season, p. 13.

[27] The Great Lakes-St. Lawrence Seaway Winter Navigation Board, Third Annual Report, 1975, pp. 40-47.

[28] Bureau of Labor Statistics, U.S., Department of Labor, Monthly Labor Review (Washington: U.S. Government Printing Office, April, 1975).

Selected Bibliography

I. Books and Reports

Canadian Marine Transportation Administration. Review of Recent Canadian Activities for the Extension of the Navigation Season - Gulf of St. Lawrence to Great Lakes, 1972.

Carr, D. Wm., & Associates, Ltd. Review Report of EBSMC Study of Alternative Seaway Improvements, 1969.

EBS Management Consultants, Inc. An Economic Analysis of Improvement Alternatives to the St. Lawrence Seaway System: Final Report. Washington: 1969.

Great Lakes Pilotage Administration, U.S. Department of Commerce, "Great Lakes Pilotage." Washington: U.S. Government Printing Office, 1966.

The Great Lakes-St. Lawrence Seaway Winter Navigation Board. First Annual Report. Detroit: U.S. Department of the Army, 1973.

_____. Second Annual Report. Detroit: U.S. Department of the Army, 1974.

_____. Third Annual Report. Detroit: U.S. Department of the Army, 1975.

Larrowe, Charles P. Maritime Labor Relations on the Great Lakes. Michigan State University: Labor and Industrial Relations Center, 1959.

National Oceanic and Atmospheric Administration. U.S. Department of Commerce. Great Lakes Pilot 1973. Washington: U.S. Government Printing Office, 1973.

Port of Montreal Authority. Highlights on the Economic Impact of the Port of Montreal. Montreal: Port of Montreal Authority, 1974.

Reymond, R.D., and Fesler, E.V. Fourth Coast - Seaway System Requirements Analysis, Volume II. Washington, 1972.

The Seaway Development Institute, Inc. "Applications of Baltic Ice Information and Ice Control Techniques to the Extension of the Great Lakes-St. Lawrence Seaway Navigation Season," prepared for St. Lawrence Seaway Development Corporation, Contract No. STL-7-247 (neg) , March 1971.

Schenker, Eric, et. al. The Economic Merits of Extending the
    St. Lawrence Seaway Navigation Season. Milwaukee: Center
    for Great Lakes Studies, University of Wisconsin-Milwaukee,
    1972.

_____. Extending the St. Lawrence Seaway
    Navigation Season - A Cost-Benefit Approach. Milwaukee:
    Center for Great Lakes Studies, University of Wisconsin-
    Milwaukee, 1972.

Schenker, Eric. "St. Lawrence Seaway To Date - and Its Future."
    Proceedings of the Eleventh Conference on Great Lakes
    Research. Toronto: 1968, pp. 640-657.

U.S. Department of the Army, Corps of Engineers. Great Lakes
    and St. Lawrence Seaway Navigation Season Extension.
    Detroit: U.S. Department of the Army, 1969.

U.S. Coast Guard, U.S. Department of Transportation, St.
    Lawrence Seaway Task Force. Report of the Technical
    Subgroup. 1968.

U.S. Maritime Administration, U.S. Department of Commerce.
    The Great Lakes and St. Lawrence Seaway Study of Insurance
    Rates. Washington: U.S. Government Printing Office, 1972.

Winter Navigation Board and Department of the Army. Proceedings
    of the Great Lakes-St. Lawrence Seaway Winter Navigation
    Seminar. Detroit: December 5-6, 1972.

II. Articles

A. Journals and Magazines

Bureau of Labor Statistics, U.S. Department of Labor. Monthly
    Labor Review. Washington: U.S. Government Printing
    Office, April 1975.

"Extending the Shipping Season in the Great Lakes-St. Lawrence
    Seaway System: The Realities After a Three Year Evaluation."
    Seaway Review, September 1974. pp. 11-21.

"The New Great Lakes Fleet." Business Week. May 18, 1974.

"World's Most Versatile Cargo Ship." Marine Engineering/Log,
    February 1975, pp. 48-49.

B. Newspapers

Journal of Commerce. "Seaway Project Results Hailed," March 7,
    1975.

_____. "Seaway Traffic Dropped in '74," March 24,
    1975.

Milwaukee Sentinel. "Year Round Shipping Advocates Confident,"
    April 14, 1975.

III.   Interviews and Conversations

Kubic, Douglas. Local 815, Milwaukee, International Long-
    shoremen's Association, June 25, 1975.

Sullivan, Patrick J. Great Lakes District, International
    Longshoremen's Association, June 24, 1975.

IV.   Federal Legislation

Public Law 89-298. The Rivers and Harbors Act of 1965.

Public Law 91-611, Section 107. The Rivers and Harbors Act
    of 1970.

Public Law 93-25, Section 70. The Water Resources Development
    Act of 1974.

V.   Unpublished Studies

Port of Milwaukee. "Transit Time Study on 228 Voyages from
    the Port of Milwaukee to the First Port of Call Over-
    seas from April 19 to November 30, 1970." Milwaukee:
    1971. (Mimeographed).

Regional Economic Analysis Division, Bureau of Economic Analysis.
    Social and Economic Statistics Administration. U.S.
    Department of Commerce. "Economic Effects of an Extension
    of Great Lakes-St. Lawrence Shipping Season on General
    Cargo and Related Industries: A Summary Report." 1974.
    (Mimeographed).

U.S. Department of Transportation. Great Lakes Pilotage Review.
    (Draft Staff Report), 1972.

V.

The Energy Crisis and
Great Lakes Shipping

Introduction

The Great Lakes serves a highly industrialized and urbanized region that constitutes one of the world's greatest consumers of energy, both for its industrial and commercial establishments and for its residential population. The Upper Great Lakes Region, north of a line connecting Georgian Bay, Bay City, Ludington and Green Bay (Figure 5.1), is one of the great resource-producing regions of the world. Iron ore, limestone, copper and forest products are its major resources. The Great Lakes System serves as a connecting link between two complementary regions--the predominantly resource-producing Upper Great Lakes and the predominantly resource-consuming Lower Great Lakes. The energy requirements of the Great Lakes Region depend heavily upon efficient, low cost transportation between the Upper and Lower Great Lakes, between the western and eastern areas and between the Great Lakes Region and the rest of the world.

It is important to recognize: (1) the energy requirements of the transportation system designed to fulfill these needs and (2) the total energy requirements of the region. A primary consideration is the ability of the transportation system, particularly Great Lakes shipping, to handle the needs of the region for fuel and resource movement. Among the major commodities moved on the Great Lakes, coal constitutes between 15 and 20 per cent of the total tonnage, while petroleum products represent about 4 per cent of the total.

In recent years, there have been two developing situations that many people believe constitute crises. One is the rising price and limited availability of fossil fuels, particularly petroleum. This situation has given rise to the economic recession that affects fuel-using industries, the general demand for transportation, and the specific demand for the movement of fossil fuels. The second crisis involves the impact of new developments on the environment. Here, again, the utilization of energy is particularly critical because all fuel-using energy results in the emission of waste matter into the air, water or land. Often these effluents may be pollutants.

Transportation is a major user of energy. About 25 per cent of all energy consumed in the United States is used in transportation; and of that about 95 per cent is petroleum in one form or another. Water transportation is almost completely dependent upon petroleum. Some of the older vessels in the Great Lakes represent virtually the last surviving coal-burning ships. They are rapidly being retrofitted, where economically feasible, with either oil-fired boilers or diesel engines. Those not economically amenable to such modifications are being retired.

INDUSTRIAL CORE REGION OF THE UNITED STATES AND CANADA

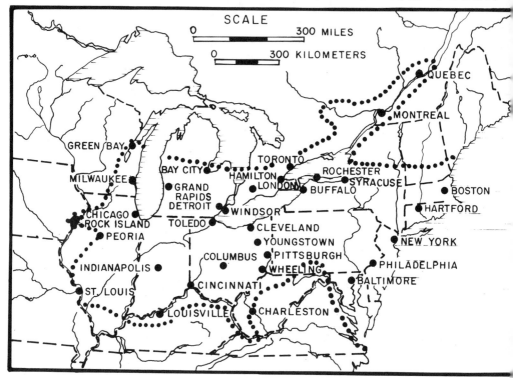

Figure 5.1

Because of the rising costs and limited supplies of
fossil fuels, a major consideration in the movement of
commodities is the relative efficiency of the various modes
of transportation. In general, within the United States
and Canada, and particularly within the area tributary to
the Great Lakes, the sources of fossil fuels and the markets
for them are widely separated. Except where pipelines are
available, transportation by water, in terms of energy
efficiency per ton-mile, is considerably more efficient than
by any other mode. However, water transportation is not
everywhere available, and where it is, its circuity may be
sufficiently greater than that of the land modes to diminish
its energy effectiveness.

Sources of energy not involving fossil fuels are now
being developed. Natural Gas is a major source of energy
for some industries and for residential use in the Great
Lakes Region, which is served by a system of pipelines.
Although Liquified Natural Gas (LNG) ships are in service
and under construction for ocean movement, it is unlikely that
they would be utilized extensively, if at all, within the
Great Lakes. At the moment, the only practicable prospect
in the Great Lakes is nuclear power. While the electric
utility industry is developing nuclear power extensively in
the Great Lakes Region as elsewhere, the "state of the art"
indicates that nuclear propulsion of vessels in the Great
Lakes does not appear to be practicable within the foreseeable
future.

For many years, the use of coal has been declining, but
recently interest in its utilization has revived. However,
most of the available coal in the Great Lakes Region has a
high sulphur content and therefore is either undesirable or
illegal for environmental reasons. Because most of the low
sulphur coal must be carried long distances at substantial
transportation cost, the minimization of such cost is critical.
This concern for the environmental consequences of coal is
currently responsible for major shifts in coal movement on
the Great Lakes.

Petroleum continues to be the dominant fuel for many
purposes despite its high cost and prospects for its reduced
availability. Although the movement of petroleum products
represents a small percentage of total traffic on the Great
Lakes, in some instances it is locally significant. Developments in transportation technology in both water transportation
and competing overland modes are also contributing to shifts
in the volume and the geographic flow pattern for both coal
and petroleum products. In the case of coal, the major force
in recent years has been the rise and current dominance of
trainload movements, and particularly the unit-train. Having
reduced the freight rates of railroad-hauled coal, these
movements diverted coal traffic from the Great Lakes. At the
same time, opportunities have been opened for relatively low-

cost, rail-lake, intermodal movement of coal.

Another set of technological developments affecting the volume and geographic pattern of coal movements is in the field of electric power transmission by wire. This has expedited the development of electric power generation at mine heads, with consequent transmission of electric power by wire as a substitute for the movement of coal by rail or water.

Another possibility is the movement of coal by pipeline in the form of a slurry, in which the coal is suspended in a liquid medium. One pipeline was actually built two decades ago across eastern Ohio, but it ceased operation when the parallel railroads initiated competitive rates.

Other possible sources of energy for the Great Lakes lie in the more distant future. These include nuclear fusion, geo-thermal power, solar power, methane and hydrogen power.

It is now the policy of the United States, and of Canada to a major extent, to reduce to the maximum possible extent their dependence upon foreign sources of fossil fuels. This policy may very well reinforce a shift of industry from seacoast regions largely dependent on imported fuel to interior locations, such as the Great Lakes Region, either in proximity to domestic sources of fuel or situated where domestic fuel can be transported to consumers at relatively low cost. This trend may substantially increase the movement of fuels in the Great Lakes Region, although not necessarily on the Lakes.

The Energy Crisis and the Regional Economic Base

In recent years, the Lower Great Lakes area has been characterized by a rate of economic growth slower than that of the rest of the United States. Nevertheless, the Region, both in the United States and in Canada, continues to be the principal locus of heavy industry in North America. The recent and current expansion of the iron and steel industry along the Great Lakes shores in both nations augurs its continued dominance. The linkages among the region's major industries are so complex, and the tertiary and quaternary activities of the region so well-developed, that the prospects are for a sustained demand for basic raw materials and for energy consumption. These activities, in turn, produce a multiplier effect, one that culminates in support of large populations which, in turn, require vast amounts of energy, not only for transportation but also for most other activities. Thus, any change in the character, availability and cost of the energy inputs will have massive effects upon the region's economic base and the way of life. These effects will inevitably redound on the Great Lakes shipping industry.

By mid-1975, Congress and the Administration had not yet presented a consistent national energy policy. The realization that energy resources, both national and world-wide, are not unlimited was reinforced by the Arab oil embargo and the consequent rapid rise in fuel prices in 1973.[1] On December 1, 1973, a report prepared in response to a presidential directive recommended a program designed to achieve national self-sufficiency in energy. The program was to include: (1) conservation of energy by reducing consumption and improving the technical efficiency of the conversion process; (2) increasing domestic production of oil and natural gas as rapidly as possible; (3) increasing the use of coal, first to supplement and later to replace oil and natural gas; (4) expanding the production of nuclear energy as rapidly as possible, first to supplement and later to replace fossil energy; (5) promoting, to the maximum feasible extent, the use of renewable energy sources, including hydro, geothermal and solar power; and (6) pursuing the possibilities for fusion and central station solar power. It was estimated that, if such a policy were to be adopted and implemented, the earliest date at which national energy self-sufficiency could be achieved would be 1985. By 1980, it was estimated, oil imports could be reduced to about half of the 1973 level.

Each of these program elements, if adopted and carried out, would substantially modify the demand, supply and flow patterns of Great Lakes transportation.

Neither the principles nor the specifics of such a policy and program have been uniformly accepted. One of the principal objections springs from considerations of their impact upon the environment within the United States. The environmentalists point out: (1) the costs of energy cannot be measured strictly on a private profit-and-loss basis because there are social costs and benefits; (2) some of the recommended policies and programs would entail major detrimental effects upon the environment; and (3) such effects have not been adequately considered or evaluated.[2]

Other objections question the philosophy of securing independence of energy sources at the expense of international interdependence, and the possible impact upon the oil-supplying nations should their major market for oil be reduced or cut off. Foreign investments in the United States are pointed out as one of the benefits of international energy interdependence, albeit a possible danger to the nation's security and economic well-being.[3]

Any estimate of future impact of the changing energy situation on Great Lakes shipping is, of course, contingent upon the nature of whatever national energy policies may be adopted and the devices and timing of their implementation. The range of possibilities is very wide.

Canadian energy policy is no further developed than that
of the United States. "So far, there is no indication that
any level of government in Canada is paying serious attention
to the question of conservation."[4] Canada is ambivalent
concerning its policy toward its leading trading partner,
the United States. Though it seeks greater fuel independence,
Canada wishes to export its oil and gas. At present, a major
traffic flow on the Great Lakes is Appalachian coal exported
through Lake Erie ports to utility plants and industries in
southern Ontario. Meanwhile, hydroelectric power, as well
as thermal power, is interchanged across the international
border by means of an extensive grid in the eastern Great
Lakes Region of each country.

Sources and Consumption of Energy in the Great Lakes Region

Because the Great Lakes Region is a major portion of
the United States and because it is not practicable to estimate
accurately the distribution among the sources and users of
energy in any particular region, the energy statistics for
the nation as a whole can be taken as indicative of the
Great Lakes Region itself.

Table 5.1 shows, for 1970, the sources of energy consumed
in the United States.

Oil and Gas

Oil and gas account for about one-fourth of the nation's
energy consumption. Because shortages have developed in both,
there is national concern to reduce not only consumption but
also reliance upon foreign sources. Imports of oil have
climbed from about 11 per cent of total consumption in 1970
to about 38 per cent in 1974. The vulnerability to the
vagaries of foreign policies and actions, such as the recent
Arab oil embargo, give rise to the demand in many quarters
for reduction of imports.

Coal

Coal, which for many users, had been declining in both
absolute and relative importance, is pointed out as a major
hope for improving the fuel situation in the short-run and
middle-range future. Environmental considerations have
recently inhibited, to some extent, the full utilization of
Appalachian coal because of its high sulphur content. Having
emphasized the need for application of devices and methods for
reducing the air pollution from these coals, the environmental
considerations have also stimulated the exploitation of lower-
sulphur western coals. Nevertheless, Appalachia is still
the principal source of coal consumed in the United States.
A significant proportion of the Appalachian coal is exported
through eastern coastal ports, mainly to Japan where it is
a source of coke for the metallurgical industries. Because

TABLE 5.1

SOURCES OF ENERGY USED IN THE UNITED STATES, 1970

Source	Amount (Million barrels per day oil equivalent)	Per Cent
Oil	13.9	43.99
Domestic	10.4	32.91
Imports	3.5	11.08
Gas	10.7	33.86
Domestic	10.3	32.59
Imports	0.4	1.27
Coal	6.5	20.57
Hydroelectric	0.4	1.26
Nuclear	0.1	0.32
Geo-thermal	0.0003	---
Total	31.6	100.00

Source: The Nation's Energy Future. A Report to Richard M. Nixon,
           President of the United States, submitted by Dr. Dixy Lee
           Ray, Chairman, United States Atomic Energy Commission,
           1 December, 1973 (Washington: U.S. Government Printing
           Office, 1973), p. 42.

of its coking qualities and its proximity to markets,
Appalachian coal will probably continue to find markets in
the metallurgical and other industries of the southern
Great Lakes Region. Significant   quantities are also
exported to Ontario, where the coal is utilized in the metallurgical and electric power plants of the Toronto-Hamilton
complex.

Western coal, from Montana, the Dakotas and Wyoming
in the United States and from the prairie provinces of Canada,
offers the major opportunity for expanded coal usage because
of its low sulphur content. It is beginning to move into
the Great Lakes Region in large volumes and will, in the
near future, constitute a major traffic flow on the Great
Lakes. A major problem in developing the western coalfields
is the environmental impact of large-scale strip mining.
Conformance to federal and state requirements, existing and
prospective, will result in some additional costs for mining
the coal. These costs, added to those involved in transporting
it the long distances to eastern and Great Lakes regional,
markets, must be considered competitively with innovations
that may make the higher-sulphur Appalachian and eastern
interior coals environmentally compatible. Another potentially
competitive element is the possible gasification of western
coals, albeit distant in the future.

Hydroelectric Power

Hydroelectric power is significant in the eastern Great
Lakes and St. Lawrence River areas where the flow of Great
Lakes water, the runoff of the rivers from the Laurentian
Shield, and the long-distance transmission of power from
northern Quebec and Labrador constitute major contributions
to the eastern power grid. Principal developments are at
Niagara Falls in both Canada and the United States, at the
several stations along the St. Lawrence Seaway, at the edge
of the Laurentian Shield along the north shore of the St.
Lawrence River and the Gulf of St. Lawrence, at Churchill
Falls in Labrador and, in the future, at the massive development in northern Quebec east of Hudson Bay.

Of major consequence in the development of shipping
patterns is the fact that hydroelectric power potential made
the St. Lawrence Seaway Project politically and economically
feasible. Revenues from sale of power exceed by a considerable
margin those from vessel tolls in the Seaway, and all the
cost of joint navigation-power features of the Seaway were
charged entirely to power generation. As a result, the
benefit-cost ratio of Seaway navigation features are much
more attractive than would otherwise be the case.

Nuclear Power

The Great Lakes Region is the locus of a major development of nuclear power plants, with additional ones under construction or committed (See Figure 5.2). There are several reasons for the rapidly growing importance of nuclear power in the Region. One is the large industrial and domestic market of the Region. Another is the virtually unlimited availability of water for the reactors which are located, subject to environmental constraints, on lake-shore sites.

Because nuclear power competes with thermal power and, unlike the latter, does not utilize fossil fuels, the short-run effects of nuclear power development on Great Lakes shipping are negative. However, in the long run, the net effects could be to stimulate Great Lakes traffic by furnishing power needed for industrial development within the Region.

Geo-thermal Power

Geo-thermal power is in the early stages of technological development. Geological conditions in the Great Lakes Region indicate that geo-thermal power will not be significant in the Region in the foreseeable future, if ever.

Uses of Energy

Tables 5.2 and 5.3 show the uses of energy in the United States. Nearly one-third of the energy is consumed in industry, about one-fourth in transportation and almost the same amount in residential and commercial uses, principally space heating, air conditioning, etc. A significant proportion is used in electric power generation itself. Of the energy consumed in transportation, over 95 per cent is supplied by petroleum, about 4 per cent by natural gas, and about one-tenth of 1 per cent each by coal and electricity.[5] Transportation, in turn, consumes over half of all the oil used in the United States. Of the energy consumed in transportation, slightly over one-third is used for freight movements other than military, and slightly over one-fourth for transportation by water.

The Energy Crisis and Great Lakes Movement of Fossil Fuel

Oil and Gas

Oil and gas together produce nearly one-fourth of the total energy consumed in the United States. Although the major sources of both are generally distant from the Great Lakes Region, both are still produced in minor quantities within

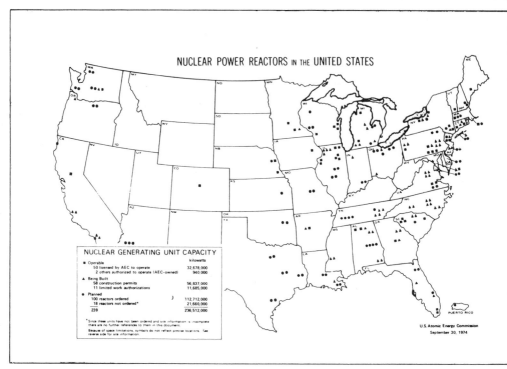

FIGURE 5.2

SOURCE: Radiation Data and Reports,
Volume 15 (December 1974),
Figure 1. p. 842.

TABLE 5.2

USES OF ENERGY IN THE UNITED STATES, 1970

Use	Amount (Million Barrels per day oil equivalent)	Per Cent[2]	Losses	Per Cent[3]
ustrial[1]	9.9	31.33	2.4	7.59
nsportation[1]	7.7	24.37	5.8	18.35
idential and Commercial[1]	7.5	23.73	1.9	6.01
ctrical Energy Generation	7.1	22.47	4.6	14.56
Residential and Commercial Use	-1.3	-4.11	-	-
Industrial Use	-1.2	-3.80	-	-
Transportation Use	-0.007	-0.02	-	-
-Energy Uses of Fuels	1.9	6.01	-	-
l Exports	-0.9	-	-	-
Total	31.6	100.00	14.7	46.52

E: [1]Includes use of generated electrical power.

[2]Column does not add to 100.00 per cent due to rounding error.

[3]Figures are percentages of total energy used.

rce: The Nation's Energy Future. A Report to Richard M. Nixon, President of the United States, submitted by Dr. Dixy Lee Ray, Chairman, United States Atomic Energy Commission, 1 December 1973 (Washington: U.S. Government Printing Office, 1973), p. 42.

TABLE 5.3

USES OF ENERGY BY SOURCE, UNITED STATES, 1970

Source and Use	Amount (Million barrels per day oil equivalent)[1]	Per Cent
Oil	13.9	100.0
Transportation	7.9	53.2
Residential and Commercial	2.5	18.0
Industrial	1.6	11.5
Non-Energy	1.5	10.8
Electrical Energy Generation	1.0	7.2
Gas	10.7	100.0
Industrial	4.6	43.0
Residential and Commercial	3.5	32.7
Electrical Energy Generation	1.9	17.8
Transportation	0.3	2.8
Non-Energy	0.3	2.8
Coal	7.4	100.0
Electrical Energy Generation	3.7	50.0
Industrial	2.5	33.8
Residential and Commercial	0.2	2.7
Non-Energy	0.1	1.4
(Exports)	(0.9)	12.2
Hydroelectric	0.4	100.0
Nuclear	0.1	100.0
Geo-thermal	0.0003	100.0
Total	31.60	

NOTE: [1]Individual uses of the various energy sources may not add to the total use due to rounding errors.

Source: The Nation's Energy Future. A Report to Richard M. Nixon, President of the United States, submitted by Dr. Dixy Lee Ray, Chairman, United States Atomic Energy Commission, 1 December 1973 (Washington: U.S. Government Printing Office, 1973), p. 42.

the Region. The Region's major sources of both domestic and imported oil and gas are connected to it by pipeline. Oil refineries are numerous along the shores of the Lakes, in both the United States and Canada. There is some movement of petroleum products by Lake vessel from the refineries to outlying consuming areas in the vicinity of the Lakes.

The major refining areas within the Great Lakes Region of the United States are in the Lower (southern) Great Lakes area, principally within or in proximity to the major consuming areas--the industrial metropolitan complexes bordering Lakes Erie and Michigan. Both Cleveland and Finley, Ohio, important centers of oil refining, are the headquarters of large companies involved in the petroleum industry of the Great Lakes Region and elsewhere: Standard of Ohio (Sohio) in Cleveland and Marathon in Finley. One of the largest refineries of Canada is located at Sarnia, Ontario, at the southern end of Lake Huron. On Lake Michigan, a complex of refineries is located in the metropolitan Chicago area, especially in the Calumet region of northwestern Indiana and along the Calumet-Sag navigation route to the south and southwest of Chicago. Indiana Harbor (East Chicago), Indiana, has long been the principal port for Lakewise distribution of petroleum products.

In recent years, the development of pipelines paralleling the Lakes has substantially reduced this tanker movement. A major products pipeline parallels the west shore of Lake Michigan, from the Calumet region through Milwaukee to Green Bay. In Canada, the western oilfields of Alberta and elsewhere ship their crude by pipeline to the Great Lakes. Formerly, the pipeline terminated in the Duluth-Superior area from whence the crude moved by large Lake tanker to the Sarnia refineries. Later, the pipeline was extended through Michigan to Sarnia, and some of the surplus tankers were converted to dry bulk carriers. Currently, plans are under way to extend the pipeline eastward to Montreal. This extension would remove Canada's crude oil tankers from the Lakes completely, greatly reduce the demand for products tankers and link the Montreal area refineries to the Lakes. The Montreal refineries presently import crude oil via deepwater ports of the Atlantic provinces (Newfoundland, Nova Scotia and New Brunswick) and via the pipeline from Portland, Maine. Thus with completion of the pipeline link, the Canadian area bordering the Great Lakes can utilize competitively both western Canadian (and possibly Alaskan) crude oil as well as overseas oil through the Atlantic ports.

Limitations of the St. Lawrence Seaway, of the connecting channels within the Lakes and of the principal Great Lakes ports make it impossible for large ocean-going tankers to enter the Lakes. Most likely, crude oil transportation will be non-existent within the Great Lakes in the foreseeable future. Gas tankers are rapidly being developed for inter-continental transportation of LNG (Liquified Natural Gas) and LPG

(Liquified Petroleum Gas). But such tankers probably will
never be significant in the Great Lakes trade because of:
the physical limitations of the Seaway and the Lakes; the
development of gas pipelines in the Great Lakes Region; the
extreme hazard represented by the gas tankers; and the cost
of such vessels, among the most sophisticated and expensive
of all craft.

Another type of tanker which currently participates in
Great Lakes trade, especially to and from overseas, is the
parcel tanker, which is somewhat analogous to the general
cargo vessel in that it carries a variety of products
simultaneously. Most of the parcel tankers in Great Lakes-
overseas trade operate on more-or-less regular schedules,
similar to dry cargo liners, and are available to a variety
of shippers. All are foreign-flag. In addition to petroleum
products, they carry a variety of other liquid cargoes, such
as lard outbound and palm oil inbound. Given their nature
and the demand for continuous flow of petroleum products,
parcel tankers will probably not participate to any extent
in the movement of such products to, from or within the Great
Lakes.

Thus, consideration of oil and gas in relation to Great
Lakes shipping does not involve, to any significant degree,
either crude or products as cargoes to, from or within the
Lakes. On the other hand, petroleum is significant in two
contexts: (1) as bunker fuel for vessels within the Great
Lakes and the Great Lakes-overseas trades; and (2) as a fuel
for industrial, utility and other uses competitive with coal,
which is, and should continue to be, a major Great Lakes
cargo.

Coal

Although oil and gas together are now by far the most
dominant fuels, the geographic conditions within and surrounding
the Great Lakes Region place special emphasis upon coal. Many
of the Region's basic industries are especially dependent
upon coal. Its electric utilities, in spite of recent expansion of nuclear power, still rely primarily on coal.
Although there is no single source of information on the
proportions of the various fuels this industry consumes,
a recent Interstate Commerce Commission publication stated
that, of the fossil fuels used for electric power generation
in the East Northcentral Region (Ohio, Indiana, Illinois,
Michigan and Wisconsin), coal accounted for 96 per cent in
1960 and 93 per cent in 1969, as contrasted with 4 per cent
for gas in 1960, 6 per cent in 1969, and 1 per cent oil in
1969.[6] This is the highest percentage of coal use by electric
utilities in any region of the nation.

Coal is also vital to the steel and cement industries, both of which are heavily concentrated in the Great Lakes Region. The iron and steel industry is also overwhelmingly concentrated in the Great Lakes Region, both in the United States and in Canada.[7] This concentration can be attributed to not only the demand for its products by the region's numerous durable goods industries, which in turn depend upon the iron and steel industry, but also the availability of lake transportation of iron ore, limestone and, to a lesser degree, coal. In addition, Lake waters are utilized for cooling and provide the opportunity for landfill, not only to dispose of slag from the plants but also to create land for plant expansion.

The iron and steel industry is the dominant factor in generating Lake movements of two of the four principal bulk commodities within the Great Lakes--iron ore and limestone. It is relatively less significant as a generator of coal traffic. Coal is used by the industry mainly for making of coke; less than 10 per cent of the coal used by the industry is for heat and power. Principally from Appalachia, coking coal is transported to the steel industry of the eastern Great Lakes mainly by rail or, in the case of plants along the Ohio River and its tributaries, by barge. Steel plants on and near the shores of Lake Michigan formerly received coal from Appalachia by Lake vessel, but that traffic has virtually terminated. Technological changes in the steel industry indicate that, in spite of prospects for increased iron and steel production, the industry's demand for coal will not substantially increase and may decrease. These technological developments include increased use of concentrated ores and improvements in blast furnace efficiency resulting from injection of oil, gas or powdered coal at lower costs. The increased use of the basic oxygen process, which is largely replacing the open hearth furnace, will reduce the demand for scrap relative to pig iron and, at the same time, reduce the need for coal.

Another industry which is highly localized in the Great Lakes Region and which consumes substantial amounts of fuel is the cement industry. Because cement is a bulky commodity, plants generally are located close to the markets, except where cheap transportation by water is available. Also, since limestone, a flux in blast furnaces, is a basic raw material in cement plants, there is a locational association between large primary iron and steel plants and cement plants. One of the world's largest cement plants is United States Steel Corporation's Buffington plant in Gary, Indiana, adjacent to the Gary Steel Works. Limestone--over two million tons in 1973--from quarries on the northern part of Michigan's southern peninsula is shipped from northern Lake Huron to this plant with a private harbor. Because both the symbiotically-related steel plants and the markets for cement in the southern Great Lakes Region are located not far from the inland

coal field, relatively little coal but many millions of tons
of limestone moves to the cement plants along the Lakes by
vessel. Vessels are used extensively as well in the
distribution of processed cement throughout the Great Lakes
Region.

The trend for the past two or three decades in the cement
industry has been toward larger and more efficient plants
which, in turn, require larger inputs of energy. The increased
energy requirements, however, have not been proportionate to
the increased production. Coal is still the main type of fuel
although gas and oil are also used.[8]

The movement of coal on the Great Lakes by three
industries (electric utilities, iron and steel, and cement
manufacturing) consists dominantly of three components:
(1) movement from the ports along the southern shore of Lake
Erie to the Detroit River and northward; (2) movement from
the Lake Erie ports to nearby Canadian ports, principally
those on Lake Ontario through the Welland Ship Canal; and (3)
movement from South Chicago to utility plants on both shores
of Lake Michigan in Wisconsin and Michigan, with some movement into Lake Superior. The coal which moves through the Lake
Erie ports is mined in Appalachia: western Pennsylvania,
West Virginia and southeastern Ohio. Its movement to the
ports is by rail (Chessie System, Norfolk & Western, Penn
Central and Bessemer and Lake Erie) and, in some instances,
is complementary with the southbound movement of ore from the
Lake Erie ports to the iron and steel industries of the Ohio
River and its tributaries including, among others, the
Pittsburgh, Youngstown, Canton, Middletown and Ironton areas.
The ports that transfer the coal from these interior areas
to Lake vessels are: Conneaut, Ashtabula, Lorain, Sandusky
and Toledo. Each of these ports is served by one or more of
the railroads.

For many years Toledo has been the leading coal port on
the Lakes and one of the largest coal-shipping ports in the
world, but recently its traffic volume has declined. In 1953,
Toledo handled 23.8 million tons of coal but by 1973 only
14.4 million tons, which was below the depression years
figures of the 1930's. In 1935, for example, Toledo shipped
16 million tons.[9] The other Lake Erie ports have experienced
similar declines. Several of the ports that formerly handled
coal shipments in considerable volume no longer do so and
have removed their coal-loading facilities. Cleveland, for
example, handled over two million tons of coal shipments
annually during the 1920's but no longer loads any. The total
movement of bituminous coal from Lake Erie ports by Lake
vessel in 1973 was 34.1 million tons, as compared with 55 million
tons in the peak year of 1944.

The Lake Erie coal moves in two directions: (1) to and beyond the Detroit River, terminating mainly in utility plants of the Detroit metropolitan area and the Upper Great Lakes: Huron, Michigan and Superior; and (2) to and beyond the Welland Ship Canal, terminating mainly in the industrial plants and especially the electric plants of the Toronto-Hamilton urban complex and the steel mills of Hamilton, Ontario.

Figure 5.3 shows the routes of coal movement between the Appalachian fields and the Lake Erie ports as well as the flows of coal on the Lakes. All of the coal loaded at ports along the south shore of Lake Erie reaches those ports by rail, although a solids pipeline was completed along the Ohio River between Liverpool and Cleveland in 1958. The pipeline ceased operations in 1963, when the railroads lowered their rates under the impetus of the pipeline competition.[10]

The industrial and population growth of southern Ontario is responsible for a sustained movement of coal between the Lake Erie ports and the ports of southern Ontario, in contrast with a declining movement of Lake-borne coal to United States destinations. In 1973, exports of coal from the Lake Erie ports to Canada represented 46.3 per cent of the total coal shipments from those ports. This figure compares favorably with 27.3 per cent in 1953 and 24.3 per cent in 1963. On Lake Ontario, the coal that is exported from the United States through the Welland Ship Canal competes with coal from Atlantic Canada that moves up the St. Lawrence Seaway. Currently, a massive industrial complex, including large steel plants and electric power plants, is under development on the north shore of Lake Erie at Naticote, Ontario, west of the Welland Canal. This complex will tend to favor receipt of United States coal, eliminating the time and cost of transit through the Welland Canal and greatly facilitating the turn-around of the Lake vessels.

A third movement, but one of declining importance, is that from the ports along the south shore of Lake Erie into the Upper Great Lakes. In 1953, coal shipments from Lake Erie to Lake Michigan totalled 9.7 million tons whereas shipments in 1973 were only 2.1 million tons. Shipments from Lake Erie to Lake Superior declined from 5.4 million tons in 1953 to 2.8 million tons 20 years later. A similar decline took place in shipments to Lake Huron ports of both the United States and Canada.

Coal shipments on Lake Michigan are overwhelmingly from South Chicago, where coal is transferred from trains origi-nating in western Kentucky, Indiana and southern and central Illinois for Lake movement to utility plants primarily along both shores of Lake Michigan in Wisconsin and Michigan. Although they have fluctuated from year to year, there has been a gradual decline in coal shipments from South Chicago, from a peak of 8 million tons in 1963 to 4 million tons in

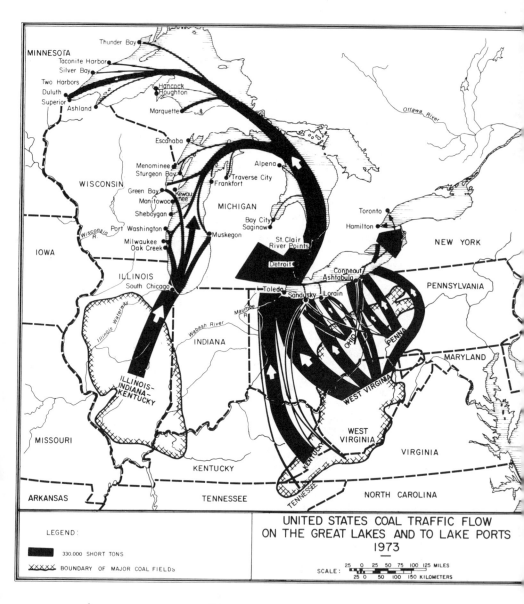

UNITED STATES COAL TRAFFIC FLOW
ON THE GREAT LAKES AND TO LAKE PORTS
1973

LEGEND:

▬ 330,000 SHORT TONS

XXXXX BOUNDARY OF MAJOR COAL FIELDS

SCALE: 25 0 25 50 75 100 125 MILES
25 0 50 100 150 KILOMETERS

Figure 5.3

116

1974. Similarly, receipts at Lake Michigan ports have been
declining. At Milwaukee, for example, bituminous coal
receipts by vessel (other than by car ferry) totalled 1.9
million tons in 1960, 1.7 million tons in 1963, and 1.1 million
tons in 1973. Oak Creek, Wisconsin, a private harbor operated
by a utility company, received 2.3 million tons in 1963 but
only two shiploads in 1974.

The environmental regulations combine with the energy
crisis to stimulate a new major flow of low sulphur, western
coal across the Great Lakes from the Lake Superior ports. In
1973, the beginnings of the movement were manifest in shipments of 127,000 tons of coal from Duluth-Superior. This
movement increased to 1.1 million tons in 1974.[11] Prospects
suggest a new major commodity movement annually, of millions
of tons of western, low sulphur coal from Lake Superior to
southerly and easterly destinations. This is a complete
reversal in the predominant direction of past Lake-borne
coal movements.

One manifestation of the prospective massive movement of
western coal from lakehead to the Lower Great Lakes Region is
the commitment for construction of a large facility for rail-
lake vessel transfer of coal at Superior, Wisconsin.[12]
Originating in Wyoming, Montana and North Dakota, the coal
will be transported by unit-trains on the Burlington Northern
to the planned facility at Superior, from whence it will be
moved by Lake vessel to utility plants. Initially, the major
movement will be to the facilities of Detroit Edison Company.
In anticipation of the movement, one Lake carrier has ordered
construction of at least two new large vessels, one with
40,000 ton capacity and another of 60,000 tons, with additional
vessels under consideration. The Burlington Northern, in
turn, is planning extensive investment in new cars and locomotives for its unit-trains. Each train will carry a total
of 10,000 tons in its 100 cars of 100 ton capacity each.

The transfer facility at Superior, costing 30 million
dollars, is expected to transship at least 4 million tons of
coal in 1976, 8 million tons in 1978, and eventually 20
million tons per year. It is anticipated that the facility
will handle an average of 2-1/2 trains per day, transferring
3,500 tons per hour. During the shipping season, it is
expected that 37,500 tons per day will be loaded aboard vessels.

A similar development of providing western coal for
eastern markets is occurring in Canada. At the Canadian
lakehead port of Thunder Bay, a facility for transfer of coal
from rail to water carriers is under construction. Initially
it will receive coal from six unit-trains daily. Averaging
100 cars of 100 ton capacity, these trains will operate over
both the Canadian National and Canadian Pacific railways
from Saskatchewan, Alberta and British Columbia on six-and
seven-day turnaround time. The terminal is expected to receive
its initial traffic late in 1976 for movement on the Lakes at
the start of the 1977 shipping season. At the beginning, the

terminal should transfer 3 million tons per year.13 This
prospective movement of coal to be utilized in Ontario and
eastern Canada indicates possible eventual competition of
western Canadian coal with imported United States coal from
Appalachia in the Toronto-Hamilton area and elsewhere in
eastern Canada. Such competition may affect the present
heavy movement, mentioned earlier, of coal between ports on
the south shore of Lake Erie and destinations in southern
Ontario on both sides of the Welland Ship Canal.

There are several negative factors involved in the
substitution of western, low sulphur coal for Appalachian
coal, in spite of the latter's higher sulphur content. One
is the greater distance from origins to markets, as previously
discussed. Despite the widespread use of unit-trains and
efficient low-cost Lake transportation, as energy costs
continue to rise, the cost of energy-consuming transportation
of the fuels will also rise. Still, the cost of western coal
including its transportation will be in competition with that
of Appalachian coal because the latter coal is more expensive
to mine and requires the additional costs of utility companies'
installing and operating equipment designed to reduce the
sulphur content at the stack to an acceptable level.

Another consideration is the fact that the heat
production of low sulphur coal is considerably less than that
of higher sulphur coal mined in Appalachia. The sulphur content of coal is measured in relation to its weight. Air
quality regulations, on the other hand, are based on heat
content. Typical western coal produces about 8,000 BTUs
per pound and Appalachian coal about 12,000 BTUs per pound.
Thus, it is necessary to use, and hence to transport, about
50 per cent more western coal to produce the same heat output.

Still another inhibiting consideration in the use of
western coal is the series of environmental constraints upon
widespread strip mining, the economical method of producing
most of the western coal. Furthermore, existing utility
plants will require extensive modifications in order to
utilize the low sulphur coal.

In spite of these constraints, it is very likely that
downbound movement of coal from Lake Superior, both in the
United States and in Canada, will soon be one of great
importance, possibly amounting to 30 or 40 million tons per
year within the next decade. Not only are the terminals under
development in both countries but a new generation of efficient,
self-unloading, large Lake vessels is under construction and
committed to handle this new traffic.

The potential for large coal movements by Lake vessels
will not necessarily be realized. The several modes of transportation are in competition for the available traffic. Since
coal is a commodity that is very sensitive to variations in
transportation cost, competitive rates which often reflect the

technological efficiency of the various optional routes
and modes will eventually determine the geographic patterns
and modes of coal movement.

The principal competitor of Great Lakes shipping for
the coal movement within the Great Lakes region is the
unit-train.[14] The unit-train is:

> --a management technique that permits effi-
> cient planning through long range contractual
> commitment of producer and consumer and dedication
> of the equipment. Specifically, a unit-train
> consists of a dedicated' set of haulage equipment
> loaded at one origin, unloaded at one destination
> each trip, and moving in both directions on a pre-
> determined schedule. The unit-train combines three
> principal factors: design efficiency, equipment
> balance, and intensive use. To achieve the lowest
> possible transportation costs, all elements of the
> operation must be in balance; the loading, haulage,
> and unloading facilities must be designed and
> scheduled for intensive use but not to a degree
> that would bring intolerable maintenance costs;
> the haulage capacity must be in balance with supply,
> with the consumer's needs, and with amortization
> requirements.[15]

A relatively recent innovation, the unit-train has enabled the
railroads to reduce substantially the costs of transporting
many bulk commodities which move in large volume.[16] By far,
the preponderant number of unit-trains transport coal.
Approximately 20 per cent of all coal mined in the United
States moves by unit-train. The Interstate Commerce Commission
estimates that by 1980 about 85 per cent of the nation's
domestic coal traffic will move under annual volume, concentration, trainload or unit-train concepts.[17]

Unit-train rates cover movements between origin and
destination. In the case of coal moving to destinations
within the Great Lakes Region from Appalachian origins, the
unit-train rates and operations are, for the moment, directly
by all-rail routes between the mines and the consumers. The
latter are principally electric utility plants, many of which
directly occupy shoreline sites and could use Lake transportation for the final portion of the movement if the rates
were favorable. Understandably, the railroads are unwilling
to short-haul themselves by installing unit-train rates
between mines and Lake ports for transshipments to water
carriers.

The result has been a rapid growth of all-rail, unit-
train movements between Appalachian mines and Lake destinations that bypass the traditional coal-loading ports on
the south shore of Lake Erie. The 60-mile movement from
Toledo to Detroit, for example, by Lake vessel has declined

in volume as the result of favorable unit-train rates
directly from mine to utility plant. Similarly reduced or
threatened are the movements of coal from western Kentucky
and southern and central Illinois by rail to South Chicago
for transshipment to Lake vessel and subsequent water movement to Lake Michigan shoreline plants such as Oak Creek,
Milwaukee, to other Wisconsin ports and to Michigan ports
such as Muskegon. Litigation before regulatory bodies and
the courts has been in progress for several years with a view
toward possible initiation of unit-train rates between the
mines and the Lake ports, for joint rail-water movement.

Another mode of transportation which could possibly be
competitive with Great Lakes transportation of coal in the
future is solids pipelining. As mentioned earlier, one such
pipeline was actually built to a Great Lakes port, but its
operation ceased when the railroads reduced their rates. Given
future pipeline technology, it is possible though unlikely that
such a mode could become competitive.18

Another competitive mode, in some instances, is the high-
voltage electric transmission line. Generation of electric
power at the coal mines is practicable since advances in the
technology of high voltage transmission make it economically
feasible, in some instances, to market the power at substantial
distances, sometimes many hundreds of miles from the source.

Vessel Bunkering and Relative Fuel Efficiencies of Competing Modes

With the cost of fuel rising at a rapid rate, the relationship between fuel costs and other elements of cost in providing
transportation service is changing. The higher costs and
limited availability of fuel affects the several transportation
modes to differing extents. An increasing emphasis is placed
upon relative fuel efficiency of the modes, as an element in
cost, and hence of choice of mode by the shipper.

Table 5.4 shows the average fuel efficiency of the several
modes of transporting goods, in terms of BTUs per ton-mile, and
in terms of the number of ton-miles of goods moved per gallon
of fuel consumed by the carrier. In this table, the "waterway"
refers presumably to towboat and barge combinations which, in
the United States, operate principally on the Mississippi
River System of inland waterways. It will be noted that waterway transportation is the most efficient of the several modes,
except for pipelines where they are available. As noted earlier
in this section, pipelines have made substantial inroads into
petroleum products traffic on the Great Lakes and similarly on
other inland waterways. However, because of the large size of
the transportation units on the waterways, it is practicable
to use them only for large-volume shipments, primarily of
bulk commodities.

TABLE 5.4

RELATIVE ENERGY EFFICIENCY OF
FREIGHT TRANSPORTATION BY MODE

Mode	BTU's per ton-mile	Ton-miles per gallon
Pipeline	---	300.0
Waterway (Barge-Towboat)	500	250.0
Railroad	750	200.0
Truck	2,400	58.0
Airplane	63,000	3.7

Source: BTU's per ton-mile: William E. Mooz, "Energy Trends and Their Future Effects Upon Transportation," Proceedings, Fourteenth Annual Meeting, Transportation Research Forum, Cleveland, Ohio, October 15-17, 1973 (Chicago, 1973), p. 707.

Ton-miles per gallon: Thomas D. Larson and Roger E. Carrier, "Energy for Transportation - How to Anticipate the Future," Proceedings, Fourteenth Annual Meeting, Transportation Research Forum, Cleveland, Ohio, October 15-17, 1973 (Chicago, 1973), p. 764.

Great Lakes vessel transportation is even more energy-efficient than inland waterway towboat and barge transportation. Though statistics on ton-miles moved per gallon of fuel are very difficult to obtain, the following has been documented: a large fleet on the Great Lakes averages 495 ton-miles per gallon, including the fuel consumed in empty back-hauls; a new 680 foot vessel with 25,000 tons capacity moved 722.5 ton-miles per gallon; and two of the largest new vessels in Great Lakes service moved 647 and 656 ton-miles per gallon, respectively.[19] These are averages for a season, derived by dividing fuel consumption (including fuel consumed on back-hauls) into total cargo hauled for the navigation season.

It is not accurate to compare directly the ton-mile fuel efficiency of the various transportation modes, since they vary widely with respect to route circuity. Water routes are considerably more circuitous than routes of other modes, especially on the Great Lakes. This is especially true because of the circumvention of the lower peninsula of Michigan between Lake Michigan ports and the Lower Great Lakes and the southerly circumvention of peninsular Ontario between the Upper Great Lakes and both Lake Ontario and the St. Lawrence River.

Table 5.5 presents a rough comparison of the fuel efficiency of Lake vessel transportation compared with that of rail and joint rail-lake movements between characteristic origins and destinations in the Great Lakes Region. Mileages are those of the short main-line railroad and highway routes and the normally-used Great Lakes navigation routes. Fuel efficiency, calculated in terms of gallons consumed per ton-miles, is derived from Table 5.4; 200 ton-miles per gallon for the average railroad freight train, 58 for highway trucks and 600 for a typical modern Lake carrier including, in the latter instance, the fuel consumed in back-hauls, whether the vessel is full or empty. Table 5.5 shows that, for each example given, the fuel consumed per ton in moving the goods by Lake, or by Lake in combination with rail, is considerably less than for overland movement by either rail or highway. In a few instances, substantial mileage can be saved and fuel economies realized by the use of ferries across Lake Michigan, but these savings are not entered in the table because the ferry services are infrequent and are threatened with imminent abandonment.

The opening of the enlarged St. Lawrence Seaway in 1959 provided an alternative route between the Great Lakes Region and overseas that by-passed the salt-water coastal ports. The economies of scale resulting from employment of medium-sized, ocean-going vessels penetrating into the interior of the continent produce cost savings for bulk and general cargo movements where time is not significant. The use of the route, in contrast with combination rail or truck and ocean carriers, also produces noteworthy savings in fuel consumption.

TABLE 5.5 - FUEL EFFICIENCY OF TYPICAL CARGO MOVEMENTS
VIA RAIL, HIGHWAY, LAKES AND RAIL-LAKES TRANSFER

Origin-Destination and Route	Distance (Statute Miles)				Gallons Consumed Per Ton			
	via Rail	via High-way	via Lakes	via Rail-Lakes	via Rail	via High-way	via Lakes	via Rail-Lakes
Chicago-Buffalo	534[a]	520	893	--	2.67	8.97	1.79	--
Duluth-Montreal	1441	1051	1337	--	7.21	18.12	2.67	--
Cleveland-Toronto	261[b]	288[b]	217	--	1.30	4.97	0.43	--
Milwaukee-Detroit	356[c]	368[c]	568	--	1.78	6.34	1.14	--
Minneapolis-Detroit	705[c]	671[d]	--	900[e]	3.53	11.57	--	2.25
Chicago-New York								
via Buffalo	960	828[f]	--	1295	4.80	14.28	--	3.80
via Pittsburgh	907	828[f]	--	--	4.54	14.28	--	--

Fuel: Ton-miles per gallon:

Rail   200
Highway   58
Lake Vessel   600

NOTE: [a]via Penn Central: Toledo and Cleveland
       [b]via Buffalo and Hamilton
       [c]via Chicago
       [d]via Mackinac Bridge
       [e]via Duluth
       [f]via I-80 across Pennsylvania

Mileage from: Official Railway Guide, Rand
McNally Handy Railroad Atlas of the United
States, World Almanac and official state
highway maps, and U.S. Army Corps of Engineers.

Representative savings in fuel by utilizing the St. Lawrence Seaway route between Chicago and various ports, as contrasted with combination rail-water movement through coastal ports, are indicated in Table 5.6. For the rail movement between Chicago and a coastal port, the short-line rail mileage is given. It is assumed, from Table 5.4, that 200 ton-miles per gallon are moved for the rail portion. For the ocean portion as well as for the total water movement through the St. Lawrence Seaway, an assumed vessel of 16,421 deadweight tons capacity at 15 knots (17.25 statute miles per hour) consumes 50 tons of bunker C fuel per 24-hour day.[20] At this rate, it moves 509.88 ton-miles per gallon.

It can be seen from the table that in the instances of movement from Chicago to Hamburg, representative of northern European destinations, and Cape Town, representative of South African and many Indian Ocean destinations, the Seaway movement consumes substantially less fuel than do any of the principal rail routes through coast ports. In the case of Yokahama, representative of transpacific destinations, the Seaway fuel consumption per ton is higher than by most of the rail-water routes, except New York (representative of Atlantic coastal ports), because of the extreme circuity posed by the St. Lawrence Seaway and either the Panama or Suez canals. Although in the latter two instances, the distances are more than halfway around the world, both liner and tramp vessels frequently utilize these routes from Chicago and other Great Lakes ports.

It is believed that the relationships among the various routes, including the comparison between rail-water and all-water, are essentially correct despite the approximated calculations. However, it is recognized that the cost differences would be somewhat reduced by use of larger vessels for the ocean movement to and from coastal ports.

Policy Considerations

The unconventional nature of solar power, wind power, gasification of coal, oil shales, geo-thermal activity and the prospects for the decreased availability and higher prices of fossil fuel argue the necessity for conservation of petroleum and coal, which are non-renewable resources. Since one-quarter of all fuel consumption is for transportation, a substantial portion of which involves movement of goods, the necessity for utilizing the mode most efficient in fuel output is obvious.

Water transportation, including that on the Great Lakes, is under-utilized. It is true that other economic and non-economic considerations help to determine choice of transportation mode, but it is also true that the economical use of fuel will assume greater weight in future choices. Because

124

TABLE 5.6 – COMPARISON OF FUEL CONSUMPTION TO MOVE A TON OF CARGO FROM CHICAGO TO REPRESENTATION OVERSEAS DESTINATIONS VIA ALTERNATIVE RAIL-WATER AND ALL WATER ROUTES

Destination	Via	Rail + water = total statute miles	Gallons consumed per ton from Chicago to destination
Hamburg	New York Seaway	908 + 4,225 = 5,133	4.54 + 8.29 = 12.83
		5,307	10.40
	Rail: Montreal	850 + 4,063 = 4,913	4.25 + 7.98 = 12.23
Cape Town	New York Seaway	908 + 7,803 = 8,711	4.54 + 15.33 = 19.87
		9,429	18.52
	Rail: Montreal	850 + 8,185 = 9,035	4.25 + 16.08 = 20.33
Yokahama	New York and Panama	908 + 11,154 = 12,062	4.54 + 21.91 = 26.45
	New York and Suez	908 + 15,001 = 15,909	4.54 + 29.47 = 34.01
	New Orleans and Panama	921 + 10,482 = 11,403	4.61 + 20.59 = 25.20
	Seattle	2,141 + 4,892 = 7,033	10.70 + 9.61 = 20.31
	Seaway and Panama	13,762	27.04
	Seaway and Suez	16,207	31.84

Basis of calculation: Mileages: Rail statute miles from Official Railway Guide and Rand McNally Handy Railroad Atlas of the United States, (Chicago: Rand McNally & Co.), shortest main line route; Seaway distances from U.S. Army Corps of Engineers; Ocean distances from U.S. Navy Oceanographic Office, H.O. 151, Distances Between Ports (Washington: U.S. Government Printing Office, 1965), nautical miles converted to statute miles. Gallons consumed per ton from origin to destination: miles from above sources, consumption calculated for rail distances as 200 ton-miles per gallon; for ocean and seaway distances on basis of 508.99 ton-miles per gallon for a vessel of 16,421 dwt at 15 knots (17.25 statute miles per hour), consuming 50 tons of bunker C fuel per 24-hour day.

water transportation is more fuel-efficient then other modes, in spite of the circuity of many water routes, it follows that public policy should be directed, in part, to those actions tending to channel, where feasible, the movement of goods toward water carriers. With regard to Great Lakes shipping, there are several policies that, if adopted, would further this end.

One such action would be a general reduction of government regulation of common carriers and of many of the contract carriers that are currently under rate and service regulation, in order to maximize the particular advantages of each mode. The present feeling in many quarters is that government regulations need to be completely overhauled and revised. Some experts argue complete de-regulation as benefiting most transportation, and the economy as a whole. Not supporting total de-regulation, most experts do believe that some reduction of regulation would facilitate more economic allocation of traffic among modes and carriers. The water carriers, including those on the Great Lakes as well as those in direct Great Lakes-overseas services, would benefit to at least some extent, because water transportation is generally lower-cost than competitive modes and because, among other advantages, it is more fuel-efficient. Lake and ocean ships are especially economical for transportation of bulk commodities. The St. Lawrence Seaway enables the utilizing of the most economic transportation mode for the longest distance penetration into the heart of the continent; only one of the Seaway's advantages, this one has been only partially exploited.

There are several ways in which the public could facilitate use of the Great Lakes and the St. Lawrence Seaway for transportation of bulk commodities, as well as some general cargo.

One such way is through the inauguration of more import-export rates on international traffic through Great Lakes ports. The fact that much of the overseas traffic through competitive coastal ports moves on such rates, which are lower than domestic rates between inland points (including those on the Great Lakes) and the respective port cities, gives the coastal ports a decided rate advantage. Similarly, the greater use of unit-trains and the initiation of unit-train rates on both domestic and international (U.S.-Canada) movements by rail in combination with Lake carriers should be encouraged. For, as pointed out earlier, Lake vessels are more fuel-efficient than railroads, even including the very efficient unit-trains.

Passenger traffic has virtually disappeared from the Great Lakes except for a few local ferry services and the cross-Lake Michigan railroad car ferries which are in danger of termination. Growing constraints on the availability of motor vehicle fuel or its price could well revive passenger vessel traffic within the Great Lakes. Such passenger travel, with or without automobiles, on many possible inter-city routes, would not result in savings of distance. But even if the land-water distance were somewhat greater, the water portion of the overall trip could result in total fuel savings between many origins and destinations.

Finally, government subsidies to water carriers could well be extended beyond present levels in order to save fuel, among other objectives. Often the cost of maintaining a shipping route by water may be considerably less than the cost of building or maintaining a highway of comparable distance. Subsidies that would unfavorably affect those carriers, especially the railroads, now maintaining and operating fixed routes must, however, be carefully avoided.

Footnotes

[1]The Nation's Energy Future. A Report to Richard M. Nixon, President of the United States, submitted by Dr. Dixy Lee Ray, Chairman, United States Atomic Energy Commission, 1 December 1973 (Washington: U.S. Government Printing Office, 1973), 171 pp.

[2]For Example: John V. Krutilla and R. Talbot Page, "Towards a Responsible Energy Policy," Policy Analysis, Vol. 1, No. 1 (Winter, 1975), pp.

[3]Douglas R. Bohl and Milton Russell, U.S. Energy Policy: Alternatives for Security (Baltimore: The Johns Hopkins University Press for Resources for the Future, 1975).

[4]Lawson A. W. Hunter, Energy Policies of the World: Canada (Newark, Del.: Center for the Study of Marine Policy, College of Marine Studies, University of Delaware, 1975), p. 58.

[5]William E. Mooz, "Energy Trends and Their Future Effects Upon Transportation," Proceedings, Fourteenth Annual Meeting, Transportation Research Forum (Chicago: 1973), p. 706.

[6]Interstate Commerce Commission, ExParte No. 270(Sub-No. 4) Investigation of Railroad Freight Rate Structure - Coal, Decided December 3, 1974 (Washington: U.S. Government Printing Office, 1975), p. 86.

[7]Gunnar Alexandersson, Geography of Manufacturing (Englewood Cliffs, N.J.: Prentice-Hall, 1967), pp. 32 ff.; also: Gunnar Alexandersson, "Changes in the Location Pattern of the Anglo-American Steel Industry, 1948-1959," Economic Geography, Vol. 37, No. 2 (April, 1961), pp. 95-114.

[8]U.S. Department of Labor, Technological Trends in Major American Industries (Washington: U.S. Government Printing Office, 1966), p. 59.

[9]Lake Carriers Association, Annual Report, 1953, p. 85; Lake Carriers Association, Annual Report, 1973, p. 40; U.S. Army Corps of Engineers, Transportation on the Great Lakes, 1937, p. 315.

[10]Gus Welty, "Coal by Pipeline: A Challenge to the Unit Train," Railway Age, Vol. 176, No. 9 (May 12, 1975), pp. 16-17; David G. Osborn, Geographical Features of the Automation of Industry (University of Chicago Department of Geography, Research Paper No. 30, 1953), p. 43-48.

[11]The Great Lakes Newsletter (Ann Arbor: Great Lakes Commission) ol. 19, No. 2, November-December 1974, p. 3.

[12]The Superior Terminal: New Access to Half the Nation's Coal Fairfield, N.J.: Orba Corporation, n.d., ca. 1975), brochure. lso Journal of Commerce, March 31, 1975.

[13]"Canada Maps Big New Unit-Train Coal Moves," Railway Age, Vol. 75, No. 20 (October 28, 1974), p. 48.

[14]John T. Starr, Jr., "Electric Utility Fuel Requirements and he Future of Unit Trains," Proceedings, Fourteenth Annual Meeting, ransportation Research Forum (Chicago: 1973), pp. 762-772.

[15]T. O. Glover, et. al., Unit Train Transportation of Coal: echnology and Description of Nine Representative Operations, Inforation Circular No. 8444 (Washington: U.S. Dept. of the Interior, ureau of Mines, 1970), p. 1.

[16]John T. Starr, Jr., The Evolution of Unit Train Operation in he United States: 1960-1969: A Decade of Experience (University f Chicago Department of Geography, Research Paper No. 158, 1975).

[17]Interstate Commerce Commission, p. 107.

[18]Welty, pp. 16-17.

[19]Letter from Vice Admiral Paul E. Trimble, President, Lake arrier's Association, June 23, 1975; also telephone conversation.

[20]This is an actual representative vessel of a type employed n world-wide tramping and physically capable of transiting the t. Lawrence Seaway.

Bibliography

Aase, James H. "Transportation of Iron Ore, Limestone, and Bituminous Coal on the Great Lakes Waterway System, with Projections to 1995." Information Circular 8461, U.S. Bureau of Mines. Washington: U.S. Government Printing Office, 1970, 61 pp.

American Iron and Steel Institute. Annual Statistical Report. Washington: American Iron and Steel Institute, annual.

Barry, James P. The Fate of the Lakes. Grand Rapids, Michigan: Baker Book House, 1972. (Chapter 4: "Power," pp. 81-99).

Bell, Harold S., ed. Petroleum Transportation Handbook. New York: McGraw-Hill Book Co., 1963, 484 pp.

Bohl, Douglas R., and Russell, Milton. U.S. Energy Policy: Alternatives for Security. Baltimore: The Johns Hopkins University Press for Resources for the Future, 1975, 141 pp.

Chesser, Al H. Transportation and Energy. Cleveland: United Transportation Union. n.d., ca. 1975, 84 pp.

Coal Traffic Annual. Washington: National Coal Association, annual.

"The Economics of Coal Traffic Flow." 79th Congress, 1st Session, Senate Document No. 82. Washington: U.S. Government Printing Office, 1945, 103 pp.

"Energy," Science, Vol. 184, No. 4,134, 19 April 1974, pp. 247-386.

Fitch, Littleton H. "Planning Transportation Use in Petroleum Distribution," in Papers, Tenth Annual Meeting, Transportation Research Forum. Chicago: 1969, pp. 173-181.

Glover, T. O., et. al. Unit Train Transportation of Coal, Technology and Description of Nine Representative Operations. U.S. Dept. of the Interior, Bureau of Mines. Washington: U.S. Government Printing Office, 1970, 109 pp.

Gordon, Richard L. U.S. Coal and the Electric Power Industry. Baltimore: The Johns Hopkins Press for Resources for the Future, 1975, 227 pp.

Guyol, Nathaniel B. Energy in the Perspective of Geography. Englewood Cliffs, N.J.: Prentice Hall, 1971, 156 pp.

Harbeson, Robert W. "Some Transport Policy Implications of Energy Shortages," Land Economics, Vol. 50, No. 4 (November, 1974), pp. 387-396.

auser, L. G. "Electric Utility Energy Sources--An Overview," in Energy Conservation Options for Illinois Proceedings of the Second Annual Illinois Energy Conference. Chicago: Energy Resources Center of the University of Illinois at Chicago Circle, 1974, pp. 109-121.

unter, Lawson A. W. Energy Policies of the World: Canada. Newark, Delaware: Center for the Study of Marine Policy, College of Marine Studies, University of Delaware, 1975, 64 pp.

nterstate Commerce Commission. Ex Parte No. 270(Sub-No. 4), Investigation of Railroad Freight Rate Structure-Coal, Decided December 3, 1974. Washington: U.S. Government Printing Office, 1975, 409 pp.

eystone Coal Industry Manual. New York: McGraw-Hill Inc., annual.

ing, L., Cassetti, E., Odland, J., and Semple, K. "Optimal Transportation Patterns of Coal in the Great Lakes Region," Economic Geography, Vol. 47, No. 3 (July, 1971), pp. 401-413.

rutilla, John V., and Page, R. Talbot. "Towards a Responsible Energy Policy," Policy Analysis, Vol. 1, No. 1 (Winter, 1975), pp.

ake Carriers' Association. Annual Report. Cleveland: Lake Carriers' Association, annual.

Lake Superior 1974 Coal Shipments Over a Million Tons," The Great Lakes News Letter, Great Lakes Commission, Vol. 19, No. 2 (November-December, 1974), p. 3.

arson, Thomas D., and Carrier, Roger E. "Energy for Transportation - How to Anticipate the Future," in Proceedings, Fourteenth Annual Meeting, Transportation Research Forum. Chicago: 1973, pp. 749-766.

anners, Gerald. The Geography of Energy. Chicago: Aldine Publishing Company, 1967. (Chapters 3-5, "Transport," pp. 42-115).

ayer, Harold M. "Energy Policy in Freight Transportation," in Energy Conservation Policy Options for Illinois, Proceedings of the Second Annual Illinois Energy Conference. Chicago: Energy Resources Center of the University of Illinois at Chicago Circle, 1974, pp. 153-160.

ooz, William E. "Energy Trends and their Future Effect Upon Transportation," in Proceedings, Fourteenth Annual Meeting, Transportation Research Forum. Chicago: 1973, pp. 703-715.

131

_____. "Transportation and Energy," in _Energy Problems in Illinois_, Proceedings of the First Annual Illinois Energy Conference. Chicago: Department of Energy Engineering of the College of Engineering in cooperation with the Office of Extension of the University of Illinois at Chicago Circle, 1973, pp. 271-286.

Munro, John M., and Constable, G.A. "Energy Use in Canadian Transportation: The Patterns of Future Adjustment," in _Proceedings Fifteenth Annual Meeting, Transportation Research Forum_. Chicago 1974, pp. 589-602.

Mutschler, Paul H., Evans, R. J., and Larwood, G. M. _Comparative Transportation Costs of Supplying Low-Sulphur Fuels to Midwestern and Eastern Domestic Energy Markets_. Washington: U.S. Bureau of Mines, 1973, 54 pp.

National Coal Association. _Coal Traffic Annual_. Washington: annual

The Nation's Energy Future. A Report to Richard M. Nixon, President of the United States, submitted by Dr. Dixy Lee Ray, Chairman, United States Atomic Energy Commission, 1 December 1973. Washington: U.S. Government Printing Office, 1973, 171 pp.

"Nuclear Power Reactors in the United States, September 30, 1974," _Radiation Data and Reports_, Vol. 15, No. 12 (December, 1974), pp. 842-845.

Peach, W. N. _The Energy Outlook for the 1980's_. A study prepared for the use of the Subcommittee on Economic Progress of the Joint Economic Committee, Congress of the United States, 93rd Congress, 1st session. Washington: U.S. Government Printing Office, 1973, 39 pp.

Petroleum Facts and Figures. New York: American Petroleum Institute annual.

Sloss, James. "Competitive Railroad Rates and Services Applied to the Movement of Bituminous Coal," in _Transportation: A Service_. Sesquicentiennial Forum on Transportation Engineering. New York: New York Academy of Sciences, 1967, pp. 144-152.

Starr, John T., Jr. "Electric Utility Fuel Requirements and the Future of Unit Coal Trains," in _Proceedings, Fourteenth Annual Meeting, Transportation Research Forum_. Chicago: 1973, pp. 767-772.

Steinhart, Carol and John. _Energy: Sources, Use, and Role in Human Affairs_. North Scituate, Mass.: Duxbury Press, 1974, 362 pp.

ihansky, Dennis P. "Predicting Total Energy Requirements of
Freight Transportation in the United States," in Proceedings,
Fourteenth Annual Meeting, Transportation Research Forum.
Chicago: 1973, pp. 717-736.

ower, Kenneth. "Hydroelectric Power in the Great Lakes-St.
Lawrence Basin," in Pincus, Howard J., ed., Great Lakes Basin.
Washington: American Association for the Advancement of
Science, 1962, pp. 195-212.

The Unit Train: Key to Coal's Survival?" Railway Age, Vol. 155,
No. 18 (November 4, 1963), pp. 40-42.

.S. Army, Corps of Engineers. Origin-Destination Study of Bulk
Commodity Movement, Upper Great Lakes Region, under Cooperative
Agreement with Upper Great Lakes Regional Commission. Chicago:
U.S. Army Engineer Division, North Central, June 1972, various
pages.

_____. Transportation on the Great Lakes.
Transportation Series No. 1. Washington: U.S. Government
Printing Office, revised 1937, 441 pp.

_____. Waterborne Commerce of the United
States, Part 3, Waterways and Harbors, Great Lakes. Chicago:
District Engineer, U.S. Army Engineer District, annual.

.S. Atomic Energy Commission. The Nation's Energy Future. A
Report to Richard M. Nixon, President of the United States,
submitted by Dr. Dixy Lee Ray, Chairman, United States Atomic
Energy Commission, 1 December 1973. Washington: U.S. Government Printing Office, 171 pp.

.S. Bureau of Mines. Unit Train Transportation of Coal: Technology
and Description of Nine Representative Operations. Information
Circular 8444. Washington: U.S. Government Printing Office,
1970, 109 pp.

hynot, G. Keith. "Some Business Aspects of Tanker Transportation
in the Great Lakes and St. Lawrence River Areas," Inland Seas,
Vol. 30, No. 4 (Winter, 1974), pp. 268 and 277-286.

VI.

Great Lakes-Overseas
General Cargo Traffic
and Port Hinterlands

Introduction

The U.S. Bureau of the Census, in 1972, released the results of a survey of the 1970 general cargo traffic between the
United States and overseas origins and destinations.[1] The data
were made available to the public on magnetic tapes, subject to
the constraint of nondisclosure policies. This chapter summarizes a recent detailed analysis of a subset of that data pertaining to movements, and potentially available movements,
through Great Lakes ports.[2] A previous attempt at such an analysis in 1967 was based on 1956 data and provided little detail.
In contrast, the details of the data collected in the new survey
permitted analysis of specific commodity movements and specific
ports, as well as determination of a hinterland on a tonnage per
state basis and identification of the general overseas area that
a given port served. For each shipment selected for the sample,
the following information was collected: the commodity type,
its weight and value, the manner of shipping, its points of origin and destination, the domestic and international means of
transportation, the United States port of entry or exit and the
distances included in the United States portions of the movement.

Data collected in the sample describe "liner-type" commodities moving in foreign trade during 1970 through ports
within the 48 contiguous states and transported on the international leg by water or air. This definition results in the
exclusion of land transportation between the United States and
both Canada and Mexico. Excluding major bulk commodities, it
restricts analysis to general cargo and certain other commodities with bulk-like characteristics, which are classified as
general cargo, such as iron and steel, and scrap. The Census
Survey selected vessel shipments for the sample with a probability proportional to shipment weight. All very large shipments were included because weight was considered the single
most important characteristic. An unfortunate result of the
sample design is that the information is biased toward heavy
shipments. Since the relationship between the distribution of
weight (for vessel shipments) and other characteristics of the
traffic population is unknown, the sample cannot describe re-
liably some important characteristics. For example, it cannot
provide an adequate estimate of the actual distribution of destinations of a particular import within the United States since
the sample bias would result in an unreliable relationship between points receiving large shipments and those attracting
primarily small shipments.

Recognition of the data limitations narrows the scope of
this study to a description of commodity-specific and port-
specific hinterlands defined by state. Because of the limitations of the data, the findings of this study cannot be gener-
alized and must be used only with extreme caution. Despite the
data limitations, the effort devoted to the hinterland analysis
was deemed justified on the basis of the uniqueness of the data.
This data base is the only detailed information source concerning

domestic movements of exports and imports in over a decade. Though the information is incomplete, no other source describes individual shipments as well. This type of information is extremely important to every individual and agency engaged in international cargo movements. For example, this analysis may permit ports to enhance the efficiency of their marketing efforts, which are conducted on a limited budget, by concentrating them both geographically and by commodity.

Specific Commodity Analyses

Thirteen export commodities and 15 import commodities important to the Great Lakes Region were selected for analysis. Five commodities were common to both lists. The selected commodities are listed in Tables 6.1 and 6.2.

In addition to the dangers of generalizing the results of the commodity analyses, given their data limitations, there are additional factors to which the reader should be alerted. Because the data were generated in 1970 during the Vietnam War, a period when many government-impelled cargoes moved through Great Lakes ports, several of the results must be interpreted with extra care. Some specific ports may have had trade increases of only a temporary nature. Particular commodity movements may be inordinately high, and Southeast Asia may rank abnormally high as a destination for exports. Also, related to government-impelled cargoes is the requirement that at least 50 per cent of such cargo be moved in U.S.-flag vessels. No U.S.-flag cargo liners served the Great Lakes for overseas movements during the period 1969 through 1974. However, a low level of scheduled cargo liner service under the United States flag resumed in 1975. This change must be considered in assessing the state of Great Lakes overseas shipping. Lastly, the effects of fewer overall sailings and increasingly strong competition from capital-intensive coastal ports must be recognized.

Tables 6.3 and 6.4 summarize the coast of interface for the international leg of the trip for Great Lakes-related shipments, including the 13 export commodities and the 15 import commodities. From Table 6.3, it can be seen that the Great Lakes Coast was dominant only in the cases of Crude Fertilizers and Minerals (SBR-27) and Metalliferous Ores and Metal Scrap (SBR-28) for exports. Canada (World Area 1) attracted over 60 per cent of the exported weight for SBR-27. However, the Great Lakes played a lesser role in the other commodities bound primarily for Canada. These were Petroleum and Petroleum Products (SBR-33) and Manufactured Fertilizers and Fertilizer Materials (SBR-56).

The sample shipments of SBR-28 were found to have originated very close to the major Great Lakes ports. If this were the reason for the use of the Great Lakes ports, one would have expected SBR-67, Iron and Steel, to be more

TABLE 6.1

RANKINGS OF EXPORT COMMODITY GROUPS

Commodity (SBR)	Shipments	Value	Weight
Cereals and Cereal Preparations (04)	4	5	6
Feeding-stuff for Animals (08)	1	2	2
Miscellaneous Food Preparations (09)	–	8	10
Crude Fertilizers and Minerals (27)	7	9	5
Metalliferous Ores and Metal Scrap (28)	3	3	3
Petroleum and Petroleum By-Products (33)	6	7	4
Animal Oils and Fats (41)	10	–	–
Fixed Vegetable Oils and Fats (42)	–	4	7
Chemical Elements and Compounds (51)	9	10	9
Manufactured Fertilizers and Fertilizer Materials (56)	–	–	8
Iron and Steel (67)	2	1	1
Non-Electric Machinery (71)	5	6	–
Transport Equipment (73)	8	–	–

Source: Analysis of International Great Lakes Shipping and Hinterland, Special Report No. 23, April, 1975, Center for Great Lakes Studies, Table 2.1, p. II-2.

Note: The 2-digit SBR numbers refer to Schedule B Subgroup commodity codes used by U.S. Department of Commerce, Bureau of the Census, for collection of foreign trade statistics.

TABLE 6.2

RANKINGS OF IMPORT COMMODITY GROUPS

Commodity (SAR)	Shipments	Value	Weight
Fruits and Vegetables (05)	7	–	–
Sugar, Sugar Preparations, and Honey (06)	3	9	4
Coffee, Cocoa, Tea, Spices and Manufactures Thereof (07)	10	6	–
Crude Rubber (23)	9	–	–
Wood, Lumber and Cork (24)	–	–	9
Pulp and Waste Paper (25)	–	8	8
Crude Fertilizers and Minerals (27)	2	7	2
Chemical Elements and Compounds (51)	–	3	3
Manufactured Fertilizers and Fertilizer Materials (56)	–	–	7
Paper, Paperboard, and Manufactures Thereof (64)	6	2	5
Non-Metallic Mineral Manufactures (66)	5	–	6
Iron and Steel (67)	1	1	1
Nonferrous Metals (68)	–	5	–
Non-Electric Machinery (71)	8	10	–
Transport Equipment (73)	4	4	10

Source: Analysis of International Great Lakes Shipping and Hinterland, Special Report No. 23, April, 1975, Center for Great Lakes Studies, Table 2.2, p. II-3.

Note: The 2-digit SAR numbers refer to Schedule A Subgroup commodity codes used by U.S. Department of Commerce, Bureau of the Census, for collection of foreign trade statistics.

TABLE 6.3

WEIGHT AND PER CENT OF TOTAL WEIGHT OF GREAT LAKES
RELATED EXPORTS THROUGH INDIVIDUAL COASTS

(In Thousands of Tons)

COMMODITY (SBR)	Great Lakes Weight	%	East Weight	%	Gulf Weight	%	West Weight	%
Cereals and Cereal Preparations (04)	65	14.96	22	5.16	333	76.85	13	3.03
Feeding-stuff for Animals (08)	564	28.02	457	22.73	986	49.03	1	0.07
Miscellaneous Food Preparations (09)	24	44.65	3	6.42	26	47.66	1	1.28
Crude Fertilizers and Minerals (27)	447	87.99	11	2.09	45	8.78	6	1.15
Metalliferous Ores and Metal Scrap (28)	802	59.47	395	29.29	152	11.24	-	0.00
Petroleum and Petroleum Products (33)	296	48.76	85	13.96	214	35.24	12	2.04
Animal Oils and Fats (41)	20	42.47	6	12.01	19	40.27	2	5.15
Fixed Vegetable Oils and Fats (42)	1	0.38	*	0.09	167	99.03	-	0.00
Chemical Elements and Compounds (51)	8	20.63	9	23.30	23	55.87	*	0.19
Manufactured Fertilizers and Fertilizer Materials (56)	5	20.17	2	7.76	17	72.07	-	0.00
Iron and Steel (67)	786	31.95	225	9.17	1,447	58.88	-	0.00
Non-Electric Machinery (71)	1	6.66	10	66.60	2	15.48	2	11.26
Transport Equipment (73)	*	4.08	3	61.11	1	20.29	1	14.52

* Significantly less than one thousand tons, but non-zero

Source: Analysis of International Great Lakes Shipping and Hinterland, Special Report No. 23, April, 1975, Center for Great Lakes Studies, Table 2.62, pp. II-153, 154.

Note: The 2-digit SBR numbers refer to Schedule B Subgroups commodity codes used by the U.S. Department of Commerce, Bureau of the Census, for collection of foreign trade statistics.

TABLE 6.4 - WEIGHT AND PERCENT OF TOTAL WEIGHT OF GREAT LAKES
RELATED IMPORTS THROUGH INDIVIDUAL COASTS
(In Thousands of Tons)

COMMODITY (SAR)	Great Lakes Weight	%	East Weight	%	Gulf Weight	%	West Weight	%
Fruits and Vegetables (05)	1	13.43	6	63.87	1	10.46	1	12.24
Sugar, Sugar Preparations and Honey (06)	9	2.29	177	43.83	218	53.88	-	0.00
Coffee, Cocoa, Tea, Spices and Manufactures Thereof (07)	4	14.49	17	67.07	4	16.14	1	2.30
Crude Rubber (23)	2	16.76	7	59.92	1	9.96	1	13.36
Wood, Lumber and Cork (24)	-	0.00	52	93.54	1	1.26	3	5.20
Pulp and Waste Paper (25)	44	82.51	9	17.49	-	0.00	-	0.00
Crude Fertilizers and Minerals (27)	790	85.63	63	6.79	70	7.58	*	0.00
Chemical Elements and Compounds (51)	48	10.72	3	0.69	121	26.96	277	61.63
Manufactured Fertilizers and Fertilizer Material (56)	35	45.46	20	25.35	23	29.19	-	0.00
Paper, Paperboard and Manufactures Thereof (64)	305	96.80	4	1.27	4	1.17	2	0.75
Non-Metallic Mineral Manufactures (66)	262	81.29	60	18.55	*	0.13	*	0.04
Iron and Steel (67)	1,199	82.88	19	1.30	223	15.45	5	0.37
Nonferrous Metals (68)	12	36.36	9	26.25	13	37.39	-	0.00
Non-Electric Machinery (71)	6	14.88	24	64.17	3	8.51	5	12.44
Transport Equipment (73)	10	26.06	9	22.55	5	13.56	15	37.82

* Significantly less than one thousand tons, but non-zero

Source: Analysis of International Great Lakes Shipping and Hinterland, Special Report No. 23, April, 1975,
Center for Great Lakes Studies, Table 2.63, pp. II-155, 156.

Note: The 2-digit SAR numbers refer to Schedule A Subgroup commodity codes used by the U.S. Department
of Commerce, Bureau of the Census for collection of foreign trade statistics

strongly held to that coast. That they moved through the Gulf Coast instead is a fact that lies beyond the explanatory power of these data.

From Table 6.4, it can be seen that the Great Lakes overwhelmingly dominated in serving five of the 15 import commodities analyzed: Pulp and Waste Paper (SAR-25); Crude Fertilizers and Minerals (SAR-27); Paper, Paperboard and Manufactures Thereof (SAR-64); Non-Metallic Mineral Manu-factures (SAR-66); and Iron and Steel (SAR-67). For these five, Canada (World Area 1) was found to be the dominant World Area of origin for all but Iron and Steel. Manufac-tured Fertilizers and Fertilizer Materials (SAR-56) was another commodity for which the Great Lakes Coast had a strong attraction. This commodity also originated largely in Canada, as did Wood, Lumber and Cork (SAR-24). Interestingly, many of the shipments of SAR-24 (51 per cent) were containerized, but these shipments represented only 5 per cent of the sample value and 3 per cent of the sample weight. A high proportion of the shipments of SAR-24 passed through the East Coast ports of the states of New York and Pennsylvania, which are unique in having both Great Lakes and East Coast ports.

Iron and Steel (SAR-67) imports seem to have been drawn to the Great Lakes ports not so much by their origins as by their destinations, which were predominantly in Illinois and Michigan.

The summary information compiled for each of the 28 commodities analyzed included tons per shipment and value per ton for shipments moving through ports on each of the four coasts. Those figures were ranked for each commodity. The average of the ranks assigned the Great Lakes Coast for tons per shipment was 1.89. This compared with an average rank of 2.79 for value per ton. The same analysis was repeated but restricted to the previously cited seven commodities dominated by the Great Lakes. In this case, the average rank for tons per shipment fell to 1.14 whereas the average rank for value per ton rose to 3.0. This analysis indicates that (relative to the other coasts) the Great Lakes attracted commodities of low unit value moving in large shipments. Although the shippers' choices revealed in these data are the result of a consideration of many factors, the Great Lakes relative lack of success in compet-ing for commodities of higher unit value probably stems in part from the inherent disadvantage of the Great Lakes-St. Lawrence Seaway System.

Specific hinterlands for the 12 most important commodity movements analyzed are shown on maps (see Appendix 6-A to this chapter) depicting the Great Lakes-related tonnage that passed through each of the four United States coasts: East, Gulf, West and Great Lakes. These maps provide a visual mea-sure of the relative competitive position of the Great Lakes

Coast. They also reveal the individual differences of the various commodity hinterlands, many of them a scattered configuration of states.

Analysis of Specific Ports or Port Clusters

Six Great Lakes ports, or port clusters, were selected for analysis of their respective hinterlands: 1) Chicago, 2) Cleveland (including Lorain), 3) Detroit, 4) Duluth, 5) Milwaukee (including Kenosha and Racine), and 6) Toledo.[3] Port clusters were chosen only because the data for the clustered ports were inseparable on the tapes. Aggregation of this type constitutes another shortcoming of the data that affected the analysis attempted.

The analysis of the ports or port clusters included a determination of the number of shipments, value and weight of the major export and import commodities handled by each port cluster. Also, a determination of the states served by each was made. Concluding the analysis was a determination of the World Areas served by each port cluster.

Tables 6.5 and 6.6 show that the six Great Lakes port clusters can be placed into two very general categories by the key measure--weight--with Chicago and Detroit classified as large, and the rest much smaller. Chicago and Detroit together accounted for over 73 per cent of the sample weight exported. Duluth ranked a distant third, accounting for less than 9 per cent. Although the absolute size of the gap between the first and second ranked port clusters was essentially the same as that between the second and third, the magnitude of the relative weights warrants the two-category classification.

Tables 6.7 and 6.8 depict a pattern found to be typical of all six port clusters: namely that an overwhelming percentage of the sample tonnage was accounted for by five or fewer commodities. The dominating commodities varied among the ports, thereby implying a specialization which reflected differences among their respective hinterlands.

Maps 6.1* and 6.2* show the combined hinterlands of each port or cluster in terms of the states served. They reveal that each hinterland is dominated by the state in which the port or ports are located. The extent of this dominance is quantified by determining the percentage of the

---

*Source: Analysis of International Great Lakes Shipping and Hinterland, Special Report No. 23, April, 1975, Center for Great Lakes Studies, Map 15, p. III-6, and Map 16, p. III-26.

TABLE 6.5

MAJOR GREAT LAKES PORT CLUSTERS RANKED BY WEIGHT
OF GENERAL CARGO EXPORTS

Rank	Port Clusters	Weight (Short Tons)	Per Cent of Sample
1	Chicago	1,392,242	47.45
2	Detroit	794,049	27.06
3	Duluth	239,407	8.16
4	Cleveland-Lorain	201,106	6.85
5	Milwaukee-Kenosha-Racine	182,082	6.21
6	Toledo	125,443	4.28
	TOTAL	2,934,329	100.00 *

Source: Analysis of International Great Lakes Shipping and Hinterland, Special Report No. 23, April, 1975, Center for Great Lakes Studies, Table 3.1, p. III-4.

*Totals may not add due to rounding.

TABLE 6.6

MAJOR GREAT LAKES PORT CLUSTERS RANKED BY WEIGHT
OF GENERAL CARGO IMPORTS

Rank	Port Clusters	Weight (Short Tons)	Per Cent of Sample
1	Detroit	854,063	37.33
2	Chicago	835,680	36.35
3	Cleveland-Lorain	201,631	8.81
4	Toledo	185,208	8.10
5	Milwaukee-Kenosha-Racine	183,945	8.04
6	Duluth	27,098	1.18
	TOTAL	2,287,625	100.00*

Source: Analysis of International Great Lakes Shipping
and Hinterland, Special Report No. 23, April,
1975, Center for Great Lakes Studies, Table 3.12,
p. III-24.

*Totals may not add due to rounding.

146

TABLE 6.7

SOME IMPORTANT GREAT LAKES EXPORT COMMODITIES BY WEIGHT

SBR	Description	Percentage of Sample Weight
28	Metalliferous Ores and Metal Scrap	26.09
67	Iron and Steel	24.83
8	Feeding-stuff for Animals	19.21
27	Crude Fertilizers and Minerals	15.22
33	Petroleum and Petroleum Products	9.94
	TOTAL	95.29

Source: Analysis of International Great Lakes Shipping and Hinterland, Special Report No. 23, April, 1975, Center for Great Lakes Studies, Table 3.2, p. III-5.

147

TABLE 6.8

SOME IMPORTANT GREAT LAKES IMPORT COMMODITIES BY WEIGHT

SAR	Description	Percentage of Sample Weight
67	Iron and Steel	49.70
27	Crude Fertilizers and Minerals	27.20
64	Paper, Paperboard and Manufactures Thereof	12.56
	TOTAL	89.46

Source: Analysis of International Great Lakes Shipping and Hinterland, Special Report No. 23, April, 1975, Center for Great Lakes Studies, Table 3.13, p. III-25.

PLACE OF ACQUISITION OF GREAT LAKES RELATED EXPORTS
THROUGH GREAT LAKES PORTS -- M A P   6.1

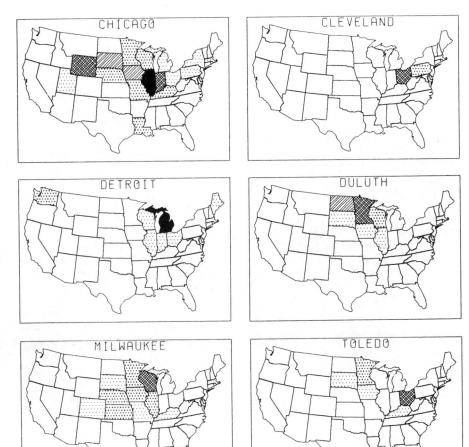

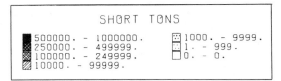

PLACE OF DESTINATION OF GREAT LAKES RELATED IMPORTS
THROUGH GREAT LAKES PORTS -- MAP 6.2

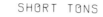

SHORT TONS

■	500000. - 1000000.	▦ 1000. - 9999.
▨	250000. - 499999.	▨ 1. - 999.
▥	100000. - 249999.	□ 0. - 0.
▧	10000. - 99999.	

sample weight exported or imported through each port or cluster that was located in the same state as the place of acquisition[4] or place of destination. These percentages are presented in Tables 6.9 and 6.10. Only Chicago's export hinterland extended to a significant degree into more than one state.

As indicated in Appendix 6-A of this chapter, certain shipments can be considered only as statistical aberrations that cannot be explained on the basis of the data. For example, on Map 6.1 the shipment acquired in the state of Washington for export through Detroit was shown to be destined for Southeast Asia. The rationale for such a movement is neither apparent nor determinable from the data. Although such shipments contributed to a curious hinterland pattern, a review of the tonnages and number of shipments involved revealed that such anomalies were insignificant.

The last element of the port analysis involved a determination of the World Area each port or cluster served. Tables 6.11 and 6.12 contain the 1970 sample export and import tonnages, respectively, of liner-type commodities handled by each of the six ports as subtotaled by 12 specified World Areas. A comparison of the World Area subtotals reveals substantially different patterns for exports and for imports, although the same two, Northern North America (i.e., Canada) and West-Central Europe, dominated traffic in both directions.

There was some tendency toward specialization in movements between certain World Areas and specific ports or clusters, especially for exports. That the various ports were not competing with each other for this traffic is consistent with the phenomenon of home-state dominance discussed earlier.

Summary and Conclusions

The initial intent of the study summarized in this chapter was to determine the competitive hinterland of the Great Lakes-St. Lawrence Seaway System as defined in terms of those states which are served by the System to some significant extent. Such an analysis is particularly important at the present time because decisions concerning future investment in the System are being made, based in part on a hinterland defined in 1967 according to 1956 data. The data source utilized in the new study was the Public Use Tapes available from the U.S. Department of Commerce, Bureau of the Census, entitled Domestic and International Transportation of U.S. Foreign Trade: 1970. These data are confined to international movements of "liner-type" commodities.

Although the data are both comprehensive and unique, and therefore inherently valuable, the strongest conclusions

TABLE 6.9

MEASURE OF HOME STATE DOMINANCE--EXPORTS

Port	Home State	Percentage of Port's Sample Export Tonnage From Home State	Percentage From All Other States Excluding Foreign Country
Chicago	Illinois	59.64	31.57
Cleveland-Lorain	Ohio	93.05	3.11
Detroit	Michigan	93.48	0.18
Duluth	Minnesota	90.16	9.76
Milwaukee-Kenosha-Racine	Wisconsin	83.17	10.60
Toledo	Ohio	98.79	1.15

Source: Analysis of International Great Lakes Shipping and Hinterland, Special Report No. 23, April, 1975, Center for Great Lakes Studies, Table 3.4, p. III-8.

TABLE 6.10

MEASURE OF HOME STATE DOMINANCE--IMPORTS

Port	Home State	Percentage of Port's Sample Import Tonnage To Home State	Percentage to All Other States Excluding Foreign Country
Chicago	Illinois	83.88	11.34
Cleveland-Lorain	Ohio	79.02	14.17
Detroit	Michigan	88.66	2.94
Duluth	Minnesota	87.52	12.25
Milwaukee-Kenosha-Racine	Wisconsin	86.33	1.03
Toledo	Ohio	83.33	13.23

Source: Analysis of International Great Lakes Shipping and Hinterland, Special Report No. 23, April, 1975, Center for Great Lakes Studies, Table 3.15, p. III-28.

TABLE 6.11

WORLD AREA DESTINATIONS OF EXPORTS THROUGH GREAT LAKES PORTS, BY TONNAGE

No.	World Area	Chicago	Detroit	Duluth	Cleveland (including Lorain)	Toledo	Milwaukee (including Racine & Kenosha)	World Area Total*
1.	Northern North America	304,701	237,276	4,660	53,584	74,796	0	675,017
2.	Southern North America	1,340	0	231	0	0	331	1,902
3.	North & East South America	77	216	1,020	0	0	0	1,313
4.	West South America	0	0	857	0	0	0	857
5.	United Kingdom & Ireland	246,123	90,547	17,527	43,544	360	12,823	410,929
6.	Northwest Europe	6,841	27,420	0	0	0	393	34,654
7.	West-Central Europe	592,338	130,800	140,262	74,070	32,017	3,167	972,654
8.	Southern Europe & Mediterranean	118,653	163,076	17,910	28,012	2,918	62,234	392,803
9.	Eastern Europe	6,547	13,228	0	0	0	1,332	21,107
10.	Southeast Asia & Australia	16,244	1,694	8,101	1,896	0	15,720	43,655
11.	East-Central Asia	96,631	129,775	48,605	0	15,353	82,139	372,503
12.	Africa, except Mediterranean	2,752	21	231	0	0	3,937	6,941
	Port Total*	1,392,247	794,053	239,404	201,106	125,444	182,081	2,934,335

Source: Analysis of International Great Lakes Shipping and Hinterland, Special Report No. 23, April, 1975, Center for Great Lakes Studies, Table 3.23, p. III-46.

* Totals may not add due to rounding.

TABLE 6.12

WORLD AREA ORIGINS OF IMPORTS THROUGH GREAT LAKES PORTS, BY TONNAGE

No.	World Area	Port							World Area Total*
		Chicago	Detroit	Duluth	Cleveland (including Lorain)	Toledo	Milwaukee (including Racine & Kenosha)		
1.	Northern North America	486,033	351,748	21,696	41,228	76,030	101,680		1,078,415
2.	Southern North America	0	3,000	0	21,167	9,234	0		33,401
3.	North & East South America	2,063	2,170	0	0	254	0		4,487
4.	West South America	2,406	0	0	0	1,060	0		3,466
5.	United Kingdom & Ireland	11,581	44,113	2,028	8,948	6,032	15,581		88,283
6.	Northwest Europe	816	39	0	155	0	658		1,668
7.	West-Central Europe	193,621	276,086	2,483	95,727	39,122	1,599		608,638
8.	Southern Europe & Mediterranean	16,128	70,317	0	15,637	40,989	142		143,713
9.	Eastern Europe	1,125	635	0	570	0	0		2,330
10.	Southeast Asia & Australia	117	7,669	119	613	154	5,516		14,188
11.	East-Central Asia	119,161	92,365	173	17,578	12,337	52,895		294,509
12.	Africa, except Mediterranean	2,638	5,429	600	0	0	5,875		14,542
	Port Total*	835,689	854,071	27,099	201,623	185,212	183,946		2,287,640

Source: Analysis of International Great Lakes Shipping and Hinterland, Special Report No. 23, April, 1975, Center for Great Lakes Studies, Table 3.26, p. III-54.

* Totals may not add due to rounding.

of the report concern the inadequate sampling procedure.
A sampling procedure that is biased toward a particular
characteristic, as described, permits very accurate estimates
of that characteristic for the population or universe. In
this study, the sample on the Public Use Tapes is biased
toward shipment weight for vessel movements. However, since
the relationship between the distribution of weight and
other characteristics of the population of movements is
unknown, one can use this sample to describe these other
characteristics with confidence only in association with
estimates of highly aggregated categories of vessel shipment
weight.

For example, it is possible that one would wish to
estimate the distribution of destinations within the United
States for a particular category of import. In this case,
since the sample is biased toward large shipments, one may
expect an unreliable relationship between ports serving
primarily large shipments and those serving mostly small
shipments. Or one might want to analyze the flows of container movements within the United States or the amount of
containerization in movements of a particular commodity or
along a single route. However, since the relationship
between weight and a given commodity, route or destination
is unknown for containerized shipments, any conclusions
drawn from this sample could be misleading. In general,
though the sample will yield theoretically unbiased estimates
when aggregating over smaller geographic areas or greater
commodity detail, the sampling variability may exceed
tolerances thereby resulting in estimates inadequately
reliable for many potential uses.

In addition to the problems with the basic sample,
there are instances of data coded in a manner not defined
in the Public Use Tapes documentation. This discrepancy
necessitates caution in the interpretation of results.
Despite these serious limitations, the survey is the best
available. Because many private and public agencies have
already used it as a data source, it was considered necessary to explain the contents of the tapes.

The previously mentioned 1967 study is entitled <u>Great
Lakes-Overseas General Cargo Analysis</u> and was conducted by
the U.S. Army Corps of Engineers. Because of its wide
acceptance and use, it became the basis for segregating the
Great Lakes-related data for analysis. The Corps study
defined a nineteen-state region consisting of the eight
border states of Illinois, Indiana, Michigan, Minnesota,
western New York, Ohio, western Pennsylvania and Wisconsin;
plus the 11 contiguous states of Colorado, Iowa, Kansas,
Kentucky, Missouri, Montana, Nebraska, North Dakota, South
Dakota, West Virginia and Wyoming.

Based on this region, some significant summary statistics
concerning aggregate exports and imports were generated. For

exports, a shipment has the possibility of having been
produced within and/or acquired within the hinterland, and/
or exported through a Great Lakes port. The most interesting
cases are those in which the place of production and/or the
place of acquisition were within the hinterland, but the
port of export was not. These cases represent potential
traffic which could have been served by a Great Lakes port
but was not. It was found that 84 per cent of the sample
weight was produced in the hinterland, 82 per cent was
acquired there, but only 40 per cent was exported through a
Great Lakes port.

For imports, the most significant situation occurs when
shipments destined for the Great Lakes area enter the United
States through a non-Great Lakes port. Again, these shipments represent potential Great Lakes port traffic. Of the
total import sample weight, it was found that 93 per cent was
destined to a place within the hinterland whereas 74 per cent
was imported through a Great Lakes port. It should be noted
that all traffic passing through a Great Lakes port is not
necessarily destined for the defined hinterland.

Maps 6.3 and 6.4 show the breakdowns by coast for all
commodity movements which are Great Lakes related. These
maps describe the Great Lakes hinterland primarily as those
states which border the Lakes. This description applies to
the shipments contained on the tapes, but it is cautioned
that it need not be true for all shipments.

It was concluded that the dominant commodities exported
through the Great Lakes Coast were Metalliferous Ores and
Metal Scrap (SBR-28), Iron and Steel (SBR-67), Feeding-stuff
for Animals (SBR-08), Crude Fertilizers and Minerals (SBR-27)
and Petroleum and Petroleum Products (SBR-33). Among imports,
the dominant commodities were Iron and Steel (SAR-67), Crude
Fertilizers and Minerals (SAR-27) and Paper, Paperboard and
Manufactures Thereof (SAR-64).

For exports, the existence of Canada as a destination
was found to be an important element in use of the Great
Lakes, but by no means did it insure its use. The acquisition
of shipments near a major Great Lakes port was not an overwhelming factor in movement through that port. In order to
analyze these movements fully, it would be necessary to
include other factors beyond the scope of this study:
primarily, sailing schedules and rates of competing domestic
and international modes, and season of movement.

With respect to imports, the Great Lakes Coast seemed
to dominate in the movement of bulk-like commodities originating in Canada. The domestic destinations of Iron and Steel
(SAR-67) movements, the major exception to this observation,
are highly concentrated within the Great Lakes border states.

It was found that when using sample weight as the
criterion, Chicago and Detroit dominated the other four

157

PLACE ØF ACQUISITIØN ØF ALL GREAT LAKES RELATED
EXPØRTS THRØUGH MAJØR CØASTS - - MAP 6.3

Source: Analysis of International Great Lakes Shipping and Hinterland,
Special Report No. 23, April, 1975, Center for Great Lakes Studies,
Map 17, p. IV-4.

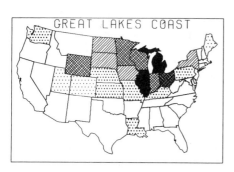

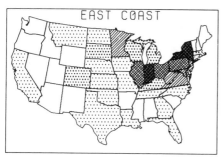

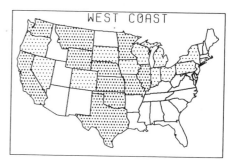

```
         SHØRT TØNS

█  750000. - 1250000.
▓  300000. -  749999.
▒  100000. -  299999.
▨   10000. -   99999.
░    1000. -    9999.
·       1. -     999.
□       0. -       0.
```

PLACE OF DESTINATION OF ALL GREAT LAKES RELATED
IMPORTS THROUGH MAJOR COASTS -- M A P 6.4

Source: Analysis of International Great Lakes Shipping and Hinterland,
Special Report No. 23, April, 1975, Center for Great Lakes Studies,
Map 18, p. IV-5.

GREAT LAKES COAST

GULF COAST

EAST COAST

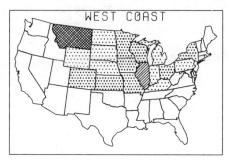
WEST COAST

SHORT TONS

750000. - 1250000.
300000. - 749999.
100000. - 299999.
10000. - 99999.
1000. - 9999.
1. - 999.
0. - 0.

identified major Great Lakes ports and clusters for both
exports and imports. The most important general conclusion
was that, with the exception of export traffic through
Chicago, each port's hinterland was found to be home-state
specific largely for both exports and imports. Table 6.13
contains a summary of the port hinterland analyses. For
exports, it contains the sample tonnage that was acquired in
the five home states of the six major ports or clusters
stated as a percentage of the entire sample tonnage exported
through those six ports as well as the same percentage for
the Great Lakes Coast. For imports, it contains the sample
tonnage that was destined for the five home states of the
six major ports or clusters stated as a percentage of the
entire sample tonnage imported through those six ports as
well as the same percentage for the Great Lakes Coast. For
both exports and imports, the percentages are repeated considering the addition of Indiana to the five-home-state
hinterland. The magnitude of the percentages clearly sup-
ports the conclusion of the available data: that the
effective hinterland of the major Great Lakes ports, and thus
of the Great Lakes as a whole, is the six contiguous states
that border the Lakes (Minnesota, Wisconsin, Illinois,
Indiana, Michigan and Ohio). Here again are raised cautions
against generalizing conclusions based on biased data.
Nevertheless, the results strongly suggest that further
research and additional information are needed to determine
the extent of the competitive hinterland of the Great Lakes-
St. Lawrence Seaway System.

TABLE 6.13

PERCENTAGE OF SAMPLE TONNAGE MOVING THROUGH 6 MAJOR GREAT LAKES
PORTS AND PORT CLUSTERS AND THE GREAT LAKES COAST
GENERATED BY 5-STATE AND 6-STATE HINTERLAND

Hinterland	Exports		Imports	
	Major Ports	Great Lakes Coast	Major Ports	Great Lakes Coast
5 State*	77.62%	75.44%	88.23%	74.03%
6 State**	82.21%	79.90%	91.41%	76.69%

*5 states: Minnesota, Wisconsin, Illinois, Michigan and Ohio
**6 states: Same plus Indiana

Source: Analysis of International Great Lakes Shipping and Hinterland,
Special Report No. 23, April, 1975, Center for Great Lakes
Studies, Table 4.1, p. IV-8.

Footnotes

[1]U.S., Department of Commerce, Bureau of the Census, Domestic and International Transportation of U.S. Foreign Trade: 1970 (Washington, D.C.: U.S. Government Printing Office, 1972).

[2]Margaret Balfe, Ronald Heilmann, James Johnson and Wayne Wendling, Analysis of International Great Lakes Shipping and Hinterland (Milwaukee: University of Wisconsin-Milwaukee, Center for Great Lakes Studies, Special Report No. 23, April, 1975).

[3]Chicago excludes the nearby ports in Indiana; Duluth excludes adjacent Superior, Wisconsin. Cleveland and Lorain are actually separate ports, as are Milwaukee, Kenosha and Racine.

[4]Only minor differences exist between place of acquisition and place of production because 64 per cent of all export shipments in the sample were acquired within 100 miles of the place of production.

Appendix 6-A

The maps that follow display, for each of the 12 most important commodity movements analyzed, the Great Lakes-related tonnage that passed through each of the four United States coasts--East, Gulf, West and Great Lakes. Maps A through F show export movements, and Maps G through L show import movements.

Each commodity movement has a unique hinterland that reflects, to some extent, the variation in the industrial economies of the states. Some of the hinterlands, especially those of the Great Lakes, tend to cluster in the vicinity of the Lakes, whereas others are scattered.

A curious phenomenon is the inclusion of some states distant from the Lakes and/or comprising a part of one of the three competitive coasts. In some instances, these inclusions result from the definition used to segregate the Great Lakes-related international movements from the population of all international movements contained on the 1970 Public Use Tapes. For example, consider Texas in the Gulf Coast portion of Map A. The dense shading indicates that between 100,000 tons and 249,999 tons of Great Lakes-related Cereal Preparations were acquired in Texas for export through the Gulf Coast. This tonnage is considered Great Lakes related and hence potential Great Lakes traffic because it was produced in the Great Lakes hinterland. Other movements are beyond the explanatory power of the data. For example, consider California, Delaware and New Jersey in the Gulf Coast portion of Map K. The shading indicates that between 1 ton and 999 tons of Great Lakes-related Iron and Steel were imported through the Gulf Coast and destined for those states. The nature of the Great Lakes relationship is viewed as a statistical anomaly and left unexplained. These may be errors in the original data, or in its processing. Despite such anomalies, the maps do provide a visual measure of the competitive position of the Great Lakes in the international movement of the various commodities.

PLACE OF ACQUISITION OF GREAT LAKES RELATED EXPORTS
OF CEREAL PREPARATIONS (SBR 4) -- MAP A

Source: Analysis of International Great Lakes Shipping and Hinterland,
Special Report No.23, April, 1975, Center for Great Lakes Studies,
Map 3, p. II-13.

GREAT LAKES COAST

GULF COAST

EAST COAST

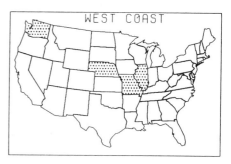

WEST COAST

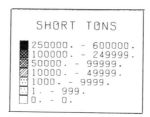

SHORT TONS

250000. - 600000.
100000. - 249999.
50000. - 99999.
10000. - 49999.
1000. - 9999.
1. - 999.
0. - 0.

PLACE OF ACQUISITION OF GREAT LAKES RELATED EXPORTS
OF FEEDING STUFF FOR ANIMALS (SBR 8) -- MAP B

Source: Analysis of International Great Lakes Shipping and Hinterland,
        Special Report No. 23, April, 1975, Center for Great Lakes Studies,
        Map 4, p. II-19.

```
            SHORT TONS
    ████  250000. - 600000.
          100000. - 249999.
    ▓▓▓▓  50000. - 99999.
    ////  10000. - 49999.
    ::::  1000. - 9999.
          1. - 999.
          0. - 0.
```

PLACE OF ACQUISITION OF GREAT LAKES RELATED EXPORTS
OF FERTILIZERS AND MINERALS (SBR 27)-- M A P C

Source: Analysis of International Great Lakes Shipping and Hinterland,
Special Report No. 23, April, 1975, Center for Great Lakes Studies,
Map 5, p. II-29.

GREAT LAKES COAST

GULF COAST

EAST COAST

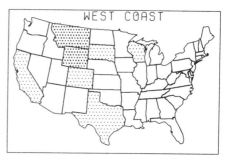

WEST COAST

SHORT TONS

250000. - 600000.
100000. - 249999.
50000. - 99999.
10000. - 49999.
1000. - 9999.
1. - 999.
0. - 0.

PLACE OF ACQUISITION OF GREAT LAKES RELATED EXPORTS
OF METALLIFEROUS ORES AND SCRAP (SBR 28)-- M A P D

Source: Analysis of International Great Lakes Shipping and Hinterland,
         Special Report No. 23, April, 1975, Center for Great Lakes Studies,
         Map 6, p. II-35.

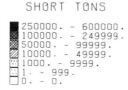

SHORT TONS

250000. - 600000.
100000. - 249999.
50000. - 99999.
10000. - 49999.
1000. - 9999.
1. - 999.
0. - 0.

PLACE OF ACQUISITION OF GREAT LAKES RELATED EXPORTS
OF PETROLEUM PRODUCTS (SBR 33) -- M A P E

Source: Analysis of International Great Lakes Shipping and Hinterland,
          Special Report No. 23, April, 1975, Center for Great Lakes Studies,
          Map 7, p. II-41.

SHORT TONS

250000. - 600000.
100000. - 249999.
50000. - 99999.
10000. - 49999.
1000. - 9999.
1. - 999.
0. - 0.

PLACE OF ACQUISITION OF GREAT LAKES RELATED EXPORTS
OF IRON AND STEEL (SBR 67) -- M A P   F

Source: Analysis of International Great Lakes Shipping and Hinterland,
         Special Report No. 23, April, 1975, Center for Great Lakes Studies,
         Map 8, p. II-64.

SHORT TONS

250000. - 600000.
100000. - 249999.
50000. - 99999.
10000. - 49999.
1000. - 9999.
1. - 999.
0. - 0.

PLACE OF DESTINATION OF GREAT LAKES RELATED IMPORTS
OF SUGAR DERIVATIVES (SAR 6) -- M A P G.

Source: Analysis of International Great Lakes Shipping and Hinterland,
          Special Report No. 23, April, 1975, Center for Great Lakes Studies,
          Map 9, p. II-84.

SHORT TONS

■	250000. - 600000.
▨	100000. - 249999.
▧	50000. - 99999.
▨	10000. - 49999.
⠿	1000. - 9999.
	1. - 999.
□	0. - 0.

170

PLACE OF DESTINATION OF GREAT LAKES RELATED IMPORTS
OF FERTILIZERS AND MINERALS (SAR 27) -- MAP H

Source: Analysis of International Great Lakes Shipping and Hinterland,
Special Report No. 23, April, 1975, Center for Great Lakes Studies,
Map 10, p. II-108.

GREAT LAKES COAST

GULF COAST

EAST COAST

WEST COAST

SHORT TONS

250000. - 600000.
100000. - 249999.
50000. - 99999.
10000. - 49999.
1000. - 9999.
1. - 999.
0. - 0.

PLACE OF DESTINATION OF GREAT LAKES RELATED IMPORTS
OF CHEMICALS (SAR 51) -- MAP I

Source: Analysis of International Great Lakes Shipping and Hinterland,
Special Report No. 23, April, 1975, Center for Great Lakes Studies,
Map 11, p. II-114.

GREAT LAKES COAST

GULF COAST

EAST COAST

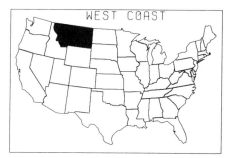

WEST COAST

SHORT TONS

250000. - 600000.
100000. -.249999.
50000. - 99999.
10000. - 49999.
1000. - 9999.
1. - 999.
0. - 0.

PLACE OF DESTINATION OF GREAT LAKES RELATED IMPORTS
OF PAPER AND PAPER PRODUCTS (SAR 64) -- MAP J

Source: Analysis of International Great Lakes Shipping and Hinterland,
Special Report No. 23, April, 1975, Center for Great Lakes Studies,
Map 12, p. II-124.

GREAT LAKES COAST

GULF COAST

EAST COAST

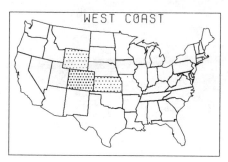

WEST COAST

SHORT TONS

- 250000. - 600000.
- 100000. - 249999.
- 50000. - 99999.
- 10000. - 49999.
- 1000. - 9999.
- 1. - 999.
- 0. - 0.

PLACE OF DESTINATION OF GREAT LAKES RELATED IMPORTS
OF IRON AND STEEL (SAR 67) -- MAP K

Source: Analysis of International Great Lakes Shipping and Hinterland,
Special Report No. 23, April, 1975, Center for Great Lakes Studies,
Map 13, p. II-134.

GREAT LAKES COAST

GULF COAST

EAST COAST

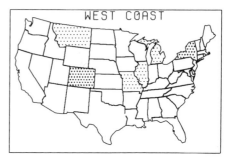

WEST COAST

SHORT TONS

250000. - 600000.
100000. - 249999.
50000. - 99999.
10000. - 49999.
1000. - 9999.
1. - 999.
0. - 0.

PLACE OF DESTINATION OF GREAT LAKES RELATED IMPORTS
OF TRANSPORT EQUIPMENT (SAR 73) -- **M A P L**

Source: Analysis of International Great Lakes Shipping and Hinterland,
          Special Report No. 23, April, 1975, Center for Great Lakes Studies,
          Map 14, p. II-149.

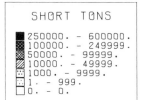

SHORT TONS

■	250000. - 600000.
▓	100000. - 249999.
▓	50000. - 99999.
▨	10000. - 49999.
⦂	1000. - 9999.
∴	1. - 999.
□	0. - 0.

Bibliography

Balfe, Margaret; Heilmann, Ronald; Johnson, James; and
    Wendling, Wayne. Analysis of International Great Lakes
    Shipping and Hinterland. Special Report No. 23.
    Milwaukee: University of Wisconsin-Milwaukee, Center
    for Great Lakes Studies, April, 1975.

Bird, James. Seaports and Seaport Terminals. London:
    Hutchinson and Company, 1971.

Drain, Edwin H. Import Traffic of Chicago and Its Hinter-
    land. Chicago: Department of Geography, The University
    of Chicago, 1963.

Frankel, Ernest G., and Marcus, Henry S. Ocean Transportation.
    Cambridge, Massachusetts: Massachusetts Institute of
    Technology, 1973.

Kaufman, Milton J. "American Experiences with Maritime Data
    Problems." Paper presented at the second seminar on
    Maritime Transport Data for Marketing, Research and
    Development, co-sponsored by the Maritime Research
    Centre, the Hague, and the Institute for Shipping
    Research of Bergen, Norway, the Hague, September 14,
    1973.

Laboratory for Computer Graphics and Spatial Analysis,
    Harvard University. Calform Manual, Version 1.1.
    Cambridge, Massachusetts: Laboratory for Computer
    Graphics and Spatial Analysis, 1972.

Schenker, Eric. The Port of Milwaukee. Madison, Wisconsin:
    University of Wisconsin Press, 1967.

U.S. Army Corps of Engineers, North Central Division. Great
    Lakes-Overseas General Cargo Traffic Analysis. Chicago:
    Illinois: U.S. Army Corps of Engineers, North Central
    Division, 1967.

U.S. Bureau of the Census. Domestic and International
    Transportation of U.S. Foreign Trade: 1970. Washington,
    D.C.: U.S. Government Printing Office, 1972.

_____. Public Use Tapes and User's Manual: Domestic and
    International Transportation of U.S. Foreign Trade.
    Washington, D.C.: Data User Services Office Staff,
    Bureau of the Census, 1972.

_____. U.S. Foreign Trade Statistics: Classifications
    and Cross-Classifications: 1970. Washington, D.C.:
    U.S. Government Printing Office, 1971.

U.S. Maritime Administration. Essential Foreign Trade
    Routes. Washington, D.C.: U.S. Government Printing
    Office, 1969.

176

VII.

Commodity Flows
and Projections

Introduction

A relatively small number of commodities dominate
traffic on the Great Lakes-St. Lawrence Seaway System. This
chapter analyzes each major commodity's flow patterns through
the System. Specific attention is devoted to the origins
and destinations of each commodity and to its prospective
supply and demand.

There have been a number of recent projections of traffic
flows for each of the major commodities. The United States
Army Corps of Engineers, as part of its legal responsibility
to make traffic projections, is a major source for the funding
of such studies. The existing projections vary in their
time span from 10 to 50 years. They also vary with respect
to their basic assumptions and their projection methodology.
In this chapter these projections are reviewed and trend
projections for the 1975-1985 period for the major commodities
are presented. The trend projections encompass only a ten-
year time span, since the accuracy of a longer-range projection is seriously affected by unforeseen changes in exogenous variables.

The additional projections made for this chapter are
based upon the assumption that future levels of traffic will,
in general, correspond to the trends observed in past years.
For many commodities, the trend has been one of a gradual
increase. However, for other commodities the past few years
have shown substantial deviations; in these cases, it must
be determined whether the deviant years are aberrations or
the first signs of sustained change.

In the following section, projections are presented for
both Lake traffic in iron ore, coal, limestone, grain and
petroleum products and for Seaway movements of iron ore, grain,
petroleum products and general cargo (both including and excluding iron and steel products). The projected Great Lakes
shipments are based on 1900-1974 data from the Lake Carriers
Association for United States and Canadian traffic.[1] For
these projections "iron ore" was defined as all shipments of
iron ore and concentrates which moved on the Great Lakes;
"coal" consisted of both anthracite and bituminous coal
(although the movement of anthracite was extremely small);
"stone" included only limestone; "grain" consisted of wheat,
oats, barley, corn, rye, flax, soybeans, buckwheat, sorghums,
and "screenings" and "sample grains"; "petroleum" was made
up of crude petroleum and selected petroleum products which
moved as bulk cargo.

The projections of traffic on the St. Lawrence Seaway
are based on levels of tonnage on the Montreal-Lake Ontario
section between 1959 and 1974.[2] "General cargo" was defined
as all shipments which moved under the general rate for Seaway

tolls and includes iron and steel bars, rods, slabs, nails and any other manufactured iron and steel in the "general" classification. Grain consists of bulk shipments of wheat, corn, rye, oats, barley and soybeans. The classification of Seaway petroleum includes bulk and general cargo shipments of crude petroleum, gasoline, fuel oil, lubricating oils and greases and other petroleum products.

The four sets of trend projections for each classification of cargo are based on differing assumptions about the importance of the immediate past as an indication of a basic change in pattern. The first projection assumes that all years are of equal importance. Each succeeding projection gives more weight to the immediate past and assumes more strongly that any recent deviations from the general trend are not random but indicative of a significant change that is expected to continue. (See Appendix 7A)

The projections for each commodity are described and evaluated separately. Because no new locks can be opened for traffic before 1985, all of the evaluations assume no major changes in the waterway system itself.

Iron Ore and Concentrates

Shipments of iron ore and concentrates exceed the shipments of any other commodity transported on the Great Lakes. In 1973, a net total of 98.5 million short tons of iron ore and concentrates was shipped on the Great Lakes to and from United States ports. This movement represented over 40 per cent of all tonnage shipped on the Great Lakes for that year.[3]

Commodity Flow

The movement of iron ore and concentrates on the Great Lakes is closely related to the production of iron and steel in the United States and Canada. Iron ore is a basic raw material that is combined with limestone and coke in blast furnaces to make molten pig iron. Either basic oxygen or open hearth furnaces turn the molten pig iron into steel.

In the Great Lakes Region, the major iron ore deposits of the United States are in Minnesota, Wisconsin and Upper Michigan--generally northwest and south of Lake Superior. The Mesabi Range in upper Minnesota, by far the largest iron ore deposit, accounted in 1973 for over 82 per cent of the total iron ore and concentrates shipped from the portion of the Great Lakes Region in the United States.[4] Since the iron ore of the Mesabi Range is near the earth's surface, open pit mining operations are extensive. The depletion of a large portion of the Mesabi Range's high grade ores has necessitated the mining of lower grade ores, or taconite, the supply of which is substantial. However, lower grade ores must be sent to "beneficiation" plants that upgrade the ores by screening, crunching, washing and agglomerating them. The end product of the process is a taconite pellet that is about two-thirds iron and will yield more pig iron with less blast furnace cost than will other ores. Therefore, less taconite needs to be shipped on the Great Lakes in order to maintain the same pig iron production. In the future, the beneficiation process may produce products with an even greater iron content, perhaps even 90 per cent iron, and further reduce transportation volumes. Still, its advantages must be counterbalanced somewhat by its cost. Extensive investments have been made in beneficiation plants near the iron ore deposits of the Region.

Currently, about 89 per cent of the iron ore transported on the Great Lakes is shipped as aggregates and concentrates.[5] The iron ore is moved primarily by railroad from the deposits to coastal beneficiation plants and/or lakehead ports, the latter having sophisticated facilities that transfer the ore to dry bulk lakers for movement to the lower lakes. The major Lake Superior ports that handle iron ore are: Taconite Harbor, Silver Bay, Two Harbors, Duluth-Superior and Marquette Harbor. Over 32.9 million tons of iron ore were shipped from Duluth-Superior in 1973 to other Great Lakes ports in the United States. That same year, shipments of Great Lakes iron ore and concentrates from the United States totalled 76.3 million tons. Of this total, 97.8 per cent was received at destinations in the United States.[6]

The most important Canadian iron ore deposits are located in Ontario and in the Quebec-Labrador area. In 1973, over 11 million tons of iron ore, or 23 per cent of the total Canadian shipments, were sent from Steep Rock and other deposits in northwestern Ontario.[7] Over 73 per cent originated in the Labrador Trough,[8] which extends from the estuary of the St. Lawrence northward to Ungava Bay. The commercial exploitation of these deposits in the late 1950's followed the construction of the St. Lawrence Seaway, which enabled the Canadian ores to be shipped to iron and steel producing centers in the United States and Canada. A series of railroads was built in the 1950's in order to connect the iron ore deposits in the Quebec-Labrador area with ports on the north shore of the Gulf of St. Lawrence.

The major iron ore handling Canadian port on Lake Superior is Thunder Bay, which moved over 5 million tons in 1973. A series of three ports (Pointe Noire, Port Cartier and Sept Isles) handles the bulk of iron ore transported from the Labrador Trough. In 1973, over 50 per cent of the iron ore from the Labrador Trough and over 34 per cent of the Ontario ores were destined to points in the United States.[9] A substantial portion of this ore moves coastwise to U.S. Atlantic ports, in addition to the Seaway movement.

The iron ore deposits of Canada and the United States supply the vast steel complexes of the two nations. The iron and steel production of the United States is largely concentrated in the Chicago-Gary-Burns Harbor, Detroit, Cleveland, Buffalo and Youngstown-Pittsburgh areas. The Canadian steel production center is at Hamilton, Ontario, with a new development underway at Naticote, Ontario, west of the Welland Ship Canal. In 1973, iron and steel plants in the United States used 96.2 million tons of iron ore and concentrates from the Great Lakes Region. Of this total, 17.9 million tons or 18.6 per cent came from the Quebec-Labrador deposits, 3.8 million tons or 3.9 per cent came from Ontario, and the remainder came from the domestic portion of the Great Lakes Region.[10] Some steel plants are located along the Lake while others are further inland and receive iron ore from the Lake ports by railroad. The construction of the St. Lawrence Seaway made the Labrador ores competitive with United States ores at major steel producing centers. In 1973, Buffalo received 27.7 per cent (7.7 million tons) and Cleveland 23.0 per cent (18.1 million tons) of its iron ore from Canada. Other major iron ore receiving ports on Lake Erie are Conneaut, Ashtabula, Lorain, Huron and Toledo. In 1973, the Port of Detroit received over 11 million tons of iron ore, and ports in the Chicago-Gary-Burns Harbor complex approximately 30 million tons.[11]

During the season that the Great Lakes-St. Lawrence Seaway System is closed to navigation, iron and steel companies in the Great Lakes Region must rely upon stockpiles of raw materials (including iron ore) in order to maintain production. The alternatives to stockpiling would be either an extension of the shipping season on the Great Lakes or the use of unit trains directly from iron ore deposit areas to steel plants. However, water transportation on the Great Lakes remains less costly than direct rail transportation for the vast majority of steel plants in proximity to the Lakes.

Projections

In 1970, the United States Bureau of Mines published forecasts of United States Great Lakes shipments of iron ore through 1995.[12] The Bureau assumed that there would be an annual rate of growth of 2 per cent in the demand for steel which would imply an increase in ore shipments of 1.5 per cent per year based upon the increasing ore content of taconite. Of these shipments, 91 per cent were presumed to be Lake movements. The International Great Lakes Levels Board extrapolated the Bureau of Mines projections to 2020 and formed higher and lower sets of projections based respectively on the assumption of 3 per cent and 1.5 per cent annual growth in demand for steel[13] and the proportionate growth in iron ore shipments. The IGLLB included Canadian coastwise traffic in its projections. The medium projections are shown in Figure 7.1.

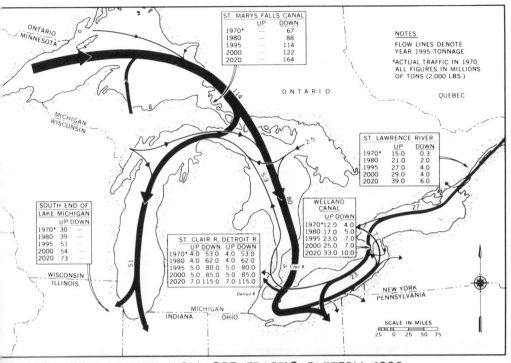

Figure 7.1 ANTICIPATED IRON ORE TRAFFIC PATTERN, 1995

SOURCE: James H. Aase, <u>Transportation of Iron Ore, Limestone and Bituminous Coal on the Great Lakes Waterway System</u>, U.S. Bureau of Mines, Information Circular 8461, Washington, D.C.: U.S. Department of the Interior, 1970, p. 8.

Reebie and Associates based their projections of future levels of United States Lake iron ore traffic on a similar methodology.[14] They used forecasts of United States iron ore requirements[15] and calculated that these needs will be met by, at most, a 15 per cent increase by 1980 in Great Lakes shipping, with two-thirds or less of the increase coming from United States sources and the remainder from Canadian sources.

The projections of A.T. Kearney, Inc., for movements of iron ore and concentrates on the Great Lakes were based on a cross-sectional multiple regression analysis to determine the domestic commodity market and on the assumption that 98 per cent of the iron ore marketed in the Great Lakes Region will be moved on the Lakes.[16]

The EBS projections of iron ore shipments in 1980 assume that 0.95 tons of iron ore will be required per ton of pig iron produced and that the iron ore in use will have an iron content of 65 to 68 per cent.[17]

Table 7.1 and Figure 7.2 summarize all of these projections. The differences among them range from about 26 million tons for 1975 to almost 90 million tons in 2000. These differences can be primarily characterized as differences in the expected demand for steel.

They both forecast the level of iron ore imports to the United States through the Great Lakes. In 1971, Reebie projected that 15.6 million tons of iron ore would be imported to the United States through the Great Lakes in 1980. However, in 1973, the United States imported, primarily from Canada, over 20 million tons of iron ore. The IGLLB projected that iron ore imports to the United States would equal 25.3 million tons in 1980 and 44 million tons in 2000.

The trend projections for Lake and Seaway traffic, shown in Table 7.2, are quite comparable to those made in the previous studies. The similarity in the trend projections makes it difficult to choose among them.

Projections of iron ore movements based entirely upon forecasts of future steel production or past trends may fail to consider some important factors. As mentioned earlier, approximately 90 per cent of iron ore and taconite from United States deposits is pelletized at beneficiation plants. In contrast, only 46.1 per cent of Quebec-Labrador deposits shipped in 1973 was pelletized. Should pressures and legal challenges by environmental groups in the United States force the closing of certain iron-ore beneficiation plants that fail to meet air and water quality standards, its steel industry may receive a greater proportion of its iron ore requirements from the Canadian and Labrador areas.

TABLE 7.1

PROJECTIONS OF U.S. GREAT LAKES SHIPMENTS OF IRON ORES

(Millions of Short Tons)

		1970	1975	1980	1985	1990	1995	2000	2020
(1)	Bureau of Mines (1970)	103.3	111.2	118.7	127.1	135.9	145.6	--	--
(2)	IGLLB -High (1973)	106.4	--	134.0	--	--	179.0	200.0	360.0
(3)	-Medium	106.4	--	123.8	--	--	153.7	164.0	221.0
(4)	-Low	91.0	--	98.6	--	--	107.0	111.0	150.0
(5)	Reebie -High (1971)	--	--	105.3	--	--	--	134.4	--
(6)	-Low	--	--	105.3	--	--	--	123.2	--
(7)	Kearney (1974)	--	85.3	93.0	104.9	117.4	132.8	150.3	--
	EBS (1969)	--	--	113.9	--	--	--	--	--

NOTE: IGLLB projections contain Canadian coastwise traffic and
are not strictly comparable. The Kearney projections are
for domestic movements only.

Source: See Text

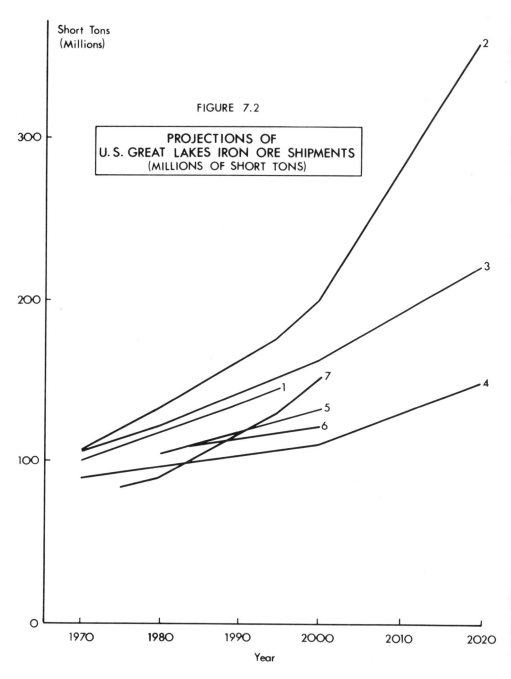

Short Tons
(Millions)

FIGURE 7.2

PROJECTIONS OF
U. S. GREAT LAKES IRON ORE SHIPMENTS
(MILLIONS OF SHORT TONS)

NOTE: NUMBERS CORRESPOND TO PROJECTION NUMBERS IN TABLE 7.1

Year

TABLE 7.2

TREND PROJECTIONS OF GREAT LAKES
AND ST. LAWRENCE SEAWAY SHIPMENTS OF IRON ORE
1975-1985

(Millions of Short Tons)

	1975	1980	1985
Great Lakes			
Unweighted trend:	98.4	102.9	107.4
Weight of immediate past:			
Slightly Stronger:	98.8	103.2	107.6
Strong:	101.6	107.8	113.9
Very Strong:	102.6	109.7	116.9
St. Lawrence Seaway			
Unweighted trend:	17.8	21.4	25.0
Weight of immediate past:			
Slightly Stronger:	15.2	16.8	18.4
Strong:	16.0	17.9	19.9
Very Strong:	15.2	16.4	17.5

Coal

On the Great Lakes in 1973, over 17.3 per cent, or 40.0 million tons, of the total shipments to or from United States ports was movements of coal. This was the second largest commodity movement on the Great Lakes for that year.[18]

Since the past and prospective patterns of coal movement on the Great Lakes are extensively discussed in Chapter 5, this section will only briefly summarize the earlier presentation and provide some projections for future movement.

Commodity Flow

Coal is extensively used by electric utility industries in the Great Lakes Region. According to a recent Interstate Commerce Commission publication, coal accounted for 93 per cent of the fossil fuels used for electric power generation in the East Northcentral region (Ohio, Indiana, Illinois, Michigan and Wisconsin). Although this figure declined from 96 per cent in 1960, it still represents the highest percentage of coal use by the electric utilities of any region in the nation.[19]

Coal is an essential raw material in the iron and steel industry, which is heavily concentrated in the Great Lakes Region. Metallurgical coal is baked in ovens until it becomes porous. This fuel, named coke, is employed in blast furnaces to make pig iron. In the blast furnace process, coke contributes carbon that reduces the iron oxide and provides the heat that is necessary for the entire process. However, the amount of metallurgical coal or coking coal needed to produce one ton of pig iron has been declining over the years as the result of: (1) improved ore charges; (2) higher blast temperatures; (3) fuel injections (natural gas, oil and tar); and (4) oxygen enrichment of the blast.[20] (Table 7.3)

The cement industry, which is also heavily concentrated in the Great Lakes Region relies on coal. A burning process chemically changes a raw materials mix, consisting of limestone, cement rock, clay and iron into a cement clinker that, in turn, is added to gypsum and ground into cement. The bulk of the industry's energy requirements is used in this burning process. In 1967, the cement industry used 8.6 million tons of coal. According to 1971 estimates, 34.7 per cent of the industry's energy needs were supplied by coal, 45.4 per cent by natural gas, and 13.6 per cent by oil. However, it is estimated that coal will supply 60.0 per cent of the industry's energy needs by 1980.[21]

The Great Lakes coal movement is generated, then, by the utilities, by the iron and steel industry, and, to a lesser degree, by the cement industry. Of the 43.6 million tons of coal moved on the Great Lakes in 1972 to destinations in the

188

TABLE 7.3

POUNDS USED PER SHORT TON OF PIG IRON

Year	Coking Coal	Coke
1913	3,247	2,173
1947	2,755	1,926
1967	1,850	1,290
1969	1,816	1,260
1971	1,827	1,260
1972	1,780	1,230
1980 (Projected)	1,450	1,000

Source: Elisabeth K. Rabitsch, "Blast Furnaces and Steel Mills - SIC 3312," in Energy Consumptions in Manufacturing, John G. Myers, et al, (editors) (Cambridge, Massachusetts: Ballinger Publishing Company, 1974), p. 429.

United States and Canada, 44.2 per cent was destined to
electric utility plants and 33.9 per cent to coke and gas
plants.[22] As mentioned in Chapter 5, the coal movements
consist of three components: (1) movement from the ports
along the southern shore of Lake Erie to the Detroit River
and northward; (2) movement from Lake Erie ports to nearby
Canadian ports, principally those on Lake Ontario that are
reached by transit through the Welland Ship Canal; and
(3) movement from South Chicago primarily to utility plants
on both the Wisconsin and Michigan shores of Lake Michigan,
with some movement to ports on Lake Superior.

Projections

The U.S. Army Corps of Engineers studied Great Lakes
shipments of coal and projected future levels of these shipments through 2015.[23] The projections were based on a
detailed study of the primary users of coal--electric utilities,
steel plants and cement plants--and upon their future outputs and locations.

The Bureau of Mines projections for United States coal
shipments on the Great Lakes assume that the use of coal
will grow with national energy requirements at a rate of
3.1 per cent per year through 1980.[24] Beyond 1980, it was
supposed that with conversion to nuclear energy this growth
rate would drop to 2.5 per cent per year even though the
technology for liquification and gasification of coal should
be available. Although this study found that about 12 per
cent of coal shipments moved on the Great Lakes in 1960,
the percentage was falling at a rate of 1.4 per cent per year
over the study period. This decline is reflected in the
Bureau's projection for United States coal traffic on the
Lakes.

In using the Bureau of Mines figures as a medium projection and extending them through 2020 the IGLLB projected
that between 1995 and 2020 shipments of coal would remain at
the 1995 level.[25] The high series assumes that U.S. production
of coal will increase 4.6 per cent annually through 1995
and remain steady from then until 2020, and the low projection
assumes annual growth of 1.25 per cent until 1995. Both
projections assume the same ratio of production to Great Lakes
shipments as do the Bureau of Mines projections.

A. T. Kearney, Inc., has forecast a continuous growth
in the market for United States domestic transportation of
coal in the Great Lakes region.[26] The Kearney report assumes
that because the potential for unit train movements of coal
has been realized, Great Lakes water carriers should be able
to maintain the 93 per cent share of this market captured in
1966.

In contrast to the Kearney study, that of R. Reebie and Associates calculated that water carriers moved only 74 per cent of the Lakes' market area consumption in 1964 and 52 per cent in 1969.[27] Although this disparity can be attributed to differences in the percentage of United States consumption considered as related to the Great Lakes, it is significant that the Reebie report concludes that rail will continue to make inroads into the Lakes' share of United States coal traffic.

EBS forecast 1980 coal shipments on the Great Lakes in light of the expected needs of the steel and electric utility industries.[28] The projections assume an annual growth rate of 5.7 per cent for electric power generation, of 0.1 per cent for coking coal and of -2.5 per cent for other consumer uses.

The IGLLB medium projection, which describes the type of movement,[29] indicates that Great Lakes coal traffic through 2020 will consist only of United States lakewise and export movements. Lakewise traffic dominates; it is expected to be 47 million tons in 1980 and to sustain a level of 52 million tons between 1995 and 2020. Export movements to Canada are projected to reach 22 million tons between 1995 and 2020, up from a 1980 level of 15 million tons. These projections are summarized in Table 7.4 and Figure 7.3.

Of the trend projections in Table 7.5, the unweighted series which forecasts the largest increases in future coal traffic seems most likely. This choice is based on three factors: the nature of future unit train movements, the new traffic in western coal and the development of nuclear power. The unit train is the principal competitor of Great Lakes shipping for movement of coal within the Great Lakes Region. The railroads have not introduced unit train rates, however, for movements between mines and lake ports because, they contend, such operations do not generate enough scale economies to justify lower rates. The Lake Carriers Association has initiated court action in order to force such rates on the railroads. A decision favorable to the Lake Carriers may increase the future level of coal traffic on the Great Lakes.

The movement of low sulfur coal from Western mines to consuming points on the Great Lakes through Duluth-Superior will substantially increase total coal movements on the Lakes. Depending upon the ability of electric utilities in the Great Lakes to make existing plants amenable to the introduction of low sulphur coals, the downbound movement of coal from Duluth-Superior may or may not compete with the upbound movement of high sulphur coal from the Lake Erie ports. Any substantial changes in existing traffic flows would also affect the limestone and grain traffic, since many vessels that now carry coal upbound carry limestone and grain downbound to avoid movement in ballast.

TABLE 7.4

PROJECTIONS OF U.S. GREAT LAKES SHIPMENTS OF COAL

(Millions of Short Tons)

		1970	1975	1980	1985	1990	1995	2000	2005	2010	2015	2020
Corps of Engineers (1961)	(1)	83.5	93.4	106.7	114.6	124.9	130.3	135.0	139.6	143.2	148.5	--
Bureau of Mines (1970)	(2)	53.0	58.0	62.0	66.0	69.0	73.0	--	--	--	--	--
IGLLB -High (1973)	(3)	61.0	--	83.0	--	--	134.0	134.0	--	--	--	134.0
-Medium	(4)	53.0	--	62.0	--	--	74.0	74.0	--	--	--	74.0
-Low	(5)	44.0	--	43.0	--	--	43.0	43.0	--	--	--	43.0
Kearney (1974)	(6)	--	45.3	48.8	52.4	56.6	62.1	68.6	--	--	--	--
EBS (1969)		--	--	91.6	--	--	--	--	--	--	--	--

NOTE: The Kearney projections are for domestic traffic only

SOURCE: See Text

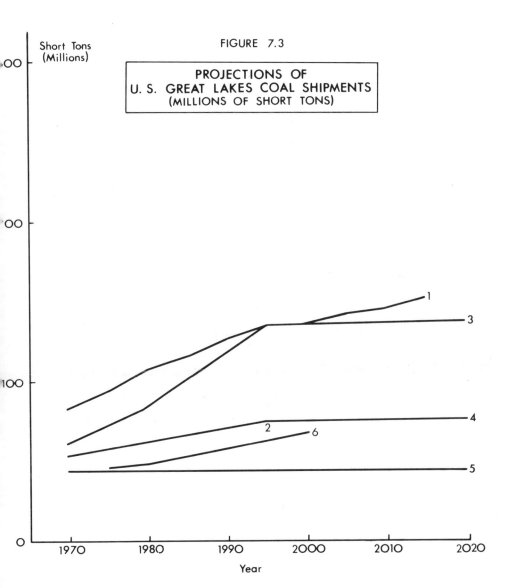

Short Tons (Millions)

FIGURE 7.3

PROJECTIONS OF
U. S. GREAT LAKES COAL SHIPMENTS
(MILLIONS OF SHORT TONS)

Year

NOTE: NUMBERS CORRESPOND TO PROJECTION NUMBERS IN TABLE 7.4

TABLE 7.5

TREND PROJECTIONS OF GREAT LAKES
SHIPMENTS OF COAL
1975-1985

(Millions of Short Tons)

Great Lakes	1975	1980	1985
Unweighted trend	58.2	60.9	63.5
Weight of immediate past:			
Slightly Stronger:	44.5	43.5	42.6
Strong:	37.8	32.7	27.6
Very Strong:	33.9	25.1	16.2

In certain cases, past projections have assumed that nuclear generation of power would increase significantly in the near future and reduce the demand for coal. Yet, because of environmental and technical problems, the future of nuclear power generation remains uncertain.

Limestone

The third largest bulk commodity movement on the Great Lakes to or from United States ports is the movement of limestone. In 1973, 36.0 million tons of limestone were transported on the Great Lakes. This accounted for 15.5 per cent of the total tonnage of shipments on the Great Lakes.[30]

Limestone constitutes 73 per cent of all crushed stone used in the United States. The major uses of limestone are: aggregates (63 per cent), cement manufacture (16 per cent), lime production (5 per cent), flux for steel production (5 per cent) and all other uses including chemical and agriculture (12 per cent).[31] Limestone is utilized in blast furnaces in order to remove the impurities (e.g. silica, aluminum and manganese) of iron ore or taconite.

Commodity Flow

Limestone is a bulky, low-value commodity that is extremely sensitive to transportation cost. Forty-seven of the 50 states have local sources of limestone that can be relied upon to serve the needs of industry in the various states. In the Great Lakes Region, limestone is plentiful in areas near the western shore of Lake Huron, the northern shore of Lake Michigan, and western Lake Erie. The proximity of this limestone to the Lakes makes Lake transportation of limestone to major industrial users feasible. Approximately 50 per cent of the fluxing stone required for steel production in the United States originates in deposits near Michigan's lake shores.[32] Michigan deposits also supply major industrial (primarily cement) and construction establishments, especially if the consumption points are in proximity to port areas. The major limestone movements on the Great Lakes, then, are related primarily to the steel industry, which consumes only 5 per cent, and the cement industry, which consumes 15 per cent of the total limestone mined in the United States. Lake movements of limestone for construction purposes (road building, etc.) and other uses have been very small to date.

Nearly all of the limestone shipped on the Great Lakes originates at six points: Port Inland, Port Dolomite, Drummond Island, Calcite Harbor, Stoneport Harbor and Marblehead Harbor. The largest volume of limestone (14.8 million tons) moved through Calcite Harbor. The major receiving ports for limestone generally correspond with the major iron ore receiving ports (Table 7.6). The Lake movement of limestone is complementary to the Lake movement of coal. Many ships that carry coal

TABLE 7.6

MAJOR SHIPPING AND RECEIVING
POINTS FOR LIMESTONE, 1973

Major Shipping Points		1973 Short Tons
1.	Port Inland, Michigan	4,367,582
2.	Port Dolomite, Michigan	3,711,083
3.	Drummond Island, Michigan	2,517,497
4.	Calcite, Michigan	14,890,067
5.	Stoneport, Michigan	8,659,304
6.	Marblehead, Ohio	2,522,768
	Total	36,668,301

Major Receiving Points		1973 Short Tons
1.	Duluth-Superior	713,726
2.	Port of Chicago, Illinois	2,253,962
3.	Indiana Harbor, Indiana	1,596,425
4.	Burns Harbor, Indiana	628,105
5.	Gary Harbor, Indiana	1,572,527
6.	Buffinton Harbor, Indiana	2,079,020
7.	Ludington Harbor, Michigan	893,334
8.	Detroit, Michigan	6,075,592
9.	Huron Harbor, Ohio	688,837
10.	Lorain, Ohio	1,738,988
11.	Cleveland, Ohio	2,814,187
12.	Fairport, Ohio	2,382,251
13.	Ashtabula, Ohio	630,609
14.	Conneaut Harbor, Ohio	2,213,855
15.	Buffalo, New York	2,041,886
	Total	28,323,304

Source: U.S., Department of the Army, Corps of Engineers, Waterborne Commerce of the United States, Calendar Year 1973, Part 3: Waterways and Harbors, Great Lakes (Chicago, Illinois: District Engineer, U.S. Army Engineer District, pp. 3-77, passim.

from Lake Erie ports to ports on Lakes Superior and Michigan
load limestone at the Lake Michigan ports listed above for
the return trip to Lake Erie.

Limestone traffic on the Great Lakes is closely tied
to steel production. The amount of limestone required per
net ton of pig iron produced in the United States declined
by 15.5 per cent between 1964 and 1973, or from .245 to
.207 gross tons.[33] This decline is primarily a result of
increased use of taconite pellets (that have some impurities
already removed) in blast furnaces. Pig iron production
must increase more than 1.6 per cent annually, before limestone requirements to maintain a constant level of production
will increase.

Projections

The Bureau of Mines projections of future United States
Great Lakes limestone traffic are based on projections of
limestone production in the State of Michigan.[34] They assume
that production of limestone in Michigan will grow at an
annual rate comparable to that maintained between 1924 and
1964, with some downward adjustment for limestone-saving
technological change in the iron and steel industry. The
actual rate of growth assumed was 2.8 per cent. The tonnage
forecasts were converted to shipment forecasts by assuming
that 84 per cent of Michigan-produced limestone was shipped
on the Great Lakes in 1960, and that this percentage would
decrease an average annual rate of 0.5 per cent.

The IGLLB projections take the Bureau of Mines projections,
add projections of Canadian domestic lakewise traffic in limestone, and extend the trend to 2020.[35] This procedure comprises
the IGLLB medium set (Figure 7.4). The high and low sets
were generated by assuming the same ratio of shipments to
production as did the Bureau of Mines and by holding Canadian
lakewise and United States import traffic at the medium level.
The high projections assume that because of its many uses,
limestone production will grow at 4 per cent a year, a rate
projected for GNP growth. The low projection assumes low
economic growth and a growth in limestone production of 1.3
per cent per year. As in the Bureau of Mines projections,
only Michigan limestone is included in this analysis.

In the Great Lakes area, Kearney projected that movements
of mining products, primarily limestone, but also sand and
gravel, will continue to be mostly by water.[36] The 88 per
cent share calculated for water transportation will continue
through 2000, the Kearney group predicted. In addition, total
tonnages will increase substantially because of the expanded
markets for steel and construction materials.

The Reebie projection is based solely on increases in
the demand for steel.[37] The EBS projection of Great Lakes
limestone movements in 1980 is similarly formulated, and it
approximates the amount which EBS calculated was moved in
1966.[38] Table 7.7 and Figure 7.5 summarize the existing projections.

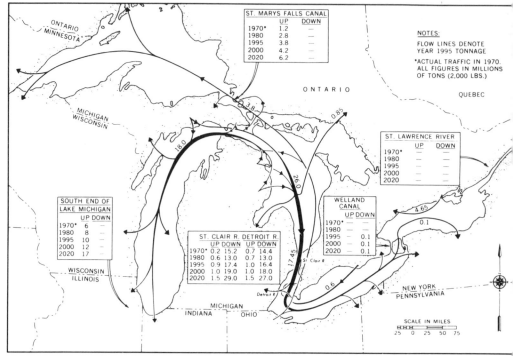

St. Marys Falls Canal

	UP	DOWN
1970*	1.2	—
1980	2.8	—
1995	3.8	—
2000	4.2	—
2020	6.2	—

NOTES:

FLOW LINES DENOTE
YEAR 1995 TONNAGE

*ACTUAL TRAFFIC IN 1970.
ALL FIGURES IN MILLIONS
OF TONS (2,000 LBS.)

St. Lawrence River

	UP	DOWN
1970*	—	—
1980	—	—
1995	—	—
2000	—	—
2020	—	—

South End of Lake Michigan

	UP	DOWN
1970*	6	—
1980	8	—
1995	10	—
2000	12	—
2020	17	—

Welland Canal

	UP	DOWN
1970*	—	—
1980	—	—
1995	—	0.1
2000	—	0.1
2020	—	0.1

St. Clair R. Detroit R.

	UP	DOWN	UP	DOWN
1970*	0.2	15.2	0.7	14.4
1980	0.6	13.0	0.7	13.0
1995	0.9	17.4	1.0	16.4
2000	1.0	19.0	1.0	18.0
2020	1.5	29.0	1.5	27.0

SCALE IN MILES
25 0 25 50 75

Figure 7.4   ANTICIPATED LIMESTONE TRAFFIC PATTERN, 1995

SOURCE: James H. Aase, Transportation of Iron Ore, Limestone, and Bituminous Coal
on the Great Lakes Waterway System, U.S. Bureau of Mines, Information
Circular 8461, Washington, D.C.: U.S. Department of the Interior, 1970,
p. 8.

TABLE 7.7

PROJECTIONS OF U.S. GREAT LAKES SHIPMENTS OF LIMESTONE

(Millions of Short Tons)

		1970	1975	1980	1985	1990	1995	2000	2020
(1)	Bureau of Mines (1970)	33.6	37.7	42.2	47.1	52.3	58.0	--	--
(2)	IGLLB –High (1973)	40.9	--	57.0	--	--	91.3	106.8	201.4
(3)	–Medium	36.8	--	46.4	--	--	63.3	70.0	103.8
(4)	–Low	32.3	--	35.9	--	--	40.8	42.6	51.1
(5)	Kearney (1974)	--	35.6	38.6	42.6	47.6	54.1	62.2	--
	Reebie (1971)	--	--	35.0	--	--	--	--	--
	EBS (1969)	--	--	34.2	--	--	--	--	--

NOTE: IGLLB figures include Canadian Coastwise traffic and are not strictly comparable. The Kearney projections include sand and gravel as well as limestone.

SOURCE: See Text

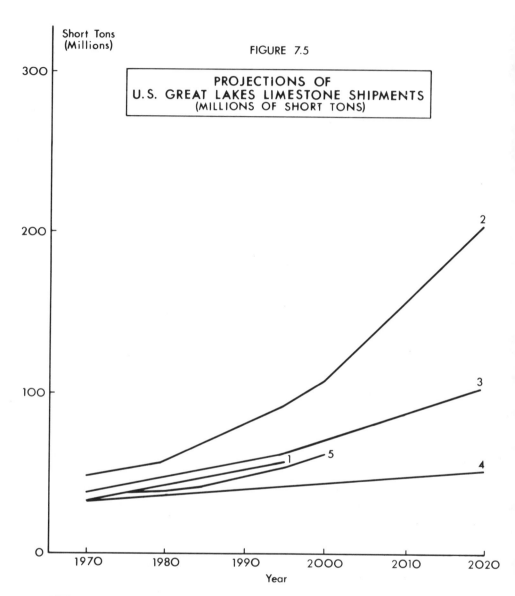

Short Tons (Millions)

FIGURE 7.5

PROJECTIONS OF
U.S. GREAT LAKES LIMESTONE SHIPMENTS
(MILLIONS OF SHORT TONS)

Year

NOTE: NUMBERS CORRESPOND TO PROJECTION NUMBERS IN TABLE 7.7

The IGLLB medium projection is broken down by type of traffic in Table 7.8. The breakdown indicates that all components of limestone traffic are expected to increase, but the relative proportions should remain nearly constant.

Table 7.9 shows trend projections for Great Lakes limestone. Because of the stability of this traffic pattern, the unweighted trend seems most likely.

Despite a possibly increased use of Michigan limestone for purposes other than as flux for iron production, the widespread availability of local limestone sources until now has made the development of such traffic unlikely. Nevertheless, future pressures and cost considerations may make additional transportation of limestone on the Great Lakes more feasible.

Another consideration, overlooked by existing projections, is the upsetting effect that shifts in the direction of coal traffic may have on the limestone traffic of the Great Lakes. The existing downbound Lake limestone traffic is complementary to the upbound movement of coal. However, if low sulphur coal movements from Duluth-Superior and Thunder Bay increase rapidly, and upbound coal movements from Lake Erie ports decrease, then the limestone movement--no longer a return cargo to avoid movements in ballast--may entail increased transportation costs.

Crude Petroleum and Selected Petroleum Products

Shipments of crude petroleum and selected petroleum products (gasoline, jet fuel, kerosene, distillate fuel oil, residual fuel oil and lubricating oil) constitute important movements on the Great Lakes. In 1973, a net total of 9.8 million tons of crude petroleum and selected petroleum products moved on the Great Lakes to or from United States ports. Of this total, crude oil constituted 5.9 per cent, gasoline 26.0 per cent, distillate fuel oil 27.2 per cent and residual fuel oil 36.9 per cent.[39]

Since movements of crude petroleum and selected petroleum products are analyzed in Chapter 5, this section summarizes earlier discussions and projects future patterns.

Numerous pipelines connect the Great Lakes Region to the major sources of oil in both the United States and Canada. Because of this extensive pipeline network and the physical limitations of the Great Lakes-St. Lawrence Seaway System, very little crude petroleum moves on the Great Lakes. The existing crude oil movements consist almost entirely of Canadian crude petroleum in Canadian tankers. The planned extension of the pipeline that links the western oil fields of Alberta to consuming regions in Canada, from Sarnia to Montreal, would divert even these movements.

TABLE 7.8

IGLLB MEDIUM PROJECTION - LIMESTONE

	1970	1980	1995	2000	2020
Lakewise	31.4	38.3	51.6	57.0	84.6
Export	1.7	2.8	4.4	4.8	7.2
Import	.5	1.1	2.0	2.2	2.3
Canadian Coastwise	3.2	4.3	5.3	6.0	8.7

Source: International Great Lakes' Levels Board, Regulation of
Great Lakes Water Levels Appendix E, Commercial
Navigation, p. E-23.

TABLE 7.9

TREND PROJECTIONS OF GREAT LAKES
SHIPMENTS OF LIMESTONE
1975-1985

(Millions of Short Tons)

	1975	1980	1985
Great Lakes			
Unweighted trend:	37.4	40.3	43.2
Weight of immediate past:			
Slightly Stronger:	41.0	44.7	48.4
Strong:	43.6	48.9	54.3
Very Strong:	43.8	52.0	58.8

On the Great Lakes, there are important movements of selected petroleum products, shipped from refineries along the shores in both the United States and Canada, to consuming areas in proximity to the Lakes. These shipments are concentrated at a few dominant nodes. In 1973, Indiana Harbor (East Chicago) accounted for over 69 per cent of the total shipment of crude petroleum and selected petroleum products between United States ports on the Great Lakes; specifically, Indiana Harbor shipped 78.3 per cent of the total gasoline, 74.5 per cent of the total jet fuel, 73.8 per cent of the total distillate fuel oil and 49.8 per cent of the total residual fuel oil.

Other Great Lakes shipping ports (with the percentage of the total movement shipped from the port during 1973 in parentheses) are: Port of Chicago (8.4), Detroit (4.2) and Toledo (8.3).[40] Thus, four ports ship 90.5 per cent of the total amount of crude petroleum and selected petroleum products moved between United States ports on the Great Lakes. The receiving ports for these shipments are scattered throughout the Lakes.

In addition to the movement of petroleum products between United States Great Lakes ports, there is considerable traffic in petroleum products between Canada and the United States and between ports in Canada. During 1973, over 1.4 million tons of residual fuel oil were imported to primarily three United States ports: Detroit (290,002 tons), Cleveland (312,756) and Oswego, New York (650,928 tons).[41]

A large amount (over 1 million tons) of crude petroleum moves downbound through the Welland Ship Canal and the St. Lawrence Seaway to refineries in Montreal.[42] There is a substantial upbound movement of refined oil products through the St. Lawrence Seaway to destinations at Lake Ontario ports and through the Welland Ship Canal to destinations at Lake Erie ports. As mentioned, the construction of a pipeline between Sarnia and Montreal may reduce movement of crude petroleum on the System.

Projections

A. T. Kearney, Inc., projected the market growth rate for United States domestic transportation of liquid fuels based on 1969 flows.[43] Assuming that water carriers maintain their 58 per cent share of the domestic Great Lakes traffic, Kearney converted these market projections to projections of future tonnages moving on the Great Lakes (Table 7.10).

R. Reebie and Associates did not make projections of actual tonnages of future Lake traffic in fuels, but they did foresee a growth in shipments that will be less than the growth in demand within the United States.[44] The extent of

TABLE 7.10

PROJECTIONS OF U.S. GREAT LAKES SHIPMENTS
OF
LIQUID FUELS

-Pipeline Movements Not Included-

(Millions of Short Tons)

	1975	1980	1985	1990	1995	2000
Kearney	5.5	6.3	7.2	8.2	9.3	10.6

Source: A. T. Kearney, Incorporated, Domestic Waterborne
Shipping Market Analysis: Great Lakes Trade Area
Report, p. II-C-14.

further development of refinery capacity in the area around the Lakes is the determinant of this more modest rate.

The trend projections in Table 7.11 show limited expansion of movements of petroleum and selected petroleum products. Assuming the expansion of pipeline traffic and continued conservation efforts, the projections which weight the immediate past slightly more strongly than other years seem most likely.

Lake movement of crude petroleum and petroleum products has difficulty competing with pipeline transportation. Because of the heavy fixed investment and economies of scale, pipeline rates are generally favorable with respect to water rates. Thus, additional pipeline construction in the Great Lakes Region will have a negative impact upon Great Lakes shipping. If Canada were to reduce sharply its currently substantial exports of petroleum products to the United States, Great Lakes shipments would decline.

Grain

During 1973, shipments of grain constituted the fourth largest commodity movement on the Great Lakes to or from United States ports. The following quantities of grain were shipped during that year: 5.4 million tons of wheat; 4.4 million tons of corn; 2.4 million tons of barley and rye; 2.0 million tons of soybeans and 758 thousand tons of oats.[45] The overall total of 15.0 million tons represented 6.5 per cent of the total commodity movements on the Great Lakes during that year.

Commodity Flow

Nearly three-fourths of the nation's grain crop is produced in states bordering the Great Lakes-St. Lawrence Seaway System or in states contiguous to them.[46] Grain moves from farms to local collector elevators at the time of harvest. From the local elevators, the grain is moved by railroad or motor carrier directly to consumption points or to ports for transshipment to other ports or to overseas destinations. The movement of grain on the Great Lakes is a function of the size of harvest, the overseas and domestic demand for United States wheat, the rates and services of competing modes of transportation, government policy and the holdover of grain in storage from previous years. As a consequence, the size of grain movements on the Great Lakes is subject to wide fluctuations, though the basic pattern is more stable.

On the Great Lakes, the United States shipments of barley (primarily a feed crop) are highly concentrated at Duluth-Superior and the Canadian shipments at Thunder Bay. During 1973, Duluth-Superior accounted for 87.5 per cent of the total barley shipments on the system, 92.7 per cent of the United

TABLE 7.11

TREND PROJECTIONS OF GREAT LAKES
AND ST. LAWRENCE SEAWAY SHIPMENTS OF
CRUDE PETROLEUM AND SELECTED PETROLEUM PRODUCTS
1975-1985

(Millions of Short Tons)

	1975	1980	1985
Great Lakes			
Unweighted trend:	14.6	15.0	15.5
Weight of immediate past:			
Slightly Stronger:	13.8	14.1	14.3
Strong:	13.6	13.7	13.9
Very Strong:	13.7	14.0	14.3
St. Lawrence Seaway			
Unweighted trend:	4.5	5.4	6.4
Weight of immediate past:			
Slightly Stronger:	3.9	4.3	4.7
Strong:	4.5	5.3	6.2
Very Strong:	4.6	5.5	6.4

States exports to Canada, 100 per cent of the direct overseas exports, and 68.5 per cent of the shipments to other United States ports. Of the total barley shipments on the Great Lakes from United States ports, 48.7 per cent is exported directly overseas (primarily to Western Europe), and 37.2 per cent is shipped to Canadian ports on the Lower St. Lawrence for probable transshipment to Western Europe. In 1973, United States exports of barley totaled 2.1 million tons, 97 per cent of which moved through the System.[47] Since Western Europe produces large quantities of barley, United States and Canadian shipments supplement the European crop and fluctuate according to European needs. In 1973, over 3.5 million tons of barley, or 11.8 per cent of the total downbound (outbound) shipments, were moved through the Montreal-Lake Ontario section of the St. Lawrence Seaway.[48] The movement of barley between United States ports on the Great Lakes is related to the brewing industry and, to a lesser degree, the distillery industry in port cities around the Great Lakes.

In 1973, Duluth-Superior accounted for approximately 98 per cent of United States wheat shipments on the Great Lakes. Of the 5.4 million tons of wheat shipped, 2.4 million tons (or 46.0 per cent) were exported to Canada (primarily for transshipment overseas), 1.5 million tons (or 24.0 per cent) were exported directly overseas and 1.4 million (or 25.0 per cent) were delivered to United States ports on the Great Lakes. In 1973, United States wheat exports totaled 40.8 million tons, 9.8 per cent of which moved through the Seaway System. Canadian wheat shipments (over 7.4 million tons in 1973) are concentrated at Thunder Bay. The combination of United States and Canadian wheat bound for overseas delivery (either directly or by transshipment at ports on the lower St. Lawrence) constitutes the dominant commodity movement downbound (or outbound) on the Montreal-Lake Ontario section of the St. Lawrence Seaway; in 1973, this wheat traffic of 11.4 million tons represented 38.2 per cent of the total downbound tonnage. Much of this wheat is bound for Europe or the U.S.S.R., areas for which the Seaway can compete with alternative routes. The total movements of wheat on the Seaway fluctuate greatly as a result of production and demand considerations as well as the rates of competitive transportation modes and routes.

Buffalo receives 1.2 million tons (or approximately 89 per cent) of the total Great Lakes shipment of United States wheat to domestic ports. Most of this wheat is utilized in the production of flour.

Corn (maize), primarily a feed crop, is exported in large quantities from United States Great Lakes ports to Canada (either for transshipment overseas or for use in Canada) or directly overseas. Of the 4.4 million tons of corn shipped from United States Great Lakes ports in 1973, 2.2 million tons (or 49.0 per cent) moved to Canadian ports in the lower

St. Lawrence, 2.1 million tons (or 48.7 per cent) moved directly overseas and only 32 thousand tons moved to other United States ports. Total United States corn exports in 1973 equaled 35.9 million tons, 12.0 per cent of which moved through the Seaway System. Movement of United States corn accounted for over 99.6 per cent of the total corn movement of 3.9 million tons downbound on the Montreal-Lake Ontario section of the St. Lawrence Seaway. The major portion of overseas exports is bound for European destinations. Four United States Great Lakes ports account for over 95 per cent of the total corn shipments: Duluth-Superior (31.6 per cent), Milwaukee (13.5 per cent), Chicago (35.0 per cent) and Toledo (15.2 per cent).

The United States produces almost 90 per cent of the non-Communist world's soybeans. Of the 2 million tons of soybeans shipped from United States Great Lakes ports in 1973, 749 thousand tons (or 37 per cent of the total) were exported to Canada and 1.2 million tons (or 61 per cent) were exported directly overseas. Total United States exports of soybeans in 1973 were 14.5 million tons, 13.6 per cent of which moved through the Seaway System. Soybean movements through the Montreal-Lake Ontario section of the St. Lawrence Seaway constituted 5.5 per cent (or 1.7 million tons) of the total downbound (or outbound) movement in 1973. The major United States shipping ports for the soybean crop were Chicago and Toledo. In 1973, Chicago handled 889 thousand tons (or 44.4 per cent) and Toledo handled 858 thousand tons (or 42.9 per cent) of the total Great Lakes shipments of soybeans.

Projections

In 1965 the United States Army Corps of Engineers projected future volumes of Great Lakes grain traffic, using a combination of methodologies that considered projections of growth in total United States exports of grains and the extent to which exports from the Great Lakes-St. Lawrence Seaway System can be expected to parallel this aggregate growth.[49] The Corps projections were broken down by type of grain and by foreign area of receipt. These breakdowns are shown in Tables 7.12 and 7.13, respectively.

EBS projections for overseas grain movements through the Seaway are also given by commodity (see Table 7.14). Although the total United States figures in Tables 7.12 and 7.14 are roughly the same, the specific commodity differences are more pronounced.[50]

The Stanford Research Institute projections of Seaway grain traffic were based on estimates of future net trade balances in the major areas of the world in view of expected changes in per capita incomes.[51] SRI does not consider that the projections for 2000 are very reliable in view of the long time period.

TABLE 7.12

PROJECTED GRAIN EXPORTS
FOR UNITED STATES GREAT LAKES PORTS
BY TYPE OF GRAIN

(Millions of Short Tons)

Commodity	1980	2015
Wheat	2.3	3.6
Corn	5.1	7.4
Oats	.3	.3
Barley-Rye	1.2	1.5
Soybeans	2.1	3.2
Flaxseed	.1	.1
Grain Sorghums	--	--
TOTAL*	11.0	16.0

---

* Totals may not add due to rounding.

Source: United States Army Corps of Engineers, Grain Traffic Analysis to Accompany Great Lakes Harbor Study, 1965, p. 78.

PROJECTED UNITED STATES FEED GRAINS EXPORTED
BY FOREIGN AREA OF DESTINATION

(Millions of Short Tons)

Area	1980			2015		
	Excluding Wheat	Wheat	Total	Excluding Wheat	Wheat	Total
Northern Europe	12.1	2.7	14.8	14.4	3.0	17.4
Mediterranean	3.7	5.9	9.6	5.5	6.0	11.5
Far East	2.7	3.8	6.5	4.3	6.0	10.3
Canada	1.1	--	1.1	1.7	--	1.7
Africa	.1	.3	.4	.2	1.5	1.7
Latin America	.1	4.2	4.3	.1	6.0	6.1
India, Persian Gulf	.1	7.2	7.3	.2	10.5	10.7
Other	.6	--	.6	.8	--	.8
TOTAL*	20.5	24.1	44.6	27.2	33.0	60.2

* Totals may not add due to rounding.

Source: United States Army Corps of Engineers, Grain Traffic Analysis to Accompany Great Lakes Harbor Study, 1965, pp. 37 and 40.

TABLE 7.14

FORECAST 1980
UNITED STATES AND CANADIAN OVERSEAS
GRAIN EXPORTS

(Thousands of Short Tons)

Commodity	United States	Canadian	Total
Wheat	1,765	7,225	8,990
Corn	6,615	--	6,615
Barley & Rye	635	555	1,190
Soybeans & Meal	2,245	--	2,245
Oats	145	105	250
Flaxseed	85	105	190
Minor Grains & Oilseeds *	5	25	30
TOTAL	11,495	8,015	19,510

* Includes rough rice, grain sorghums (NEC.), rapeseed, and oilseeds (NEC.).

Source: EBS Management Consultants, Inc., An Economic Analysis of Improvement Alternatives to the St. Lawrence Seaway System, Appendix A, Part 1.

R. Reebie and Associates forecast United States Great Lakes exports of grain by using United Nations projections of a 21.1 million ton annual demand for grain in Europe, assuming that Great Lakes exports of grain go primarily to Europe, and calculating that they will remain at a constant percentage of total United States exports.[52]

The IGLLB used the projections of United States grain traffic made by the Senate Select Committee on National Water Resources and extended these through 2020.[53] The derived Great Lakes tonnages assumed the same ratios of shipments to production used by the Corps of Engineers. The medium projections of the IGLLB are shown in Figure 7.6.

The Kearney forecasts of United States domestic grain traffic on the Lakes assume that 60 per cent (primarily wheat to Buffalo) of this traffic will move on water because of the inherent cost advantages of water transportation.[54]

In addition to the above projections, the IGLLB projections by type of traffic foresee that major Great Lakes grain movements will continue to be export and Canadian domestic shipments. The existing projections are summarized in Table 7.15.

In the trend projections in Table 7.16, the unweighted trend should be given negligible weight since it shows higher grain shipments on the Seaway than in the Great Lakes and Seaway combined--an inconsistent result. The other three trend projections are relatively similar and roughly comparable to previous projections. Nonetheless, the exogenous nature of the forces determining grain movements (i.e. government policy and crop yields) weakens the basis for making any choice among projections based on past figures.

General Cargo

According to the Federal Maritime Administration, general cargo consists of "miscellaneous goods packed in boxes, bags, bales, crates, drums, unboxed or uncrated, accepted and delivered by mark and count."[55] For statistical purposes, the definition of general cargo varies somewhat among the various authorities including the United States Army Corps of Engineers, Statistics Canada, the St. Lawrence Seaway Authority and the St. Lawrence Seaway Development Corporation. In many cases, such statistical variations complicate the comparison of general cargo traffic on the various segments of the Great Lakes-St. Lawrence Seaway System. General cargo movements, however, have particular importance to Great Lakes ports. For port communities, breakbulk general cargo generates several times the income per ton that bulk cargo does.[56] Fluctuations in general cargo movements have been substantial, and 1974 represented a post-Seaway low in such movements. In the following discussion of general cargo flows, iron and steel products including scrap, although classified as general cargo, are treated separately.

213

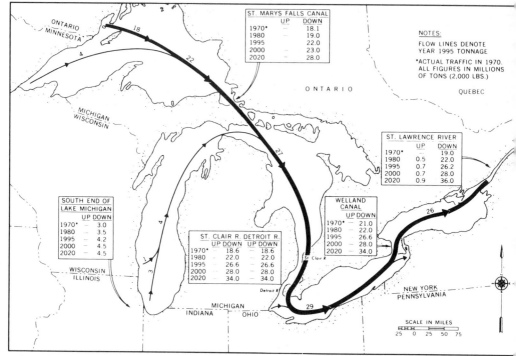

Figure 7.6   ANTICIPATED   GRAIN   TRAFFIC   PATTERN,   1995

SOURCE: International Great Lakes Levels Board, <u>Regulation of Great Lakes Water</u>
<u>Levels</u>, <u>Appendix E.</u>, <u>Commercial Navigation</u>. Report to the International
Joint Commission, 1973, p. E-30.

TABLE 7.13 = PROJECTIONS OF GREAT LAKES GRAIN SHIPMENTS
(Millions of Short Tons)

	1970	1975	1980	1985	1990	1995	2000	2015	2020
(Total U.S. and Canadian Traffic)									
IGLLB-High (1973)	--	--	28.5	--	--	36.6	39.3	--	52.1
-Medium	--	--	25.8	--	--	30.7	32.4	--	38.9
-Low	--	--	24.4	--	--	26.6	27.4	--	31.8
(U.S. and Canadian Direct Overseas Exports and Imports)									
SRI -High (1965)	16.8	18.9	21.2	--	--	--	30.0	--	--
-Low	14.0	15.3	16.7	--	--	--	20.0	--	--
EBS (1969)	--	--	19.5	--	--	--	--	--	--
(Total U.S. Traffic)									
Corps of Engineers (1965)	--	--	14.0	--	--	--	--	19.6	--
IGLLB (1973)	--	--	14.0	--	--	--	--	--	2.4
(U.S. Exports)									
Corps of Engineers (1965)	--	--	11.0	--	--	--	--	16.0	--
Reebie (1971)	--	7.5	--	8.8	--	--	--	--	--
IGLLB (1973)	--	--	11.0	--	--	13.1	13.8	--	16.7
(U.S. Lakewise)									
Corps of Engineers (1965)	--	--	3.0	--	--	--	3.6	--	--
IGLLB (1973)	--	--	3.0	--	--	3.3	3.4	--	3.7
Kearney (1974)	--	2.4	2.7	3.0	3.3	3.7	4.1	--	--

Source: See Text

TABLE 7.16

TREND PROJECTIONS OF GREAT LAKES
AND ST. LAWRENCE SEAWAY SHIPMENTS OF GRAIN
1975-1985

(Millions of Short Tons)

	1975	1980	1985
Great Lakes			
Unweighted trend:	19.6	20.6	21.6
Weight of immediate past:			
Slightly Stronger:	24.2	26.3	28.3
Strong:	25.0	27.6	30.2
Very Strong:	24.1	25.7	27.3
St. Lawrence Seaway			
Unweighted trend:	21.1	25.2	29.2
Weight of immediate past:			
Slightly Stronger:	19.0	21.1	23.3
Strong:	20.5	23.6	26.6
Very Strong:	19.7	21.8	23.9

Commodity Flows

On the Great Lakes System in 1973 approximately 8.2 million tons of iron and steel products were moved to and from United States ports. Approximately 47 per cent of this total represented receipts of iron and steel products from overseas origins.[57] This movement, then, constitutes an important element of the upbound traffic through the St. Lawrence Seaway. In 1973, approximately 14.6 per cent (or 4.2 million tons) of iron and steel products were moved (total upbound or inbound) through its Montreal-Lake Ontario section.[58] Over 73 per cent of the 3.8 million tons of iron and steel products destined for United States Great Lakes ports was received at Detroit (40.8 per cent of the combined total) and Chicago (32.3 per cent). Manufacturers in these cities find foreign steel products competitive with the products of United States companies.

Although the basic traffic patterns of iron and steel products remain stable, their total volume has decreased significantly in recent years. Between 1971 and 1973, the receipts of iron and steel products on the Great Lakes from overseas at United States ports declined by approximately 29.0 per cent, or from 5.4 million tons in 1971 to 3.8 million in 1973. Between 1973 and 1974, the movement of steel products inbound through the Montreal-Lake Ontario section declined from 4.1 to 3.2 million tons--a 22 per cent decrease. The falling volumes reflect a combination of developments: decreasing demand for foreign steel because of the recession, increasing costs of foreign steel in comparison with United States steel and the increasing competition between coastal ports and Great Lakes ports.

The major downbound (or outbound) movement of iron and steel products on the Montreal-Lake Ontario section of the St. Lawrence Seaway is scrap. In 1973, 935,043 tons of scrap (3.1 per cent of the total downbound movements) moved through the Seaway on its way to overseas destinations. Over 80 per cent of this scrap originated at three United States Great Lakes ports: Detroit (47.3 per cent), Duluth-Superior (18.9 per cent of the total scrap movements) and Milwaukee (14.0 per cent).

The movement of the leading general cargo export commodities from United States Great Lakes ports to overseas destinations substantially declined between 1971 and 1973. Exports of wheat flour, other grain mill products and prepared animal feeds declined by 14.2 per cent, or from 1.4 million tons in 1971 to 1.2 million tons in 1973. Exported meat dropped from 56.4 thousand tons in 1971 to 35.5 thousand in 1973--a 36.9 per cent decline. Overseas movement of three major non-agricultural general cargoes (non-electrical machinery, basic chemicals and products and motor vehicles and parts) from United States Great Lakes ports declined by at least 35 per cent in each case.

With the exception of basic chemicals and chemical products, the movement of leading general cargo import commodities to United States Great Lakes ports from overseas destinations substantially declined as well between 1971 and 1973. In 1971, 160.3 thousand tons of nonmetallic minerals (including mica, graphite, pumice, magnesium and abrasive materials) were shipped from overseas to United States Great Lakes ports. By 1973, this figure had declined to 97.3 thousand tons--a 39.3 per cent reduction in total shipments. Imports of crude rubber were reduced from 130.7 thousand tons in 1971 to 54.9 thousand tons in 1973--a 58.0 per cent decline. The corresponding import total for motor vehicles and parts declined from 140.6 thousand tons in 1971 to 77.0 thousand in 1973--a 45.3 per cent decline. During the same period, non-electrical machinery imports declined 21.2 per cent. Only imports of basic chemicals and chemical products to United States Great Lakes ports increased between 1971 and 1973: from 37.9 thousand tons in 1971 to 49.0 thousand tons in 1973--a 31.6 per cent increase.

Projections

The United States Army Corps of Engineers projected United States direct overseas general cargo tonnage on the basis of anticipated economic and social forces.[59] The portion of this traffic that is expected to move through the Lake System is based on the System's cost advantages, on the location and concentration of commodity consumption and production, and on the effects of the limited navigation season.[60]

Stanford Research Institute based its forecasts of Seaway general cargo traffic on the assumption that the proportion of United States and Canadian traffic moving through the Seaway would grow through 1970 and then remain constant through 2000.[61] Between 1970 and 2000, the Seaway is expected to move between 8 and 12 per cent of the general cargo exports and imports of the United States, between 20 and 30 per cent of Canadian imports and between 12 and 20 per cent of Canadian exports.

The EBS projections for each commodity for 1980 are based on specific assumptions concerning competing transportation modes.[62] The EBS projections by commodity are shown in Table 7.17.

The IGLLB low projections are based on those by the Corps of Engineers.[63] The high and medium projections assume a 3 per cent and 2 per cent rate of growth, respectively, in United States traffic between 1968 and 1980. Both assume a rate of growth of 1.4 per cent from 1980 to 1995 and of 1.0 per cent between 1995 and 2020. These post-1980 rates are those derived from the Corps projections. In each case, Canadian traffic was assumed to grow at the same rate as that of the United States. Existing projections are summarized in Table 7.18 and Figure 7.7.

(Thousands of Short Tons)

UNITED STATES EXPORTS: Commodity	1980
Dried Milk	95.0
Wheat Flour & Semolina	110.0
Other Grain Mill Products	155.0
Prepared Animal Feeds	120.0
Fresh Meat & Meat Products	85.0
Other Animal Products	650.0
Motor Vehicles & Parts	75.0
Machinery, Excluding Electrical	45.0
Chemicals & Chemical Products	50.0
Vegetables & Preparations	120.0
Soybean Meal	1,420.0
Sub-Total: Major Groups	2,925.0
Other General Cargo Commodities	325.0
Total	3,250.0

UNITED STATES IMPORTS: Commodity	1980
Nonmetallic Minerals	105.0
Motor Vehicles	130.0
Liquors and Wines	170.0
Crude Rubber	186.0
Machinery, Excluding Electrical	115.0
Glass and Glass Products	60.0
Wood Pulp	55.0
Chemicals and Chemical Products	50.0
Veneer and Plywood	100.0
Fruit and Preparations	75.0
Sub-Total: Major Groups	1,046.0
Other General Cargo Commodities	350.0
Total	1,396.0

CANADIAN EXPORTS: Commodity	1980
Soybean Oil, Cake & Meal; and Other Agricultural Products	155.0
Miscellaneous Manufactures	120.0
Chemicals	95.0
Rubber, Crude, Natural and Synthetic	75.0
Flour (Wheat)	10.0
Animal Products	12.0
Food Products	25.0
Beans and Peas	15.0
Malt	17.0
Forest Products	8.0
Newsprint	3.0
Sub-Total: Major Groups	535.0
Other General Cargo Commodities	50.0
Total	585.0
Total Iron & Steel Exports	74.0
Total System Exports	3,909.0

CANADIAN IMPORTS: Commodity	1980
Miscellaneous Manufactures	375.0
Sugar	180.0
Other Mine Products	145.0
Chemicals	65.0
Food Products	65.0
Machinery and Machines	40.0
Rubber	25.0
Agricultural Products	30.0
Forest Products	25.0
Sub-Total: Major Groups	950.0
Other General Cargo Commodities	150.0
Total	1,100.0
Total Iron and Steel Imports	4,532.0
Total System Imports	7,028.0
TOTAL OVERSEAS TRAFFIC	10,937.0

Source: EBS Management Consultants, Incorporated, An Economic Analysis of Improvement Alternatives to the St. Lawrence Seaway, Appendix A, Part IV, 1969, pp. 9-32, passim.

TABLE 7.18

PROJECTIONS OF GREAT LAKES DIRECT OVERSEAS GENERAL CARGO TRAFFIC

(Millions of Short Tons)

		1970	1975	1980	1985	1995	2000	2005	2015	2020
(1)	SRI -High (1965)	5.5	6.7	7.6	--	--	11.2	--	--	--
(2)	-Low	4.1	4.9	5.6	--	--	7.4	--	--	--
(3)	Corps of Engineers (1967)	--	5.6	--	6.7	7.6	--	8.5	9.2	--
	EBS (1969)	--	--	10.9	--	--	--	--	--	--
(4)	IGLLB-High (1973)	--	--	11.7	--	14.3	15.0	--	--	18.3
(5)	-Medium	--	--	10.5	--	12.9	13.5	--	--	16.5
(6)	-Low	--	--	7.4	--	9.1	9.5	--	--	11.5

NOTE: The Corps of Engineers Projections are for United States exports only.

Source: See Text

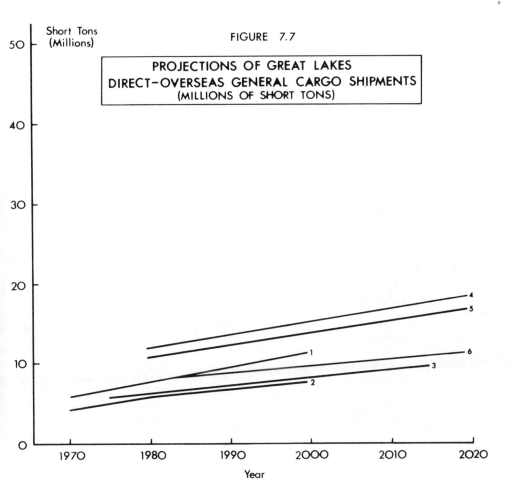

Short Tons (Millions)

FIGURE 7.7

PROJECTIONS OF GREAT LAKES
DIRECT-OVERSEAS GENERAL CARGO SHIPMENTS
(MILLIONS OF SHORT TONS)

Year

NOTE: NUMBERS CORRESPOND TO PROJECTION NUMBERS IN TABLE 7.18

The trend projections in Table 7.19 clearly reflect the decline in the early 1970's of overseas general cargo shipments, except iron and steel through the Seaway. These recent declines have resulted primarily from increased competition from coastal ports served by larger and more efficient vessels and handling increasingly greater proportions of general cargo in containers. Since these trends are likely to continue, the recent losses of general cargo traffic on the Great Lakes should be weighted strongly.

Nevertheless, the 1974 recession makes undesirable the trend projection that places a very strong weight upon the immediate past. Construction of full container facilities on the Great Lakes may attract some additional containerized cargo through the Lakes. Some Great Lakes ports have facilities that are particularly well-suited to handling certain manufactured items that are either too bulky or too heavy to move by other transportation modes. In addition, there will always remain some general cargo that is not containerized and for which Great Lakes ports can compete. In view of these considerations, the trend projection that places a strong weight upon the immediate past appears most realistic.

Summary and Conclusions

The movements of certain bulk commodities (iron ore, limestone and coal) dominate traffic within the Great Lakes while shipments of grain and iron ore are the leading commodity movements through the St. Lawrence Seaway. Although these movements should remain important in the foreseeable future, some significant variations in specific commodity flows will occur. A substantial downbound movement of western low-sulphur coal through Duluth-Superior will increase in the next few years. Iron ore shipments from the Quebec-Labrador area will become increasingly important as Canada completes construction of the Naticote steel works. Grain movements on the St. Lawrence Seaway will fluctuate in accordance with United States and Canadian production and with worldwide demand.

The major advantage of the Great Lakes-St. Lawrence Seaway System is the proximity of large industrial and resource areas to Great Lakes ports, and the complementarity of certain basic movements. Some vessels that move coal upbound from Lake Erie ports handle limestone or iron ore on the return trip. Iron ore shipments from the Quebec-Labrador area complement grain movements to lower St. Lawrence ports for transshipment overseas. The locational decisions of many iron and steel manufacturers were based upon the economies of water transportation. The System will continue to serve the resource demands of the major industries in the Great Lakes Region.

The Great Lakes-St. Lawrence Seaway System is facing stiff competition, however, from alternative transportation modes in the movement of certain bulk commodities. For

TABLE 7.19

TREND PROJECTIONS OF DIRECT OVERSEAS GENERAL CARGO TRAFFIC ON
THE ST. LAWRENCE SEAWAY, 1975-1985

(Millions of Short Tons)

	1975	1980	1985
General Cargo			
Unweighted trend	8.2	10.1	12.0
Weight of immediate past:			
Slightly Stronger:	6.9	7.8	8.6
Strong:	7.0	7.8	8.6
Very Strong:	5.8	5.4	5.0
General Cargo/ Iron and Steel			
Unweighted trend	6.2	8.0	9.9
Weight of immediate past:			
Slightly Stronger:	5.0	5.8	6.7
Strong:	5.4	6.5	7.6
Very Strong:	4.7	5.1	5.5
General Cargo/ Without Iron and Steel			
Unweighted trend	2.0	2.1	2.1
Weight of immediate past:			
Slightly Stronger:	1.9	1.9	2.0
Strong:	1.5	1.3	1.0
Very Strong:	1.0	.3	0

example, the movement of coal through Lake Erie ports has significantly decreased in recent years with the advent of transporting coal directly between the mine and point of consumption. Similarly, Lake transportation of crude petroleum and selected petroleum products has been substantially curtailed by pipeline construction in the Great Lakes Region. Competitive transportation modes are likely to make additional inroads into Great Lakes traffic in the coming years.

The sharp reduction in general cargo shipments on the St. Lawrence Seaway System during the 1970's can be attributed to several factors. The economic recession has affected shipping overall, but its impact upon general cargo shipments has been especially severe. Furthermore, Great Lakes ports have lost traffic to coastal ports that are better equipped to handle the increasing proportion of general cargo which is containerized and are able to accommodate larger, more modern container ships. The best prospect for Great Lakes ports appears to be in the handling of specialized general cargo that is either too heavy or too bulky to move by other transportation modes. Some Great Lakes ports presently have facilities specifically designed to handle such cargo.

APPENDIX 7A

Trend Projections, 1975-1985

A straight line was fitted to past levels of commodity
flows to generate the Unweighted Trend given for each
commodity in the preceding chapter. The commodity equations
are given in Table 7A.1. This single time trend explains
more than half of the variations in the commodity movements in nine of the eleven cases.

The three other sets of trend projections use expo-
nentially weighted moving averages with increasingly greater
weights given to the more recent past. The effect of this
process is to smooth out year-to-year fluctuations and to
predict a future level as an average of all past levels and
most especially of the most recent past. The set of
predictions which weights the immediate past only slightly
more strongly than other years uses x=.1. Those that give
a "strong" or "very strong" weight to more recent data use
x=.2 and x=.3, respectively. In each case, x is the fraction
of the difference between the actual value and the previous
forecasted value by which the next forecast is adjusted.[64]

TABLE 7A.1

Great Lakes	Constant (t-value)	Slope (t-value)	R^2	d
Iron Ore	30,432,390 (7.42)	894,817 (9.54)	0.55	0.92
Coal	17,682,245 (9.61)	533,078 (12.67)	0.69	0.51
Stone	1,870,964 (2.02)	581,872 (22.0)	0.89	0.63
Grain	4,631,453 (5.83)	197,334 (10.86)	0.62	0.67
Petroleum	11,514,380 (14.66)	88,350 (2.26)	0.14	0.35
Seaway				
Iron Ore	5,483,269 (3.50)	723,929 (4.46)	0.59	0.82
Grain	7,465,362 (4.67)	804,894 (4.87)	0.63	1.3
Petroleum	1,107,096 (4.84)	197,316 (8.34)	0.83	2.20
General Cargo Without Iron & Steel	1,957,625 (7.44)	5,257 (0.19)	0.03	0.42
Iron and Steel General Cargo	-74,724 (-0.14)	367,638 (6.54)	0.75	0.99
General Cargo	1,882,901 (2.47)	372,894 (4.73)	0.62	0.71

Footnotes

[1]Lake Carriers Association, Annual Report (Cleveland, Ohio: n.p., 1900-1974).

[2]St. Lawrence Seaway Authority and the Saint Lawrence Seaway Development Corporation, Traffic Report of the St. Lawrence Seaway (Cornwall, Ontario: St. Lawrence Seaway Authority, 1959-1974).

[3]U.S., Department of the Army, Corps of Engineers, Waterborne Commerce of the United States, Calender Year 1973, Part 3: Waterways and Harbors, Great Lakes (Chicago, Illinois: District Engineer, U.S. Army Engineer District), p. XII.

[4]American Iron Ore Association, Iron Ore 1973 (Cleveland, Ohio: 1973), p. 10.

[5]Robert Reebie and Associates, The Relationship of Land Transportation Economics to Great Lakes Traffic Volume, Executive Summary, Prepared for U.S. Department of Commerce, Maritime Administration (Springfield, Va.: National Technical Information Service, October, 1971), p. III-7.

[6]American Iron Ore Association, Iron Ore 1973, p. 19.

[7]Ibid., p. 11.

[8]Ibid.

[9]Ibid., p. 19.

[10]Ibid.

[11]U.S., Department of the Army, Corps of Engineers, Waterborne Commerce 1973, pp. 28-31, 61, 74.

[12]James H. Aase, Transportation of Iron Ore, Limestone, and Bituminous Coal on the Great Lakes Waterway System (Washington, D.C.: U.S. Department of the Interior, Bureau of Mines, 1970), p. 6.

[13]International Great Lakes Levels Board, Regulation of Great Lakes Water Levels--Appendix E: Commercial Navigation (Report to the International Joint Commission, 1973), p. E-15.

[14]Reebie, Land Transportation Economics, pp. 7-8.

227

[15] Hans H. Landsberg, Leonard L. Fischman, and Joseph L. Fisher, Resources in America's Future (Baltimore: Johns Hopkins Press, 1963).

[16] A. T. Kearney, Incorporated, Domestic Waterborne Shipping Market Analysis: Great Lakes Trade Area Report (Washington, D.C.: U.S. Department of Commerce Maritime Administration, 1974), p. II-C-7.

[17] EBS Management Consultants, An Economic Analysis of Improvement Alternatives to the St. Lawrence Seaway System (Washington, D.C.: EBS Management Consultants, Inc., 1969), Appendix A., p. II-B-10.

[18] U.S., Department of the Army, Corps of Engineers, Waterborne Commerce 1973, p. XII.

[19] Interstate Commerce Commission, Ex-Parte No. 270 (Sub-No. 4) Investigation of Railroad Freight Rate Structure - Coal, Decided December 3, 1974 (Washington: U.S. Government Printing Office, 1975), p. 86.

[20] Elisabeth K. Rabitsch, "Blast Furnaces and Steel Mills-SIC 3312," in Energy Consumption in Manufacturing, John G. Myers, et. al., editors (Cambridge, Mass.: Ballinger Publishing Company, 1974), p. 429.

[21] Bernard A. Gelb, "Hydraulic Cement-SIC 3241," in Energy Consumption in Manufacturing, John G. Myers, et. al., editors (Cambridge, Mass.: Ballinger Publishing Company, 1974), p. 362.

[22] L. W. Westerstrom, "Coal-Bituminous and Lignite," in Minerals Yearbook 1972, Volume I, Metals, Minerals, and Fuels, U.S. Department of the Interior, Bureau of Mines, (Washington: U.S. Government Printing Office, 1974), p. 380.

[23] U.S., Department of the Army, Corps of Engineers, Coal Traffic Analysis to Accompany Great Lakes Harbor Study (Chicago: U.S. Army Corps of Engineers, North Central Division, 1961), p. 45.

[24] Aase, p. 13.

[25] IGLLB, Regulation of Great Lakes Water Levels, p. E-19.

[26] Kearney, Domestic Waterborne Shipping, p. II-C-11. The Maritime Share is derived from these projections of future transportation of coal by all modes using the assumption stated in the report that 93% of the traffic will be on water.

[27]Reebie, <u>Land Transportation Economics</u>, p. III-10.

[28]EBS, <u>An Economic Analysis of Improvement Alternatives</u>, Appendix A, p. III-A-7 to III-A-22.

[29]IGLLB, <u>Regulation of Great Lakes Water Levels</u>, p. E-19.

[30]U.S., Department of the Army, Corps of Engineers, <u>Waterborne Commerce</u> 1973, p. XII.

[31]Reebie, <u>Land Transportation Economics</u>, p. III-16.

[32]Kearney, <u>Domestic Waterborne Shipping</u>, p. II-B-28.

[33]American Iron Ore Association, <u>Iron Ore 1973</u>, p. 61.

[34]Aase, p. 10.

[35]IGLLB, <u>Regulation of Great Lakes Water Levels</u>, p. E-23.

[36]Kearney, <u>Domestic Waterborne Shipping</u>, pp. II-B-27 through II-B-30.

[37]Reebie, <u>Land Transportation Economics</u>, p. III-17.

[38]EBS, <u>An Economic Analysis of Improvement Alternatives</u>, Appendix A, p. II-C-8.

[39]U.S., Department of the Army, Corps of Engineers, <u>Waterborne Commerce 1973</u>, p. XII.

[40]Ibid., Section 1, passim.

[41]Ibid.

[42]St. Lawrence Seaway Authority and the Saint Lawrence Seaway Development Corporation, <u>Traffic Report of the St. Lawrence Seaway</u>, 1974, pp. 29 and 51.

[43]Kearney, <u>Domestic Waterborne Shipping</u>, p. II-C-14.

[44]Reebie, <u>Land Transportation Economics</u>, p. III-20.

[45]U.S., Department of the Army, Corps of Engineers, <u>Waterborne Commerce 1973</u>, p. XII. Although barley and rye are classified together for statistical purposes, shipments and receipts in this category are almost entirely of barley.

[46] Kearney, _Domestic Waterborne Shipping_, p. III-B-6.

[47] U.S., Department of Commerce, _U.S. Exports: Commodity Groupings by World Area_ (Washington, D.C.: U.S. Government Printing Office, 1974). Further references to U.S. exports in this section are also from this source.

[48] St. Lawrence Seaway Authority and the Saint Lawrence Seaway Development Corporation, _Traffic Report of the St. Lawrence Seaway_, 1973. This and all other St. Lawrence Seaway traffic statistics in this section are from this source.

[49] U.S., Department of the Army, Corps of Engineers, _Grain Traffic Analysis to Accompany Great Lakes Harbor Study_ (Chicago: U.S. Army Corps of Engineers, North Central Division,1965), Section 5, passim.

[50] EBS, _An Economic Analysis of Improvement Alternatives_, Appendix A, Part I.

[51] Stanford Research Institute, _Economic Analysis of St. Lawrence Seaway Cargo Movements and Forecasts of Future Cargo Tonnage_ (Menlo Park, California: Stanford Research Institute, 1965), Section VI, pp. 81-100.

[52] Reebie, _Land Transportation Economics_, p. III-34.

[53] IGLLB, _Regulation of Great Lakes Water Levels_, p. E-28.

[54] Kearney, _Domestic Waterborne Shipping_, p. II-C-15.

[55] U.S., Department of Commerce, _Essential United States Foreign Trade Routes_ (Washington, D.C.: U.S. Government Printing Office, 1963), p. 70.

[56] See Chapter III of this report.

[57] U.S., Department of the Army, Corps of Engineers, _Waterborne Commerce 1973_. These and other statistics on United States Great Lakes traffic are from this source.

[58] St. Lawrence Seaway Authority and the Saint Lawrence Seaway Development Corporation, _Traffic Report of the St. Lawrence Seaway_, 1973. This and all other St. Lawrence Seaway traffic statistics are from this source.

[59] U.S., Department of the Army, Corps of Engineers, _Great Lakes-Overseas General Cargo Traffic Analysis to Accompany Great Lakes Harbor Study_ (Chicago: U.S. Army Corps of Engineers, North Central Division, 1967), Section VI, passim.

[60] Ibid., p. 128.

[61] Stanford Research Institute, Economic Analysis of Cargo Movements, p. 98.

[62] EBS, An Economic Analysis of Improvement Alternatives, Appendix A., Part IV, passim.

[63] IGLLB, Regulation of Great Lakes Water Levels, p. E-32.

[64] Elwood S. Buffa and William H. Taubert, Production Inventory Systems: Planning and Control (Homewood, Illinois: Richard D. Irwin, Inc., 1972), pp. 36-47.

Bibliography

Aase, James H. Transportation of Iron Ore, Limestone, and Bituminous Coal on the Great Lakes Waterway System. U.S. Bureau of Mines Information Circular 8461. Washington, D.C.: U.S. Department of the Interior, 1970.

Aerospace Corporation. Port System Study for the Public Ports of Washington State and Portland, Oregon. Seattle: Aerospace Corporation, 1975.

American Iron Ore Association. Iron Ore 1973. Cleveland, Ohio: 1973.

Battelle Memorial Institute. Summary Report: Market Analysis on Container Suitable Intermodal Traffic at the Port of Cleveland. Columbus, Ohio: Battelle Memorial Institute, 1967.

Blackman, A. Wade. U.S. Ocean Shipping Technology Forecast and Assessment. East Hartford, Connecticut: United Aircraft Research Laboratories, 1974.

Box, George E. P., and Jenkins, Gwilym M. Time Series Analysis forecasting and control. San Francisco: Holden-Day, Inc., 1970.

Easton, James. Transportation of Freight in the Year 2000 with Particular Reference to the Great Lakes Area. Detroit: The Developing Detroit Area Research Project, Detroit Edison Company, 1970.

EBS Management Consultants, Inc. An Economic Analysis of Improvement Alternatives to the St. Lawrence Seaway. Washington, D.C.: EBS Management Consultants, Inc., 1969.

Great Lakes Basin Commission. Great Lakes Basin Framework Study, Appendix 9, Navigation, Volume 1, Commercial Navigation. Ann Arbor, Michigan: Great Lakes Basin Commission, 1972.

Great Lakes Basin Commission. Great Lakes Basin Framework Study, Appendix 19, Economic and Demographic Studies. Ann Arbor, Michigan: Great Lakes Basin Commission, 1975.

Hazard, John L. The Great Lakes-St. Lawrence Transportation System. Problems and Potential. Washington, D.C.: Upper Great Lakes Regional Commission, 1969.

International Great Lakes Levels Board. Regulation of
    Great Lakes Water Levels, Appendix E., Commercial
    Navigation. Report to the International Joint
    Commission, 1973.

Interstate Commerce Commission. ExParte No. 270
    (Sub-No. 4), Investigation of Railroad Freight
    Rate Structure-Coal, Decided December 3, 1974.
    Washington, D.C.: Interstate Commerce Commission,
    1975.

Kearney Management Consultants. Domestic Waterborne
    Shipping Market Analysis. 11 vols. Chicago:
    Kearney Management Consultants, 1973-74.

Lake Carriers Association. Annual Report of the Lake
    Carriers Association. Detroit: Lake Carriers
    Association, 1900-1974.

Landsberg, Hans H., Fischman, Leonard L., and Fisher,
    Joseph L. Resources in America's Future. Baltimore:
    Johns Hopkins Press, 1963.

Little, Arthur D., Inc. Domestic Waterborne Shipping Market
    Analysis Appendix B, Forecasting Methodology.
    Washington, D.C.: Arthur D. Little, Inc., 1974.

Myers, John G., et. al., editors. Energy Consumption in
    Manufacturing. Cambridge, Mass.: Ballinger Publishing
    Company, 1974.

Paterson, J.H. North America, A Geography of Canada and
    the United States. New York: Oxford University Press,
    1975 (Fifth Edition).

Pounds, Norman J. G. The Geography of Iron and Steel.
    London: Hutchinson University Library, 1971.

Reebie, Robert, and Associates, Inc. Relationship of Land
    Transportation Economics to Great Lakes Traffic
    Volume. Washington, D.C.: Robert Reebie and Associates,
    Inc., 1971.

Reymond, R.D., and Fesler, E.V. Fourth Coast-Seaway Systems
    Requirement Analysis. 2 volumes. Washington, D.C.:
    U.S. Department of Transportation, 1972.

St. Lawrence Seaway Authority and the Saint Lawrence Seaway
    Development Corporation. Traffic Report of the
    St. Lawrence Seaway. Cornwall, Ontario: St. Lawrence
    Seaway Authority, 1959-74.

Schenker, Eric, and Geiger, Joseph. The Impact of the
    Port of Green Bay on the Economy of the Community.
    Sea Grant Program Technical Report No. 16. Madison:
    University of Wisconsin, 1972.

Schenker, Eric, and Kochan, James. Overseas Shipping
    at Great Lakes Ports: Projections for the Future.
    Center for Great Lakes Studies Special Report
    No. 10. Milwaukee: University of Wisconsin-
    Milwaukee, 1970.

Stanford Research Institute. Economic Analyses of
    St. Lawrence Seaway Cargo Movements and Forecasts
    of Future Cargo Tonnage. Menlo Park, California:
    Stanford Research Institute, 1965.

Starkey, Otis, P., et. al. The Anglo-American Realm.
    New York: McGraw-Hill Book Company, 1975.
    (Second Edition).

Sweet, D.C.; McGriffin, John; and Maggied, H.S.
    Industries Suited for the Upper Great Lakes Region.
    Columbus, Ohio: Battelle Memorial Institute.

U.S. Bureau of the Census. U.S. Exports/Schedule B
    Commodity Groupings by World Areas, Report FT 450,
    Annual 1973. Washington, D.C.: U.S. Government
    Printing Office, 1974.

U.S. Bureau of Mines. Outlook and Research Possibilities
    for Bituminous Coal. U.S. Bureau of Mines Information
    Circular 7554. Washington, D.C.: U.S. Government
    Printing Office, 1956.

U.S. Department of Agriculture. Potential Effects of
    St. Lawrence Seaway on Costs of Transporting Grain.
    Washington, D.C.: U.S. Government Printing Office,
    1959.

U.S. Department of the Army, Corps of Engineers, Coal
    Traffic Analysis to Accompany Great Lakes Harbors
    Study. Chicago: U.S. Army Corps of Engineers, North
    Central Division, 1961.

_____. Grain
    Traffic Analysis to Accompany Great Lakes Harbors
    Study. Chicago: U.S. Army Corps of Engineers, North
    Central Division, 1965.

_____. Grain
    Transportation in the North Central Region. Washington,D.C.:
    U.S. Army Corps of Engineers, 1961.

234

_____. Great Lakes Harbors Study. Chicago: U.S. Army Corps of Engineers, North Central Division, 1966.

_____. Great Lakes-Overseas General Cargo Traffic Analysis. Chicago: U.S. Army Corps of Engineers, North Central Division, 1967.

_____. Great Lakes-St. Lawrence Seaway Navigation Systems Study. Chicago: U.S. Army Corps of Engineers, North Central Division, 1975.

_____. Iron Ore Traffic Analysis to Accompany Great Lakes Harbors Study. Chicago: U.S. Army Corps of Engineers, North Central Division, 1958.

_____. Stone Traffic Analysis to Accompany Great Lakes Harbors Study. Chicago: U.S. Army Corps of Engineers, North Central Division, 1958.

_____. Waterborne Commerce of the United States, Calendar Year 1973, Part 3: Waterways and Harbors, Great Lakes. Chicago: U.S. Army Corps of Engineers, North Central Division, 1973.

U.S. Department of Commerce, Essential United States Foreign Trade Routes. Washington, D.C.: U.S. Government Printing Office, 1963.

U.S. Department of the Interior. Minerals Yearbook 1972, Volume I, Metals, Minerals, and Fuels. Washington, D.C.: U.S. Government Printing Office, 1974.

VIII.

Port Development Organization

Introduction

The previous chapters have indicated that Great Lakes ports face complex problems resulting from both technological advancements in shipping and cargo handling and the increasing concern with environmental impacts. The ports are being required to respond both quickly and positively to increased drafts of ships, the development of intermodal service and legislation to protect the quality of coastal lands and waters. Increased costs will be incurred in attempting to meet these challenges, and should a port default in technical progress, its traffic will be lost to a competing mode or port. Conceivably, the traditional local and private base of financial support for port development may become inadequate. There is also serious question whether the existing institutional structures of the ports will be able to administer these new developments.

At present, there exists a wide variety of institutional arrangements and organizations responsible either for navigation or for port development on the Great Lakes-St. Lawrence Seaway System. The numerous government agencies (at the international, federal, regional, state and provincial and local levels) seldom coordinate their activities. Yet port operations and functions must be viewed from a comprehensive perspective.

Port activities include: (1) harbor - consisting of navigation aids, channels, bulkheads, etc.; (2) cargo transfer facilities - docks, berths, wharves, sheds, warehouses, labor and cargo handling facilities involved in transshipment; (3) industrial areas - land and buildings that are basically not related to water transportation with the exception that products or raw materials from or to the plants may receive access or egress by water; (4) landward transportation access facilities - defined to be outside the port proper, but providing access to and egress from the port; (5) waterlanes - line haul facilities connecting the port with the foreland via the sea lanes; (6) carriers - including the vessels to be accommodated by the port; (7) cargo - the goods to be transshipped at the port; and (8) near shore water and land - not directly used in the port's functioning, but by their proximity perhaps affecting port development or influenced by concomitant outputs.

A complete concept of a port also includes its relationship with the land area it serves, or its hinterland. The term "hinterland" defines more than a fixed geographic space that is connected to the port by means of transport lines and receives goods shipped through the port. Mayer has described a port's hinterland as having three components[1]:

First, there is the immediate metropolitan hinterland, within which the port competes generally successfully with all other ports for traffic because of proximity. Within the immediate metropolitan area, however, the inland ports face the competition of other than water-borne carriers for movement to and from the seacoast. The inland ports, such as Chicago, therefore, are competitive with seacoast ports for their own metropolitan area traffic.

Second, beyond the immediate metropolitan area, there is the hinterland area, varying from time to time and for each item of freight, within which the port has a special advantage in that inland freight rates are lower than to and from any competing inland port. The extent of this non-competitive hinterland,[2] of course, depends upon the freight rate structure of the inland carriers - railroads, motor carriers and barges - and its boundaries are extended or contracted by modifications of the inland freight rates to and from the port.

Third, there is a competitive hinterland, within which a given port must compete with other ports on the basis of equal inland rates or of rates which are not sufficiently high to overcome the advantages of superior frequency and quality of service through the port concerned.

The port, then, is a gateway that serves a broader community than the immediate metropolitan area. Many factors determine the size of the community, or hinterland, served. They not only include the port's physical features, such as channel depth, floor area of warehouse space and availability of cranes, but also relate to the level of service provided by inland carriers, the conduct of aggressive trade promotion programs and the protection of the port by challenging discriminatory rate changes.[3]

Technically, a port is a physical collection of harbors, connecting channels and waterfront/terminal facilities provided by a public body or private enterprise to transfer goods between waterborne and inland carriers and/or land functions. The effectiveness of a public port is judged in the broader context of a community enterprise, for the community "recognizes the port area as an important utility service area whose growth and activities have a vital connection with development of commerce in the city and tributary area."[4] Since both the local community and hinterland are the ultimate benefactors of a healthy, viable port, the area benefiting from a public port must exercise responsibility for it.

Increasingly, it is becoming evident that a port is a
member of a larger transportation/land use system. Ports
generate traffic, provide employment and induce direct and
indirect benefits to the local community and hinterland.
Likewise, ports consume resources by requiring the construction
of facilities that occupy land and may produce undesirable
effects such as oil spills and contaminated dredge spoils.
For these reasons, ports are increasingly becoming involved
with the larger community on issues of environmental quality
and resource use. The growing realization that port functions
represent a complex system of all these elements may assist
in improving the existing institutional arrangements at all
levels of government to which ports are subject.

Federal Participation in Ports

The United States has a long history of federal participation in transportation matters, both in fostering the
development of transportation systems and in regulating
transportation practices in the interests of interstate
commerce and national defense. The history of concern for
freedom of navigation on waterways was initiated with the
Ordinance of 1787, which formed the basis for governing
the Northwest Territory. The Ordinance declared the navi-
igable waterways into and between the St. Lawrence and
Mississippi River to be common highways and forever free.
As early as 1787, Congress authorized payment for the construction of light houses, beacons, buoys and public piers.
In 1824, the first in a series of river and harbor improvement
measures was enacted.[5]

The existing federal agencies that deal with navigation
and port development are fragmented and work independently,
often at cross-purposes. The Department of Transportation
(DOT) was established in 1966 with the intent to unify all
federal transportation programs.[6] DOT, however, has not been
able to coordinate the federal government's response to water
transportation.

Two DOT operating agencies, the St. Lawrence Seaway
Development Corporation and the U.S. Coast Guard, are of
major significance to navigation interests on the Great Lakes.
In addition, the DOT's Assistant Secretary for Policy and
International Affairs has become involved in issues germane
to the Great Lakes by participating in the Seaway seasonal
extension study and by sponsoring research on the feasibility
of providing feeder shipping service on Great Lakes waters.
Yet, harbor maintenance and channel dredging are the responsibility of the Army Corps of Engineers, which is separate
from DOT. Concern for port development is within the domain
of the Maritime Administration, which is part of the Department
of Commerce. The environmental aspects of port operations
are the concern of the Environmental Protection Agency and
the National Oceanic and Atmospheric Administration, an agency

of the Department of Commerce, which is the administrative
unit that oversees the National Coastal Zone Management Act.
In view of this administrative labyrinth, it is no surprise
that the federal government has responded piecemeal to the
comprehensive issues that ports face, as evidenced in the
following discussion of some of these major federal agencies.

St. Lawrence Seaway Development Corporation

Originally, the St. Lawrence Seaway Development Corporation
was established as an independent government corporation, but
it was transferred to the Secretary of Commerce in 1958. In
1966, it became a charter member of the new DOT, charged
with the responsibility to promote, construct, operate and
maintain deep water navigation works in the International
Rapids section of the St. Lawrence River, together with
necessary dredging in the Thousands Islands area. The
Corporation works with its Canadian counterpart, the St.
Lawrence Seaway Authority of Canada, in constructing, maintaining and operating the Seaway from Lake Erie to Montreal.
Through user tolls, the Seaway was by Congressional mandate
to be self-liquidating, although this policy has proved to
be impractical. The 1970 Maritime Act forgave all interest
on the United States portion of the St. Lawrence Seaway
debt and thereby eliminated an imminent increase in tolls.[7]
The Seaway Development Corporation has promoted use of the
Seaway by providing vessel movement data, furnishing statistical and technical information, conducting economic impact
studies concerning the Seaway, investigating competitive
rate structures, providing market information to ports and
exploring potential sources of new cargo development.[8]

The entire Great Lakes-St. Lawrence Seaway System
encompasses 2,342 miles. However, the Corporation has
responsibility over only the 144-mile International section.
Hazard has stated: "The St. Lawrence Seaway Authority of
Canada has publicly disclaimed developmental activities and
the St. Lawrence Seaway Development Corporation after several
aborted attempts appears to have given up."[9] Though the
Corporation exercises little direct influence over port
development matters, the depth of the international channel
and the size of the locks do control the maximum vessel size
on the Seaway. The combined economics of vessel size and
toll levels do give the Corporation together with its Canadian
counterpart direct influence over the extent and nature of
foreign trade on the Great Lakes. Still, the Seaway cannot
function effectively without successful ports, with which
the Corporation has no power of involvement. Rather, it has
provided some promotion capabilities and sought informal,
friendly working relations with individual Great Lakes ports.

U.S. Coast Guard

The primary responsibilities of the U.S. Coast Guard
are maritime law enforcement and rescue service. Its involvement with ports pertains to providing and maintaining aids
to navigation such as lighthouses, buoys, bells, fog signals,
search and rescue, and radio beacons and also to overseeing
port security and law enforcement matters. The Coast Guard
is also responsible for the removal of derelict material,
icebreaking, control over the operation of ships in harbors
and approach channels, harbor patrols, pier and terminal
inspection, and marine casualty and accident investigations.

The Coast Guard was established as a military service
and a branch of the armed forces in 1915. Except when
operating as part of the Navy in time of war or when the
President directs, the Coast Guard is an operating agency
within DOT. Administration of certain functions concerned
with protection and preservation of navigable waterways was
transferred from the Corps of Engineers to the Coast Guard
in 1967, including issuance of permits for bridges. The
Coast Guard is also charged with administering the Great
Lakes Pilotage Act of 1960. This responsibility pertains
to registering pilots, regulating pilotage pools and establishing rates and charges for pilotage services. These
responsibilities have increased the Coast Guard's involvement
with ports and the Seaway.[10]

In its capacity of assisting marine commerce, the Coast
Guard is vital to port operations. In contrast to other modal
agencies housed within DOT, it administers only a limited
number of functions and is not responsible for promoting
maritime commerce. These promotion responsibilities are
housed with two non-DOT agencies, the Corps of Engineers
and the Federal Maritime Administration.

Corps of Engineers

The federal government exercises sizable impact on port
development by controlling channel depths and widths, turning
basin widths and depths, and constructing breakwaters. The
periodic maintenance or improvement of channels is administered
by the Corps of Engineers, an agency of the Department of the
Army, Department of Defense. The navigation involvement of
the Corps relates to its civilian functions.

Parallel to this development function are the Corps'
regulatory functions relating to the protection of harbors
and channels. Specifically, the Corps has responsibility
for:
1. establishing harbor lines and fixing the limit
   to which piers, wharves, bulkheads or other
   works may be extended into navigable waters, by
   federal permit

2. granting permits for the occupation and use of federal works under control of the Corps of Engineers.

In 1956, the Corps of Engineers was authorized to undertake a Great Lakes Harbor Study that recommended improvement of 30 existing harbors and construction of one new harbor. The study was concerned with assessing the economic justification for providing a controlling harbor depth of 27 feet commensurate with that of the Seaway. Between 1961 and 1970, the Corps of Engineers' expenditure for navigation in the Great Lakes Region averaged $40 million annually. During the 1961-65 period, routine maintenance and operations consumed approximately $10 million annually and $20 million annually between 1966 and 1970. Yet none of this money was spent in providing port facilities.[11]

The Corps also has direct involvement in environmental matters associated with ports. Dredging represents an ecological problem generated by ports, since depositing dredging spoils outside the channel can interrupt currents and also stir up spoils contaminated from municipal, industrial and agricultural waste discharges. Because many of the Great Lakes harbors are located at the mouths of rivers, spoil disposal and the construction of spoils-contained areas are of vital concern to the Region.[12] Public Law 91-611, Section 123, authorizes the "Corps of Engineers to construct, operate, and maintain contained spoil disposal facilities of sufficient capacity for a period not to exceed ten years." The section further requires that "the Secretary of the Army shall obtain the concurrence of appropriate local governments and shall consider the views and recommendations of the Administrator of the Environmental Protection Agency and shall comply with requirements of section 21 of the Federal Water Pollution Control Act and the National Environmental Policy Act of 1969." Further, local agencies must contribute 25 per cent of containment area construction costs.*[13]

These provisions will increase the cost to local bodies for dredging while the environmental assurances accompanying dredging activities may well delay needed projects and substantially raise total costs. Since maintenance of a sufficient channel depth is vital to the operations of a port, this act could have severe implications on Great Lakes port operations. Partly because of the high water level prevailing in the Great Lakes in the early 1970s, dredging and the disposal of spoiled material has not been a significant

---

* A waiver has been provided if the Administrator of the Environmental Protection Agency finds local subdivisions are participating in and in compliance with an approved plan for construction, modification, expansion, or rehabilitation of waste treatment facilities and ... applicable water quality standards are not being violated.

244

issue, and the problem is still of undefined magnitude.

River and harbor improvements, as implemented by the Corps of Engineers, do not develop in the context of a long-range, intermodal transportation plan. Many projects are initiated at a local level. Review of the Corps' project approval process indicates that from seven to ten years elapse before a project moves from inception to construction. Projects are approved by independent congressional actions on a project-by-project basis. Also, the economic feasibility of a navigation project is interwoven with general considerations of regional water resource development. Initially, the DOT legislation contained a Section 7, requiring that Corps studies of waterways, harbors and other navigation projects be made in accordance with economic standards and criteria established by DOT. This element of inter-agency coordination was never achieved.[14]

Federal Maritime Administration

The primary rationale for establishing the Federal Maritime Administration was to create an agency to administer programs authorized by the Federal Maritime Act of 1936 and subsequent related statutes that called for the development and maintenance of an efficient American Merchant Marine, one capable of meeting commercial and military needs. The present agency was originally established as a commission and reported directly to the President. In 1950, it was transferred to the Department of Commerce where it is still housed, as a Bureau. Its concerns are promoting American shipping and port development, designing new ships, granting subsidies and testing new shipping concepts. To date, the agency has been preoccupied with its shipping role, granting construction-differential subsidies to ship yards, providing operating-differential subsidies to U.S. flag ships and overseeing ship mortgage insurance and tax deferral capital construction programs.

The Merchant Marine Act of 1970 amended the Merchant Marine Act of 1936 and recognized the Great Lakes as the "fourth Sea Coast." As such, operating and construction subsidies were extended for United States vessels constructed and operated in the Great Lakes. Regulatory functions have been removed from the five member Maritime Commission, and are now exercised through an independent five member Federal Maritime Commission. The latter agency controls rates, service, routes, agreements and tariffs of waterborne common carriers which are engaged in foreign commerce and serve United States ports.

One of the Federal Maritime Administration's responsibilities is to assist United States ports in the development of more efficient and economic facilities and operations. These efforts include studies to determine the technical and economic feasibility of constructing deep-water terminals for large bulk carriers serving United States ports as well as promotion of intermodal coordination through containerization and the modernization of port facilities. The agency also serves as a consultant on maritime matters to other federal agencies, sponsors research projects that have impacts on port operations and provides technical assistance to local port bodies.[15] However, most public ports work more closely with the U.S. Corps of Engineers and the U.S. Coast Guard, as the port endeavors of the Maritime Administration are seldom "localized."

The Maritime Administration holds important respon- sibilities for the promotion of water transportation. Although the Department of Transportation is responsible for developing an overall national transportation system, this central maritime agency is housed in the Department of Commerce. Maritime interests have blocked proposals to transfer the agency to DOT, hindering effective implementation of coordinated transportation policies at the federal level. Davis has concluded the "Maritime Administration is ineffective in its present location and the Department of Transportation needs its essential programs to attain an integrated national transportation system."[16]

Environmental Protection Agency

The EPA, which coordinates government action to assure protection of the environment, becomes involved in navigation by regulating vessel sewage, establishing the criterion for disposal of dredge spoils, controlling oil and hazardous materials and determining the environmental implications of the Seaway season extension program and superport develop- ment. Its port involvement basically relates to the growing concern over environmental degradation of coastal areas.*

Economic Development Administration (U.S. Department of Commerce)

The EDA is one of the few agencies that provides direct federal support for port improvements through grants and low interest loans to local port agencies in order to allow them to purchase cargo handling equipment and construct terminal buildings. EDA funds are earmarked to communities for projects that will improve their economic base and relieve chronic unemployment. It is estimated that over $100 million have been directly invested in port facilities since 1965. Paradoxically, EDA, an economic development agency, exercised greater direct federal involvement in improving port facilities than those agencies with a statutory responsibility for ports.

---

* The National Oceanic and Atmospheric Administration (U.S. Department of Commerce) is the administrative unit to oversee the National Coastal Zone Management Act.

Miscellaneous

Several other federal agencies have responsibility for port operations. Generally, their functions are regulatory and concern the flow of cargo through a port; having little influence on port development, they do affect the day-to-day workings of a port. Such responsibilities pertain to stimulating trade, regulating commerce, overseeing the entrance of vessels and discharging and loading of cargo at ports.[17] In these activities, about 40 federal agencies directly or indirectly touch upon port operations or administration.

Summary

A comprehensive view of port functions includes not only the terminal facilities, harbors and connecting channels, but also the relationship of the port to its foreland, hinterland and the entire transportation/land use system. The federal government has not worked within this broad context. Specific federal agencies promote navigation interests (Corps of Engineers) and shipping interests (Maritime Administration). Nevertheless, the only federal agency that provides financial assistance to ports (the Economic Development Administration) was specifically designed to aid unemployment. Although the Maritime Administration has had broad statutory responsibilities for the promotion and development of ports since the Merchant Marine Act of 1920, it has traditionally favored its shipping role over an active role in port functions. Such policies have been consistent with the port industry's opposition to federal involvement.

However, the maritime industry must be viewed as a system. As Bauer has stated: "Improvements to this Nation's Merchant Marine cannot be dealt with in isolation. The tremendous cost of constructing a modern merchant fleet would be negated without a corresponding development of efficient port facilities."[18] Decisions concerning vehicle and link improvements must be correlated with levels of investment in ports and supportive land access transport systems. Though it is not clear whether ports have a greater affinity with commerce development than with other elements of transportation, all federal involvement in navigation improvements, maritime safety, environmental protection, transportation and urban planning could benefit from greater coordination.

No discussion of federal policy on waterway transportation would be complete without mentioning the periodic recommendations to impose user tolls on inland waterways to cover operating and capital improvement costs. Most recently, the National Water Commission Study called for nonfederal interests to bear, through a user charge, an appropriate share of the cost of constructing and maintaining federal inland waterway projects. Any effort to alter the traditional concept of "free navigation" raises interesting questions concerning changing federal administrative responsibilities. The report further recommends:

> "The Department of Transportation should broaden and intensify its effort to improve national transportation policy. It should develop a plan for such administrative and legislative actions as may be required to bring into being an integrated national transportation system in which all modes of transportation including waterways are utilized in such a way to reduce to a practical minimum the cost to the Nation of meeting the demands for transportation."[19]

The call for a comprehensive national transportation policy has been heard for many years. Whether by development of a comprehensive policy or by piecemeal actions, many forces are at work to restructure the traditional federal role in navigation and ports. In fact, significant new policy recommendations for federal action are being formulated as part of the recently prepared Maritime Administration report, Public Port Financing in the United States, and as part of the Maritime Transportation Research Board's study, Port Development in the United States. Since federal responsibilities can not be formulated in the context of the Great Lakes Region alone, a further discussion of them will not be included.

Regional Government Bodies and Special Interest Groups Concerned With Ports

Both regional government bodies and special interest groups have been established within the Great Lakes Region to deal with regional water quality and port development issues. Many of the government agencies have direct involvement either in navigation or in areas potentially affecting navigation.

Great Lakes Commission

The eight states bordering on the Great Lakes are parties to a compact by which they agree to work together in order to promote their joint interests in the Lakes. The Great Lakes Commission, formed by the agreement, had its origins in 1955, when the first five states ratified the compact terms. The other states followed in a few years, and Congress authorized the compact in 1968.[20] Basically fact finding and advisory in nature, the commission provides: (1) information on developments on the Great Lakes through the issuance of special reports, (2) a recognized council for joint consideration of regional problems and (3) coordination of the viewpoints and plans of member states.[21] The commission is concerned with developments relating to water resources in general and operates through five standing committees: (1) Seaway, navigation and commerce; (2) water resources; (3) fisheries and wildlife; (4) pollution control; and (5) international relations.

Relying on state funding and not including any federal representation, the Great Lakes Commission is only consultative and has formal power only to issue advisory reports to its respective state and local legislative bodies. It has been most effective as a mechanism to provide liaison among individuals concerned with the Great Lakes-St. Lawrence Seaway.

The Great Lakes Basin Commission

The Great Lakes Basin Commission, established under Title II of the Water Resources Planning Act of 1965, is engaged in the preparation of a coordinated joint plan for the development of Great Lakes waters. Federal and state agencies are members of the planning body, and the Commission benefits from direct federal financial support.[22] Its present activities concern the formulation of a comprehensive, coordinated and joint plan for the conservation, preservation, use and development of water and related land resources in the United States portion of the Great Lakes Basin. The plan will be designed to guide federal, state, interstate, local and nongovernmental agencies in the use of water and related land resources.[23] The framework report includes consideration of navigation programs and problems.

Presently, much confusion exists over the respective roles of the Great Lakes Commission and the Great Lakes Basin Commission. The latter stresses environmental concerns, and the former concentrates upon economic development. Neither organization appears to be in a position to deal effectively with the diversity of issues encountered at a regional level or to strive for a balance between economic growth and environmental quality.[24] Also, neither organization is in a position to act as a management entity, and, as concluded by the National Water Commission,[25] "the missing links seem to be mechanisms for providing overall policy guidance to integrate the things being done."

The Upper Great Lakes Regional Commission

The Upper Great Lakes Regional Commission provides liaison between the federal government and state governors in development matters that affect the Upper Great Lakes states of Michigan, Wisconsin and Minnesota. Since its establishment in 1967, in order to promote the economic development of the region,[26] the commission has been involved in the following navigation activities: (1) research on keeping the harbor of Duluth free from ice during winter months, (2) investigation of the feasibility of establishing

a joint Duluth/Superior Port Authority and (3) financing
a comprehensive study on the problems and potential of the
Great Lakes-St. Lawrence transportation system.

Miscellaneous Government Agencies

Other government agencies have responsibilities related
to the broader issues of environmental concern and water
quality. Since two-fifths of the Great Lakes Basin lies
within Canada, joint government bodies must have a significant
voice on policy matters. The International Joint Commission (IJC)
is concerned with the use, diversion and obstruction of the
flow of boundary water by one nation that might have an
impact on the other nation. The IJC reviews for approval
all proposals concerning the flow and level of boundary
waters and makes recommendations on specific problems
referred to it by either or both federal governments. Topics
such as the flow of water and evaluation of water quality all
have important implications on navigation.[27]

Associations of Port Authorities

The American Association of Port Authorities represents
both a technical society and a trade association promoting
the port industry. Its members include authorities from all
the major ports of the United States and Canada, and many
from ports in Latin America. Its major objectives are as
follows: (1) to encourage waterborne transportation by
various promotion activities; (2) to exchange technical
information on port construction, maintenance, operation
and management; (3) to promote the importance of port
authorities in their relationship to the community; (4) to
cooperate with the federal government in assuring that
channels and waterways connecting with United States ports
are properly maintained and expanded as commerce demands;
(5) to strive for uniform practices in ports as opposed to
the variations created in the past by private enterprise; and
(6) to work toward a common objective.[28]

The AAPA is represented by 15 standing committees on
topics such as port operations, port promotion, law and
legislation and environmental affairs. The AAPA takes
stands and encourages policies that affect the promotion
and maintenance of a strong, unified port industry. Although
it is not directly concerned with the Great Lakes-St.
Lawrence Seaway System, implications from its national policy
statements do have repercussions on the region.

In addition to the AAPA, there are three other port
associations: the International Association of Great Lakes
Ports, the Council of Lake Erie Ports and the Western Great
Lakes Ports Association.

Legislative Groups and Task Forces

Congressmen and senators from the eight Great Lakes states are called into conference periodically to coordinate action on legislative matters of special regional significance. Areas of concern have been: (1) designating the Great Lakes as a fourth seacoast, (2) alleged discriminatory freight rates to Great Lakes ports and (3) extending the Seaway shipping season.

At the suggestion of the conference of Great Lakes senators, a task force was established to coordinate the views of the port and shipping interests on the Great Lakes. The task force's major objectives are (1) to encourage the orderly development of the Great Lakes Region and (2) to foster and promote a quality environment for the Region. The component organizations of the task force include, among others, (1) the Council of Lake Erie Ports, (2) the Great Lakes Commission and (3) the Western Great Lakes Port Association. The task force has been active in providing a unified voice on regional matters.

Miscellaneous Special Interest Groups

Other significant groups concerned with the Great Lakes-St. Lawrence Seaway System are user or labor-oriented groups such as the International Longshoreman's Association and the Marine Engineers Beneficial Association, each of which maintains a Great Lakes district. Organizations of Great Lakes Terminal Operations and the U.S. Great Lakes Shippers Association are also active in the region. The Lake Carriers Association is designed to consider and act upon matters of concern to vessel owners engaged in the Great Lakes bulk freight and tanker trades, such as the reduction of navigation hazards and the provision of adequate channel and harbor depths, and to make known the industry's views before legislative committees and regulatory agencies. There is also a Great Lakes Fisheries Commission (federal) dealing with this resource, its research and regulation.

Summary

An analysis of the regional agencies (both government and special interest) indicates that an effective job is being done in providing communications among the various states, local ports and special interest groups. However, the multiplicity of existing agencies, none of which has a comprehensive responsibility for port functions, has a tendency to diffuse the region's viewpoint in port development issues. In addition, the organizations are basically planning, consultative and advisory, and, as such, lack powers of implementation. Many of the implementation responsibilities remain in state and local government.

State Interest in Port Development

History has shown ports generally to be unable to generate sufficient funds to cover capital improvements, development and operating costs. This fact is especially true for the Great Lakes ports, which operate under the additional handicap of a restricted navigational season.[29] Although private enterprise constructs and maintains many port facilities for its own use, public involvement has been required in many situations.

Hazard has defined the various port functions that potentially could be provided by state government: (1) informational -- port promotion and research; (2) enabling -- creation of port agencies or authorities; (3) supportive -- appropriation of funds; (4) constructive -- building of port facilities; (5) protective -- regulation of water and rail rates; (6) negotiatory -- commercial treaties, etc.[30]

Both informational and protective functions can be very significant to the overall prosperity of a port. Much can be accomplished by soliciting trade and providing assistance to insure that a port is represented before the eyes of foreign and domestic shippers. State protection and leadership in rectifying alleged discriminatory transportation rates can be vital to generating or preserving traffic flows at a port. In some cases, the state's participation is restricted to the creation of local public port bodies through the passage of enabling legislation. In other cases, states can provide supportive aid to local ports or undertake responsibility for the construction and operation of port facilities as a state enterprise. Centralization of responsibility can mean the creation of an autonomous state agency that supersedes all existing local authorities or the creation of one that plans and provides technical assistance and furnishes coordinating activities among individual ports. Some states have no government port involvement since all responsibilities for port promotion and operations are deferred to local public bodies or private interests.

A review of state involvement indicates that, based on the functions performed, port responsibilities can variously be housed in the Department of Transportation, an autonomous State Port Commission and/or Offices of Business and Development. With the recent interest in preparing integrated statewide transportation policies involving all modes of transportation, the number of State DOTs has greatly expanded. Typically DOTs are responsible for the development and coordination of adequate, safe and efficient transportation facilities including both public and private modes--airlines, railroads, water carriers, pipelines and motor vehicles. Evidence suggests that DOTs are assuming greater leadership in port functions.

The recent National Transportation Needs studies of 1972 and 1974, in requiring states to inventory the physical facilities, activity levels and cost data for ports handling over three million short tons of cargo, have done much to increase communications between state officials and independent port operators. The 1990 National Transportation Planning Study was conducted in all 50 states under the direction of the U.S. Department of Transportation to define the areas in which public and private funds will be needed through 1990 to finance highways, public transit systems, airports, railroads, waterways, pipelines and related terminal facilities. It is intended that the study provide the President and Congress with recommendations for a post-Interstate Highway program and assessments of the future of railroads, of future impacts of waterway system extensions on the trucking and railroad modes, and of the need of a federal program for terminals.

Other issues such as creating a transportation trust fund, increasing local participation in the costs of dredging and imposing user taxes might call for greater state involvement in ports. It can be expected that a formal relationship between local ports and the state, where a history of coordination is not present, will take time to consolidate. These relationships are now well defined only in those states which have asserted jurisdiction over ports.

State Port Authorities

Oregon recently undertook a study of the organizational structures and operating procedures of all state port authorities operating in 1968. The Oregon study indicated that although the eastern coastal states have taken the lead in establishing regional port authorities, only 15 states had a state port authority as of 1968.[31] The programs, objectives and scopes of the then existing port authorities varied greatly from state to state. From a sample of 13 state port authorities, the Oregon study found that some authorities were primarily coordinating agencies, while others were operating agencies that might also have involved non-water oriented commerce. In general, trade promotion and central planning were common to most state port authorities. Included in the survey were a few port authorities, such as the Delaware and New York authorities, that have multi-state responsibilities. At the time of the survey, Hawaii had one of the few DOTs with a formal responsibility for ports. As indicated by the survey, most state agencies coordinate activities with private terminal operations and, in many cases, will directly lease terminal and other facilities to them. An examination of the 13 sample port authorities suggested that seven administer other than water transportation facilities, two lease facilities to local government or private operators, 11 operate port facilities and eight oversee cargo development programs. Most of these agencies were created in the late 1940s and early 1950s.

Sources of funding also vary among the states, with strong reliance placed on revenues, revenue bonds and state tax subsidies.[32]

The Oregon study found that, as of 1968, no Great Lakes state had a state port authority. However, since the completion of Burns Harbor in 1970, through the Indiana Port Commission the State of Indiana has taken an active role in port development. Although created in 1961 by action of the Indiana State Legislature, the Port Commission was insufficiently active prior to Burns Harbor for inclusion in the Oregon tabulation. Besides Burns Harbor, the Indiana Port Commission is active in constructing a public port terminal on the Ohio River in Southeast Indiana and in conducting a feasibility analysis at a second Ohio River site.

In recent years, greater reliance has been placed on State DOTs for administrating port functions. Since the 1968 Oregon survey, the following port agencies have been integrated into State DOTs: (1) Maryland Port Authority (1972), (2) North Carolina State Port Authority (1971), (3) Maine Port Authority (1972), and (4) Oregon Ports Division created as part of DOT (1969).

In some states, involvement in ports is predicated on the argument that the operation of water terminal facilities makes a positive and worthwhile contribution to the economic base of the state and that any increase in this activity will enhance the state's economy. In these states, the key consideration then becomes the organizational structure best able to reflect the state's interest.*[33]

State Departments of Transportation

State involvement in ports, as previously noted, reflects the circumstances of the particular state. By 1973, 23 states had created a DOT organization, including the Great Lakes states of Illinois, Ohio, Pennsylvania, New York and Wisconsin. In recent years, state DOT structures have been adopted to resolve the problems of coordinating intermodal transportation planning, construction and operation. State DOTs have typically been created to: (1) unify transportation responsibilities, (2) provide effective transportation planning, and (3) administer financial matters related to development of a state transportation system.

Usually these DOTs have combined highways, public mass transit, air transportation and, to a lesser extent, water transportation functions. Most states, in undertaking state-

---

*This is not to discount an alternative philosophy that regional coordination and state involvement should not be imposed in favor of local autonomy.

wide transportation planning, have an interest in all modes, but, to date, most emphasis has been placed on highway and airport facilities. In approaching modes that rely upon private investments (i.e., railroads and private ports) and highly competitive public facilities (public ports), intermodal planning has been at best weak. Regulatory functions, outside of New York State, are housed in other agencies such as public service commissions, and a working relationship exists between the regulatory agencies and the transportation planning agency.[34]

From a recent survey of 12 state DOTs as noted in Table 8.1, five had authority to build, operate and maintain ports, four had authority to grant financial aid to ports and four had a major organizational division for waterways. Again the diversity among states can be seen; some states have direct authority and responsibility for ports or waterways, others have responsibility for intermodal transportation planning which extends to ports, and others have no port jurisdiction at all. In general, the degree of authority and organizational structure for transportation modes other than highways vary substantially. Likewise, the responsibility for different modes within the same state can greatly vary.[35]

Departments of Commerce and Economic Development

Promotion activities at the state level are performed by Offices of Business and Economic Development. These arms of state government are commonly located in a Department of Commerce or Department of Business Development. For example, the Illinois Department of Business and Economic Development provides personal contact with importers and exporters, technical assistance services and promotion devices to generate increased use of Illinois ports. It also serves as an information clearinghouse and protects the interests of shippers and ports in matters such as proceedings before regulatory agencies. Promotion activities include the maintenance of overseas and domestic offices, the scheduling of travel development conferences and tours of local ports. Port development plans are also advanced through appearances before various agencies and committees in support of proposals that benefit trade and transportation in the state.[36] In Wisconsin, the Department of Business Development provides informal support and advisory assistance to ports, which are recognized as an important ingredient in stimulating state development. However, without sources of funds specifically earmarked for port development, the operations frequently remain relatively low key.

TABLE 8.1 — AUTHORITY OF STATE DEPARTMENTS OF TRANSPORTATION TO PREPARE AND EFFECTUATE COMPREHENSIVE TRANSPORTATION PLANS

State	Authorization for Comprehensive Transportation Planning	Has a Comprehensive Transportation Plan Been Prepared? (Year)	Is Comprehensive Transportation Planning in Process?	Build/Operate/Maintain: Highways (state)	Build: Airports	Build: Ports	Build: Canals and Waterways	Build: Urban Transit	Aid: County or Municipal Roads	Aid: General Aviation Airports	Aid: Commercial Airports	Aid: Ports	Aid: Urban Transit	Reg: General Aviation Airports	Reg: Commercial Airlines	Reg: Bus Passenger Service	Reg: Rail Passenger Service	Reg: Truck Freight	Reg: Rail Freight	Reg: Urban Mass Transit	License: Motor Vehicles	License: General Aviation Airplanes
California	X		X	X	*	X	X	X	X	X	X	X	X	X	X	a	a			a	X	c
Connecticut	X	1971	X	X	X			X	X	X	X		X	X	X	X				X		X
Delaware	X	1971 [d]	X	X	X	X	X	X	X	X	X	X	X	X	X							
Florida	X	1961 [e]	X	X	X	X			X	X	X	X	X	X	X							
Hawaii	X		X	X	X					X					f	e	e			e		
Maryland	X	1968	X	X	X	X	X		X	X	X		X	X		X		X	X		X	X
New Jersey	X	1968	X	X	*	X			X	g	X		X	X								X
New York	X		X	X	X	X	X		X	X	X				h		l			j	X	
Oregon	X	1970	X	X	X				X	X	X	k	X	X							X	X
Pennsylvania	X	–	X	X	X				X	X	X				f						X	
Rhode Island	X		X	X	X		X		X	X	X	X	X	f							X	X
Wisconsin	X	E	X	X	n	X	X		X	X	X			X	X						X	c

a – State law provides authority, but by policy it is not exercised
b – Only for service under contract to state
c – Authority to register, not to license
d – In accordance with National Transportation Planning Study
e – 1961 plan has been updated for major modes, but not republished as a single document
f – For airports, but not airlines
g – For publicly owned airports only
h – Only when carrier is receiving public aid
i – New York has authority to give financial aid to Amtrak for subsidy of additions to the "basic system"
j – Commuter and urban mass transit is now provided by public authorities exempt from New York State Department of Transportation regulations
k – Authorized by implication
l – In draft stage (1971)
m – For highways and airports only
n – Authority in statutes, but cluded

Source: 1971 poll of states. Reported in Statewide Transportation Planning Needs and Requirements, NEHRP

TABLE 8.1, continued. MAJOR ORGANIZATIONAL DIVISIONS IN STATE DOT'S

State	Administration and Business Management	Planning and Research	Public Works and Maintenance	Aeronautics and Airports	Highways	Mass Transit	Special Transit Districts	Rail and Motor Carrier Services	Waterways	Motor Vehicle	Highway Patrol	Safety	Legal	Business Regulatory
California	X		X	X				X		X	X			X
Connecticut	X	X		X	X				X					
Delaware	X	X		X	X		X							
Florida		X	X[1]	X										
Hawaii				X	X	X			X					
Maryland	X	X		X	X	X			X	X		X		
New Jersey	X	X		X	X	X							X	
New York		X[2]	X[3]											
Oregon				X	X	X			X	X				
Pennsylvania	X	X		X	X	X				X		X		
Rhode Island	X	X	X[4]	X	X					X				
Wisconsin	X	X		X	X					X ·				

1 Road Operations   2 Planning and Development   3 Office of Transportation Operations

4 Maintenance Separate Department

Opposition to State Involvement

Many people believe that port functions are of a local nature and should not be administered by state government. In fact, through appropriate enabling legislation, many states have transferred port responsibilities to local governments. For example, although Ohio has recently established a DOT, it has no jurisdiction over water transportation. Rather, Ohio has established strong autonomous local port authorities, and the state's role is deferred in favor of these bodies.

Most local port bodies appear interested in discussing central funding assistance, but are reluctant to accept any associated central controls. Serious reservations are expressed about distributing the state aid equitably among all ports. Because of the competition among ports, local ports would favor no state aid over a state program that might give preferential treatment to certain ports.37

Summary

State responsibility for ports may encompass direct financial involvement, supervision of the day-to-day operations of a port and the provision of technical assistance or coordination of functions. State involvement in ports reflects: (1) the broader impacts of waterborne commerce that transcend city or county boundaries; (2) the commitment to multi-modal planning that reflects the social and economic impacts of port investments; (3) the rapid pace of technological innovations and environmental concerns that tax the finances and expertise of local port bodies; (4) the emergence of the state as a level of government well suited for comprehensive transportation planning and development. (Having taxing and bonding power to assist in capital investments, states are better able to serve the overall need for regional and metropolitan development. States already serve as the focal points for federal assistance in other domestic endeavors and can therefore provide more effective coordination with such programs as housing, law enforcement, environmental control and economic development); and (5) the need for careful planning in order to avoid making substantial duplicative or uneconomic investments. (With investment costs expanding, greatest advantage can come from making decisions based on regional benefits and need.)38

These considerations must be balanced against a history of local port autonomy and vigorous trade competition. Tradition speaks against a larger role for states in port matters: (1) concern is noted by port managers for the strings that will be associated with state aid; (2) concern is voiced over developing equitable allocation procedures so each port receives its fair share according to need; (3) competition among ports is felt to be successful in providing the best service to the shipper and rewarding, within the framework of

the free enterprise system, motivation and innovation; and
(4) extensive port operations are in private ownership,
which is not amenable to government involvement. (That ports
can operate effectively without state aid should be seen
as an additional benefit to the taxpayer.)[39]

Federal investments in navigation are well accepted.
Although federal funds are generally not earmarked for terminal facilities, many port operators are quite willing to
seek economic development grants, state loans and state promotion and protection assistance. With direct state and
federal financial responsibility well defined in competing
aviation and highway modes, the distinction that occurs at
the port boundary is difficult to rationalize. As stated
by a Maritime Administration report:

> More than ever before, other factors will
> determine the new traffic distribution
> patterns. Factors such as inland trans-
> portation facilities and highway systems,
> which are both beyond the immediate control
> of port officials, will influence the
> routing of containerized freight.[40]

Increasingly, the port operator finds his traffic trends
influenced by factors outside his control. The traditional
argument that with sufficient motivation, initiative and
innovation a port can strive for superiority in a competitive
environment must be modified. State government can provide
one level of coordination, and many state governments are
presently redefining their relationship with local port
bodies.

Local Interest in Port Development

Local participation in ports has been well accepted in
the Great Lakes Region. Not withstanding extensive private
investment, local public funds have been utilized in many
communities to develop and promote public ports. These
public investments are predicated on the fact that ports
cannot initially be self-sufficient. As a result of the
tremendous direct and indirect economic benefits to be gained,
ports should receive public assistance until financial maturity can be reached. Local financial assistance has been
extended to ports in the Great Lakes states with combinations
of revenue bonds, general bonds, taxation powers and capital
grants.

The jurisdiction of a port can take a number of forms:
an arm of local, municipal or county government, a special
purpose district or a specially designated authority. It
can also be an arm of state government through the establishment of an independent port commission or a port bureau under
the auspices of a Department of Transportation.

Local administration of municipal and/or county port agencies, which historically has been predominant in the United States, includes local officials, either appointed or elected, serving as port commissioners. Because benefits from a public port frequently extend beyond the boundaries of a single county or municipality, a district agency, consisting of a portion of a county or several counties, might be established. State administrative agencies and multistate agencies, which round out the organizational options, are currently relatively rare in the Great Lakes Region.[41]

Extensive use has been made of special districts and port authorities, or independent units of government established to administer one or more explicit functions. As special purpose units of local government, they have the advantage of not adding to constitutional debt and tax limitations. If, in the case of an authority, improvements are financed through revenue bonds, then the bonds are self liquidating through the collection of revenue for the use of facilities and services.[42] The authority's greater flexibility in debt scheduling, personnel, budget and initiation of autonomous programs has made this organizational mechanism attractive. These advantages to a local community have to be weighed against the authority's fiscal autonomy, or inability to share losses or profits with other authorities or local government. One danger is proliferation of programs, for these agencies tend to be oriented to a single-purpose, ad-hoc in design, independent of the traditional checks and balances of elected government, and self perpetuating. Schenker reported in Regional Coordination of Urban Transportation Functions in the Milwaukee Area that city after city has responded to municipal service needs by establishing a separate authority, a single purpose government. Whereas 20 years ago there were approximately 12,000 special districts in the U.S., today some 21,000 exist, operating across governmental boundary lines and usually without the checks and balances characteristic of general purpose government. This phenomenon only compounds the confusion of an already overly fragmented system of local government.[43]

Despite these inherent problems, the ability of port authorities to provide more financial and political independence and greater administrative latitude deserves consideration.[44] The basic statutory powers of a port should be drawn in sufficiently broad language to permit complete interface with various forms of transportation and should include industrial development powers and non-transportation functions related to the basic objectives of developing trade and commerce in the port area. Geographic jurisdictions should reflect the area benefiting from the port and thus logically expected to provide financial backing. As a policy, port boundaries should be determined by economic forces and not by legal definitions.

Public Aid to Local Ports

No pattern for sources of public aid currently emerges in the Great Lakes. For example, the Port of Chicago has two separate organizational structures. One is operated as an arm of city government (Navy Pier), while the other (Chicago Regional Port District) is a state-established special district. The former relies on general obligation bonds sanctioned by the city government, while the latter is required to be self-sufficient and must generate sufficient revenue to meet debt on its original bond issue of $24 million. A self-sufficiency requirement has placed severe constraints on the Chicago Regional Port District's ability to develop Lake Calumet Harbor, limiting management's flexibility in fostering experimentation with new developments. It has been difficult to sell bonds in order to undertake bold new ventures such as development of a major container port.

The Indiana Port Commission, an arm of the Indiana state government, constructed, promotes and operates Burns Harbor on the Great Lakes and one port on the Ohio River. Although Indiana provided a one-time grant for Burns Harbor, further development must be financed from operating and lease revenues. The Indiana operation is unique in the Great Lakes Region because of the direct state involvement in port ownership and operations. Other examples of indirect state involvement include Minnesota's providing Duluth with a lump sum of $6 million (matched with $1 million from the county and $3 million from the city) for initial construction of port terminal facilities. On a continuing basis, Minnesota grants the Port Authority of Duluth approximately $80,000 per year for promotion purposes. Simiarly, New York has provided an interest free loan to the Ogdensburg Bridge and Port Authority for construction of terminal facilities. The Port of Erie has received annual state appropriations to defray part of the cost of improving and maintaining public port facilities. Under Ohio enabling legislation, the Cleveland-Cuyahoga Port Authority and Toledo-Lucas County Port Authority have been granted locally-voted taxing power for port development for a renewable five-year period. General obligation and revenue bonds may also be utilized to supplement the millage rates. Ohio ports, then, enjoy a high degree of autonomy and financial flexibility by virtue of the mill tax levy that can be utilized for promotion, operations and capital improvements. One difficulty encountered by the Lorain, Ohio Port Authority is that local voters may elect not to renew the levies. The Lorain .25 mill levy expired in 1969.

Summary

In many instances, the impact of port activity is multi-county or even multi-state. Yet, port organization is often restricted to the municipal limits of a single city. Although some changes are beginning to occur, many states and localities remain committed to a narrow definition of port functions. The result may be a continued fragmentation of port agencies that are incapable of dealing with modern problems.

Future Regional, State and Local Roles in Port Development

The present organizational situation in the Great Lakes represents a collection of individualized responses divided among private interest groups and various levels of government. This section advances some suggestions for improvements on a regional, state and local level.

Recommendations for Regional Bodies

The numerous regional organizations that exist on the Great Lakes remain fragmented and lack effective powers. Numerous proposals have been offered to deal with the institutional problem of the Great Lakes at a regional level. The selection of a specific institutional arrangement will depend on financial and political considerations as well as responses to newly enacted or proposed legislation, including the Coastal Zone Management Act and National Land Use Planning Act. The continuing regional role rests in the areas of planning, coordinating and influencing federal policies. In the interim, a critical need exists to elevate transportation planning to a level commensurate with that of water resources planning, which is progressing on a regional basis.

Presently, many private organizations are actively promoting port and navigation interests at a regional level. Partly because of their numbers and diversity, confusion about their roles arises. The Great Lakes Task Force, an articulate and unified private voice in the Region, should continue to serve as a clearinghouse and point of contact for port interests. The task force or a similar group should be strengthened so that it might engage in information, protection, negotiation and coordination of activities on issues of mutual interest. A good line of communication is essential among ports as well as between environmental and port interests.

With so many challenges of mutual concern confronting the Great Lakes ports, a greater regional awareness becomes essential. Until an organization combining advisory and coordinative activities with management responsibilities can

be established, a strong port voice must make itself heard.
The following policy suggestions should be adopted:

1. The coordination among existing regional
   organizations should be strengthened and
   facilitated by improved definition of
   organizational responsibility.

2. Shipping should be viewed as both a water
   resource and transportation enterprise.
   A need exists to bring the existing bodies
   responsible for shipping into better focus
   with the transportation systems either
   competing with or supplementing water transportation.

3. The existing Great Lakes Task Force should
   be strengthened to provide a forum on issues
   of common concern to ports and other shipping
   interests.

4. All feasible avenues should be pursued so
   that coordination can be strengthened among
   Great Lakes ports in working on common
   regional problems.

Recommendations for State Bodies

   The issues presently confronting Great Lakes ports call
for creative solutions to attract new trade and to provide
a framework for effective investment decisions. The declining trade patterns make a greater reliance upon state
aid more likely.[45] The states are in a position to assess
the relative merits of further port expansion on the Great
Lakes and to insure that local port investments are wise
and prudent. When states collectively address the key
regional policy issues confronting the Great Lakes ports, a
stronger and more effective voice should be heard. Today,
proposals supporting an increased state role in local port
matters are advanced less on the basis of theory, than as
a practical approach to insure the continued economic survival
of the Great Lakes ports and shipping industry. The recently-
enacted Coastal Zone Management legislation will provide yet
another dimension of concern on issues of environment and
land use for a coordinated port organization. The legislation will undoubtedly spawn time-consuming enabling and
approval processes among states and local port bodies.

   State involvement, however, is hindered by the inherent
difficulties associated with the sharing of power between
state and local governments. Local port autonomy is zealously
defended within the membership of the port industry.[46] Local
matters are felt to be the hegemony of local government,
including decisions concerning a public port. State
involvement is resisted as meddling, a threat to local auton-

omy. A state program, local port supporters argue, will mean favoritism and public expenditures to benefit a competing port more than a home port; or to stimulate the less successful or minor ports.

In the current era of financial stress, these arguments lose their appeal. Without vessels and commerce, the potential economic benefits of a public port do not accrue to the local community. Strong cases for state support can be developed, but the state's involvement may well include the jealously guarded responsibility for economic development as well as trade solicitation, financial assistance and coordinative functions.

A relatively well-accepted role for state government is its engaging in promotion, protection and information. Through state action, resources are made available that exceed the capabilities of any local port. Because many issues currently plaguing the Great Lakes, such as alleged discriminatory inland freight rates and a restricted navigation season, are shared by most of the ports, coordination can be facilitated and duplication avoided if the states undertake leadership in dealing with these problems. State resources can assist port bodies in dealing with shared regional problems, for it is recognized that one port will not necessarily benefit at the expense of another.

It is suggested that the Great Lakes states engage in the following activities on behalf of local public ports:

1. "Promote and coordinate activities between local port bodies and federal agencies having responsibility for maintaining and enlarging channels, turning basins, navigational aids, etc."[47] Here the state provides clearinghouse and information services and becomes a liaison between local concerns and the federal navigation programs.

2. "Promote and protect local ports so they can most effectively engage in commerce and be better able to face competition in a fair and equitable manner."[48] The state should undertake studies and participate in proceedings before regulatory bodies to insure that ports are confronting fair competition and non-prejudicial rate structures.

3. Provide planning expertise and technical assistance either in house or by consultants, as requested, to assist in developing port plans, and preparing environmental impact statements.

4. Serve as a liaison between local port
bodies and other branches of state
government to insure coordination
between port activities and surface
access decisions, land use policies,
environmental regulations and economic
development plans.

5. Serve as an information clearinghouse
for industrial location decisions.
Here the availability of ports might
receive recognition along with numerous
other community and transportation services.

The state's role in constructive and supportive activities
on behalf of local public ports generates even greater
controversy evoking charges of unjust selectivity and re-
straints on local autonomy. Restrictive policies, however,
are the necessary conditions for protecting the state's
investment. Some Great Lakes states have initiated constructive and supportive programs by issuing low interest
loans or by offering outright grants to local public ports.
In most situations, the states can rely upon professional
and capable port managers for implementing constructive
responsibilities. Unless the financial crisis widens, the
state role can best be restricted to constructive assistance
with no supportive role. State investments should not
constitute operating subsidies even for state-controlled
ports. State supportive aid should be restricted, unless
it can be demonstrated that local initiative is inadequate
and the port has a definite statewide impact.

It is proposed that the Great Lakes states adopt
the following policy.

1. "It is within the jurisdiction of state
government to assist public port bodies
to expand, modernize, and improve facilities and services so operations can be
made more effective and economical."[49]
These improvements must (a) be economically justified considering both social
and economic costs, (b) be consistent
with overall state and regional transportation and landuse plans, (c) have
minimal adverse effect upon the environment and (d) demonstrate strong
local support and initiative.

2. "Efforts should be undertaken to standardize
   the funding and implementation process for
   port constructive and supportive efforts and
   make the process compatible so that it is
   followed by related transportation modes."[50]

Assurances must be generated that the local port body
represents the broad interests of the citizens and that
improvement programs have received citizen review and comment.
State constructive assistance on a matching basis would fully
test local commitment. Also, flexible funding programs
should be considered to permit state aid in the form of grants,
low interest loans or an extension of the financial credit
of the state (i.e., backing port improvement bonds with the
full credit of the state).

The state must accept the responsibility to evaluate
the local plans and judge which ones best meet local needs
and represent sound investments. Accordingly, firm investment criteria need to be established to guide state officials
in their reviews. Although investment decisions will involve
many difficult judgments, such decisions are routinely
conducted in other transportation modes. The formulating of
a state port plan is prerequisite to this review process.
To insure that local proposals are in conformance with this
plan, it should be developed to the point that it defines the
role of each port and indicates the standards required for
it to reach its full potential. Based on general guidelines,
this review can determine deficiencies and ascribe priorities
to requested physical improvements. Without the benefit of
an overall state port development plan, the evaluation process
will be subjective.

The state program should be voluntary, the state's
review powers extending only to the degree that the state
provides financial assistance and must protect its investment. If local port bodies feel that they can respond to
the challenge alone, they can elect not to seek state aid.
Projects not qualifying for state assistance can be undertaken
at the option of local governments, without reliance upon
state aid.

Funds for maintaining a state constructive program can
be derived from the general fund or from a state transportation
fund. The state port bureau should not become involved in
funding land development programs. These activities can
better be reserved for local government or other state bureaus
that have economic development as a primary mission. State
water recreation or boating programs likewise should be
funded as a separate entity.

Recommendations for Local Bodies
<hr>

Cyclic trends will be encountered on such dynamic systems as the Great Lakes-St. Lawrence Seaway. It is preferable that financial flexibility be encouraged, but within a framework of public participation, accountability and open disclosure. According to Schenker, the role of each port within the System and the position of this System in the larger shipping systems of the nation and continents must be determined. "As total resources are becoming more and more limited, it is impossible to justify any investment in any port which does not fill a definite need."[51] The days of over-expansion, high risks and unlimited competition are over. Without well conceived plans and programs that are responsive to the objectives established for public ports, public support for ports will wane. Leadership in this area requires a professional, competent staff having political autonomy, public accountability and acute sensitivity to local issues. Only then can a water transportation program remain directed at the needs and resources of the local area.

The following policies are suggested for local port bodies:

1. Public port organizations should be shaped by the functions they are expected to perform. The establishment of port goals and objectives is vital to the determination of functional and jurisdictional responsibilities.

2. Local port bodies must expand interaction and contact with regional planning bodies to provide port plans that are coordinated with related transportation and land use efforts.[52]

3. Based upon a thorough analysis of local needs and resources, ports should be permitted to engage in a variety of projects to further commerce, trade and industrial development, including:

   a. owning, acquiring and developing industrial lands for lease or sale to business and industry in compliance with a comprehensive plan. (Industrial development activities should be limited to the acquisition and development of industrial sites to promote marine terminal activity);

267

b. in some instances, constructing and
   operating marine, air and land transportation terminals and related
   facilities;

c. constructing selected facilities for
   tenants, using industrial revenue
   bonds, general obligation bonds or
   port revenues; and

d. undertaking and adopting comprehensive
   development plans.[53]

4. Selection of jurisdictional boundaries should
   reflect the fact that a port's boundaries are
   determined by economic forces and not legal
   definitions. The area directly benefiting
   from the presence of a local public port should
   be responsible for supporting the enterprise.
   In many cases, these jurisdictional boundaries
   are synonymous with a metropolitan city, a
   county or several counties; the boundaries should
   be reflected in the port's administrative and
   financial requirements.

Conclusions

Currently, organizational responsibility for ports in
the Great Lakes is dispersed among local bodies, various
levels of government and private interest groups. Noticeably
lacking is a strong regional organization, since most regional
functions are relegated to advisory and planning groups,
which are generally ad hoc and policy-oriented. In the
Great Lakes Region, the concept of autonomous local port
authorities is still very much accepted. Yet, it is clear
that the existing problems concerning traffic patterns on
the Great Lakes will necessitate basic organizational change.

From the present array of relationships, it is possible
to speculate on the emergence of alternative organizational
structures. The alternatives may be reviewed as spaces
defined by two perpendicular axes. As noted in Table 8.2,
existing organizations can be described by the functions
performed as well as by the level of government responsible.
Horizontal integration refers to the emergence of a strong
regional body for coordination and policy formulation, while
decentralization implies continued reliance upon local
autonomy. A second concept relates to vertical integration
with emphasis on the port as more than a strict transportation
function, but rather as an instrument of economic development and as an important element in defining overall environmental quality. The adoption of a comprehensive approach to

TABLE 8.2

Vertical and Horizontal Integration of Port Functions

	Governmental Level of Responsibility					
	Private	Local	State	Bi-State	Regional	Federal
Environmental Quality			State Environmental Quality Agency		Great Lakes Basin Commission	Environmental Protection Agency
Economic Development Functions		Local City County or Metropolitan Port Authority or Commission	State Economic Development Office		Upper Great Lakes Regional Commission and Great Lakes Commission	MIRAD
			State	Bi-State	Regional Spokesman Through Private Interest Groups	St. Lawrence Seaway & Corps of Engineers
Navigational Operating Functions	Private Port Industry		Harbor Commission or Port Section in State DOT	Port Authority		Coast Guard

Decentralization of Responsibility

(emphasis on private/local viewpoint)

1. Local Initiative
2. Local Autonomy
3. High Degree of Competition   Level of Responsibility

Horizontal Integration of Responsibility

(adoption of regional viewpoint)

1. Multi-modal Coordination
2. Multigovernmental Jurisdictions
3. Emphasis on Regional Planning

ports will most likely lead to greater vertical and horizontal integration. The problems faced by ports, particularly Great Lakes ports, necessitate greater reliance upon regional and state organizations, for they are more capable of relating ports to the entire transportation, land use and environmental patterns of the region.

FOOTNOTES

[1]H. Mayer, The Port of Chicago and the St. Lawrence Seaway (Chicago: University of Chicago Press, 1957), p. 120.

[2]Strictly speaking a Great Lakes port always competes, if not with another Great Lakes port, then with surface modes or with coastal ports via land bridge rail service.

[3]M. L. Fair, Port Administration in the United States (Cambridge, Mass.: Cornell Maritime Press, 1954), p. 4.

[4]Ibid., p. 6.

[5]Battelle Memorial Institute, Final Report on Port and Water Transportation Planning Study for the State of Oregon (Richland, Washington: Pacific Northwest Laboratories, December 16, 1968), pp. 13-23.

[6]G. Davis, The Department of Transportation (Lexington, Mass.: Heath Lexington Books, 1970), p. 2.

[7]Ibid., p. 130.

[8]Ibid., p. 52.

[9]J. Hazard, The Great Lakes-St. Lawrence Transportation System--Problems and Potential (Lansing, Michigan: Graduate School of Business, Michigan State University, December 1969), p. 74.

[10]Davis, p. 107.

[11]Great Lakes Basin Commission, Great Lakes Basin Framework Study, Appendix 9, Navigation, Volume 1, Commercial Navigation (Ann Arbor, Michigan: Great Lakes Basin Commission, 1974).

[12]K. Cooper, "Port for the Eighties and Beyond," paper presented at the ASCE Transportation Engineering Meeting, Milwaukee, Wisconsin, July 17-21, 1972.

[13]"River and Harbor Act of 1970," Public Law 91-611, Section 124, Title I, December 31, 1970.

[14]Battelle Memorial Institute, Port and Water Transportation Planning Study, pp. 13-25.

[15]Federal Maritime Administration, Annual Report--1972 (Washington: Federal Maritime Administration, 1973).

[16]Davis, p. 193.

[17]A. Quinn, Design and Construction of Ports and Marine Structures (New York: McGraw Hill, 1961), pp. 21-25.

[18]E. T. Bauer, "Needful Steps for Improved Future--Marad--Port Industry Relationships," paper presented before the North Atlantic Port Association, Washington, D.C., December 7, 1972.

[19]U. S. Water Resources Council, A Synopsis of the National Water Commission's Final Report (Washington, D.C.: U.S. Water Resources Council, June 15, 1973), pp. 14-15.

[20]G. Kelnhofer, Preserving the Great Lakes Resources (Fort Collins, Colorado: Development Consultants, Inc., May 1970), p. 34.

[21]Great Lakes Commission, Annual Report--1972 (Ann Arbor, Michigan: Great Lakes Commission, 1973), p. 2.

[22]Kelnhofer, p. 34.

[23]Great Lakes Basin Commission, "The Future of the Great Lakes--A Public Meeting," (Ann Arbor, Michigan: Great Lakes Basin Commission, 1972).

[24]Kelnhofer, pp. 34-35.

[25]Water Resources Council, National Water Commission's Final Report (Washington, D.C.: National Water Commission, 1972), p. 436.

[26]Hazard, p. 94.

[27]Kelnhofer, p. 31.

[28]Quinn, p. 25.

[29]E. Draine and D. Meyer, Port of Chicago Unification Study (Springfield, Illinois: State of Illinois, Commission for Economic Development, January 1970), p. 111.

[30]J. Hazard, Michigan Commerce and Commercial Policy Study (East Lansing, Michigan: Michigan State University, International Business Studies, 1965), p. 151.

[31]The states with port authorities in 1968 were: Alabama, Colorado, Connecticut, Florida, Georgia, Hawaii, Maine, Maryland, Massachusetts, New Hampshire, New Jersey, New York, North Carolina, Pennsylvania, South Carolina, Virginia.

[32]Battelle Memorial Institute, Port and Water Transportation Planning Study, p. 12-1.

[33]Battelle Memorial Institute, Port and Water Transportation Planning Study, p. 13-1.

[34]"Statewide Transportation Planning Needs and Requirements," National Cooperative Highway Research Program, Synthesis of Highway Practice, 5, 1972, p. 6.

[35]"Statewide Transportation Planning Needs and Requirements," p. 8.

[36]"Illinois Department of Business and Economic Development," Seaway Review, Vol. 2, No. 1, Spring 1971.

[37]Battelle Memorial Institute, Port and Water Transportation Planning Study, p. 13-8.

[38]N. Ashford, "The Developing Role of State Government in Transportation," Traffic Quarterly, October 1968, pp. 455-468.

[39]R. Gilman, "Views of the Port Industry," Journal of the Waterways, Harbor and Coastal Engineering Division, ASCE, Vol. 97, No. WW1, February 1971, pp. 13-18.

[40]"Deep Water Policy Issues," Hearings before the Committee on Interior and Insular Affairs, U.S. Senate, 92nd Congress, Second Session, April 25, 1972, p. 432.

[41]M. Hanson, Great Lakes Ports and Shipping Systems (Carbondale, Illinois: Southern Illinois University, October 1969), pp. 18-21.

[42]M. McPherson, Prospects for Metropolitan Water Management (New York: American Society of Civil Engineers, 1970), pp. 6-24.

[43]E. Schenker, Regional Coordination of Urban Transportation Functions in the Milwaukee Area (Springfield, Va.: National Information Technical Service, No. 206-324).

[44]Hazard, The Great Lakes-St. Lawrence Transportation System--Problems and Potential, p. 94.

[45]For example a recent statewide plan developed for the State of New York indicated the State's Great Lakes ports are presently operating at annual deficits of $1 million and have incurred an accumulated deficit of $12 million. In terms of improvement programs $29 million is needed for rehabilitation and $79 million is required for new port facilities. Fiscal needs of this magnitude for port improvements reoccur throughout the Great Lakes.

[46]Battelle Memorial Institute, Port and Water Transportation Planning Study, pp. 13-1, 2.

[47]Commonwealth of Pennsylvania, Transportation Policies for Pennsylvania (Harrisburg, Pennsylvania: Department of Transportation, Commonwealth of Pennsylvania, July 1970), p. 52.

[48]Battelle Memorial Institute, Port and Water Transportation Planning Study, pp. 13-1, 2.

[49]Commonwealth of Pennsylvania, Transportation Policies for Pennsylvania, p. 54.

[50]Battelle Memorial Institute, Port and Water Transportation Planning Study, p. 14-6.

[51]Schenker, pp. 41-42.

[52]L. Haefner, "Multimodal Transportation Needs--At Port Site--A Policy Programming Framework," Proceedings 15th Annual Meeting, Transportation Research Forum, 1974, pp. 100-103.

[53]"Public Port Districts," brochure published by the Department of Commerce and Economic Development, State of Washington, 1972.

Bibliography

Ashford, N. "The Developing Role of State Government in Transportation." Traffic Quarterly (October 1968), pp. 455-468.

_____ and **Rubins**, R. "The Role of the State in Transportation." Traffic Engineering, Vol. 42 (January 1972), pp. 13-17.

Battelle Memorial Institute. Final Report on Port and Water Transportation Planning Study for the State of Oregon. Richland, Washington: Pacific Northwest Laboratories, December 16, 1968.

Bauer, E. T. "Needful Steps for Improved Future--Marad--Port Industry Relationships." Paper presented before the North Atlantic Port Association, Washington, D.C., December 7, 1972. 6 pp.

Brockel, H. "New Forecasts Reflect Seaway Optimum." World Ports, Vol. 6 (May 1974), pp. 10-14, 27.

Cahn, D., Aliberti, A., and Seifert W. Project Bosporus, MIT Report 21. Cambridge, Mass.: MIT Press, 1970. p. 7.

Commonwealth of Pennsylvania, Department of Transportation. Transportation Policies for Pennsylvania. Harrisburg, Pa., July 1970.

Cooper, K. "Ports for the Eighties and Beyond." Paper presented at the ASCE Transportation Engineering Meeting, Milwaukee, Wisconsin, July 17-21, 1972.

Craine, L. E. Institutional Arrangements for the Great Lakes. A Report to the Great Lakes Basin Commission, March 15, 1972.

Cresap, McCormick and Paget. A Study of Organization and Development for the Duluth/Superior Ports. Washington, D.C.: Upper Great Lakes Regional Commission, May 1974.

Davis, G. The Department of Transportation. Lexington, Mass.: Heath Lexington Books, 1970.

"Deep Water Policy Issues." Hearings Before the Committee on Interior and Insular Affairs. U.S. Senate, 92nd Congress, Second Session, April 25, 1972. 687 pp.

Dicer, G. Tennessee Water Transportation Report. Knoxville, Tenn.: College of Business Administration, Department of Marketing and Transportation, University of Tennessee, June 1973.

Draine, E. and Meyer, D. Port of Chicago Unification Study.
Springfield, Illinois: State of Illinois, Commission
for Economic Development, January 1970. 149 pp.

Fair, M. L. Port Administration in the United States.
Cambridge, Maryland: Cornell Maritime Press, 1954.

Gilman, R. "Views of the Port Industry." Journal of the
Waterways, Harbor and Coastal Engineering Division, ASCE,
Vol. 97 (February 1971), pp. 3-18.

Great Lakes Basin Commission. "The Future of the Great Lakes--
A Public Meeting." Ann Arbor, Michigan, 1972.

_____. Great Lakes Basin Framework Study,
Appendix 9, Navigation, Volume 1, Commercial Navigation.
Ann Arbor, Michigan: Great Lakes Basin Commission, 1974.

Great Lakes Commission. Annual Report-1972. Ann Arbor,
Michigan, 1973.

_____. Great Lakes Commission--Informational
Brochure. Ann Arbor, Michigan.

Haefner, L. "Multimodal Transportation Needs--At Port Site--
A Policy Programming Framework." Proceedings, 15th
Annual Meeting, Transportation Research Forum, 1974, pp.
100-103.

Hanson, M. Great Lakes Port and Shipping Systems. Research
Report for Office of Port and International Systems.
Carbondale, Illinois: Southern Illinois University,
October 1969. 240 pp.

Hazard, J. "Future of U.S. Ports." Appears in Port
Planning and Development as Related to Problems of U.S.
Ports and the U.S. Coastal Environment, edited by Eric
Schenker and Harry C. Brockel. Cambridge, Maryland:
Cornell Maritime Press, 1975, pp. 301-311.

_____. The Great Lakes-St. Lawrence Transportation System
--Problems and Potential. East Lansing, Michigan:
Graduate School of Business, Michigan State University,
December 1969. 132 pp.

_____. Michigan Commerce and Commercial Policy Study.
East Lansing, Michigan: Michigan State University International Business Studies, 1965.

_____. "The Second Decade for the St. Lawrence Seaway."
Congressional Record-Senate, May 1, 1969, pp. 10965-
10968.

"Illinois' Department of Business and Economic Development."
Seaway Review, Vol. 2, No. 1 (Spring 1971).

Jursa, J. "The Flight for Cargo-A New Approach for 73." Seaway Review, Vol. 3, No. 3 (Autumn 1972), pp. 7-11.

Kelnhofer, G. Preserving the Great Lakes Resources. Fort Collins, Colorado: Development Consultants, Inc., May 1970. 73 pp.

Larson, T. "Towards--More Effective State Role in Transportation." Transportation Research Forum Proceedings, 1972, pp. 243-256.

A. D. Little, Inc. Port Management Problem Study. Washington, D.C.: Maritime Administration, U.S. Department of Commerce.

Marcus, H. "The Need for a Unified Governmental Approach to Port Planning." Transportation Research Forum Proceedings, 1973, pp. 831-839.

Mayer, H. The Port of Chicago and the St. Lawrence Seaway. Chicago: University of Chicago Press, 1957.

McPherson, M. Prospects for Metropolitan Water Management. New York: American Society of Civil Engineers, 1970.

Milwaukee River Watershed Study. Waukesha, Wisconsin: Southeastern Wisconsin Regional Planning Commission, 1970.

National Water Commission, U.S. Water Resources Council. National Water Commission's Final Report. Washington, D.C.: U.S. Government Printing Office, 1972.

_____. A Synopsis of the National Water Commission's Final Report. Washington, D.C.: U.S. Government Printing Office, June 15, 1973. 92 pp.

"Navigable Waters, Harbors and Navigation." Wisconsin Statutes, Chapter 30. 1960.

Public Law 89-670. An Act to Establish a Department of Transportation. 1966.

Public Law 91-611, Section 124, Title I. River and Harbor Act of 1970.

Quinn, A. Design and Construction of Ports and Marine Structures. New York: McGraw Hill, 1961.

Schenker, E. "The Future of U.S. Great Lakes Transportation with Particular Reference to Containerization and General Cargo." Congressional Record-Senate, June 2, 1969, pp. 14515-14518.

_____. Impact of the Port of Green Bay on the Economy of the Community. Madison, Wisconsin: University of Wisconsin Sea Grant Program, November 1972.

_____. "Port Rates and Cost Recovery." Paper presented at the Annual Meeting of the American Association of Port Authorities, Miami Beach, Florida, October 25, 1972.

_____. Regional Coordination of Urban Transportation Functions in the Milwaukee Area. Springfield, Virginia: National Information Technical Service, No. 206-324.

_____. "Southern State Port Authorities and Florida." Land Economics, Vol. 35 (February 1959), pp. 35-47.

Schenker, E., and Brockel, H., eds. Port Planning and Development as Related to Problems of U.S. Ports and the U.S. Coastal Environment. Cambridge, Maryland: Cornell Maritime Press, 1975.

Schofer, J. and Thomas, E. "Strategies of the Evaluation of Alternative Transportation Plans." National Cooperative Highway Research Program, Report No. 96.

State of New York, Department of Transportation, Office of Planning and Development. Policies and Plans for Transportation in New York State. Albany, New York, 1968.

State of Washington, Department of Commerce and Economic Development. Public Port Districts. (Brochure), 1972.

"Statewide Transportation Planning Needs and Requirements." Synthesis of Highway Practice, Vol. 5. National Cooperative Highway Research Program, 1972. 41 pp.

A Status Report of State Departments of Transportation. Highway User Federation for Safety and Mobility, Washington, D.C., December 1970. 30 pp.

U.S. Department of the Army, Corps of Engineers. Annual Report. Washington, D.C.: U.S. Government Printing Office.

_____. U.S. Deepwater Port Study-Summary and Conclusion. Washington, D.C.: Institute for Water Resources, August 1972.

U.S. Department of Commerce, Maritime Administration. Annual Report-1972. Washington, D.C.: U.S. Government Printing Office, 1973.

U.S. Department of Commerce, Maritime Administration. Office of Ports and Intermodal Systems. Public Port Financing in the United States. Washington, D.C.: U.S. Government Printing Office, June 1974.

U.S. Department of Transportation. National Transportation
Annual Manual (1970-1990), Manual D-Airport and Other
Intercity Terminals, Part 3, Washington, D.C., April
1971.

Waters, R. "Comprehensive Planning-A Vital Need." World
Ports, Vol. 6. (February 1974), pp. 16-17.

"Wingspread Conference on the Future of the St. Lawrence
Seaway." Sponsored by the University of Wisconsin Sea
Grant Program and the Center for Great Lakes Studies,
University of Wisconsin-Milwaukee, March 6, 1973. 15 pp.

IX.

Summary and Conclusions

Summary

The Great Lakes and St. Lawrence Seaway System is rapidly changing in significance as a major transportation resource. The changes are of substantial importance in terms of the need for reexamination and modification of planning and improvement programs—internationally, nationally, regionally, statewide and locally.

The changes are economic, technological and attitudinal. The roles of both internal Great Lakes transportation, and of Great Lakes-overseas transportation through the St. Lawrence Seaway have been subject to accelerating change in all those respects.

The internal Great Lakes transportation system is unique in its specialization, and its adaptation to regional resources. Three dominant commodities, iron ore, coal and limestone, are strategically located around the Great Lakes. They provide the genesis for the western hemisphere's largest concentration of iron and steel manufacture, and for other industries dependent upon iron and steel. The hinterland, both in Canada and the United States, embraces some of the most productive grain lands of the world; important centers of food processing and grain milling; and areas of dairy production and meat packing.

The lake transportation system early tailored itself to these resources. Automation of bulk cargo handling is an old story to the Great Lakes. The self-unloading ship, considered a triumph of modern technology, appeared on the Great Lakes in the early 1920s, and the concept has moved forward consistently and efficiently for the past 50 years, climaxing with the new fleet of 1000-foot vessels which are self-unloading. Similar automation was developed on shore, equally early, with the Hulett unloaders, giant coal bridges, and shoreside conveyor systems for bulk cargo. In a word, what's new on the oceans is two generations old on the Great Lakes.

Many of these systems came into being not only in response to unique resource patterns, intense industrialization of the region and large-scale agriculture, but as a necessary response to the seasonality of the system. The Great Lakes fleets were called upon to achieve delivery of a 12-month volume of materials in an 8 1/2-month shipping season. Thus emerged another characteristic of the system and the region: extensive shoreside stockpiling facilities, for iron ore and coal, grain elevators, and cement, stone, salt and pig iron storage.

From these circumstances there developed a transportation system which despite harsh climate and seasonal limitations, has quite often achieved system delivery in the range of 200 to 250 million tons per year. Within 10 years after the opening of the enlarged St. Lawrence Seaway in 1959, the

283

Great Lakes-St. Lawrence System moved cargo in the range of 50 to 53 million tons per year, including about 15 million tons of cargo directly to and from overseas, with the remaining 38 million moving within the Lakes-St. Lawrence System, primarily in Lake vessels.

The large Lake bulk freighter, operated within the confines of the five Great Lakes, adapted itself to the new opportunities of the St. Lawrence Seaway, and with great flexibility engaged in the transport of grain from the western Great Lakes to St. Lawrence River elevators, and the new westerly movement of iron ore from Quebec-Labrador back into the Great Lakes. In effect, the traditional pattern of iron ore from west to east, was partially reversed, and an important new movement of iron ore developed from east to west, with grain, coal and stone balancing out the vessel movements.

With little public awareness, there occurred one of the largest examples of bloc obsolescence of shipping in the entire history of the world. Prior to the opening of the Seaway in 1959, traffic between the Great Lakes and the St. Lawrence River had been limited to the dimensions of a 14 foot draft lock and canal system, capable of handling ships only 258 feet long and 42.5 feet wide. A fleet of about 250 of these "canalers" connected lake ports and the St. Lawrence River, busily transporting coal, grain, newsprint, and a variety of traffic between Lake ports and the St. Lawrence. With a maximum capacity of 3000 tons, and crews averaging 35, the carrier fleet was obsoleted overnight, when "upper lakers" of 30,000-ton capacity, and also with crews of 35, could deliver ten times the cargo volume per voyage. Within five years after the opening of the Seaway, the entire canal fleet of 250 vessels, practically all under the Canadian flag, had gone to the scrapyards, and the conventional Lake bulk freighter had assumed the role of these historic carriers.

The Great Lakes fleet between 1930 and 1975 shrank from 800 vessels, to fewer than 300, but those 300 transport more cargo than the 800 did at their peak. In the Lake fleet, shipboard employment has shrunk from 25,000 officers and men, to fewer than 10,000. These trends are accelerating. The giant tanker on the oceans, another phenomenon of the last 10 years, demonstrated the economies of scale for other forms of bulk transportation. Dry bulk cargo carriers on the oceans moved rapidly from the 20,000-ton vessel to the 200,000-ton concept, for coal, grain, fertilizer, iron ore and other commodities. Great Lakes-Seaway general cargo trade had already felt the impact of this revolution, and the bulk cargo trades are facing a similar metamorphosis.

With the decline of open pit iron mining in the Mesabi and other Lake Superior ranges, and with cost inflation justifying new ventures, taconite has emerged in the Great Lakes Region as a major commodity, while direct-shipping iron ore production has shifted from the western Great Lakes Region to eastern Canada.

Along with these changes in the pattern of cargo movement within the Great Lakes is a major change in the numbers
and characteristics of Lake vessels. These changes involve
the retirement of old and moderate-sized vessels; the "jumbo-
izing" of usable older Lake vessels; but most importantly,
with the building of an enlarged lock at the Sault Ste.
Marie canals, the emergence of the 1,000-foot Great Lakes
freighter of about 60,000 tons carrying capacity. Ten of
these ships are built or on order, and their effect on the
System will be profound. They will undoubtedly force the
retirement of scores of old and inefficient ships. Too large
to traverse the Welland Canal or the Seaway locks, the new
giants are landlocked within the upper four Great Lakes. We
now see the phenomenon of a modernized Great Lakes bulk fleet
too large to traverse the Seaway and container ships and
bulk carriers too large to enter the System.

Within the Great Lakes, shipping technology is responding
to shifts of resources and industrial method. Coal, traditionally a major item in Lake commerce, declined with the
advent of natural gas and petroleum. The energy crisis will
undoubtedly require maximum utilization of coal. The historic
fields south and east of the Great Lakes are already feeling
the stimulus. Low-sulfur coals, found in the western states
in huge deposits, are being commercially developed and it is
now moving easterly via Lake Superior ports to the Lower Lakes.
Even as energy becomes a more critical question, the movement
of petroleum continues to decline within the System, primarily
shifting to pipeline. A Lake tanker and barge fleet of 97
vessels in 1960 shrank to only 39 vessels in 1974.

The advent of the container ship in the middle 1960s,
and the second closing of the Suez Canal in 1967, accelerated
a revolution in world shipping and transportation technology
which has had reverberations within the Great Lakes as well.
General cargo, between the Great Lakes and overseas had reached
a peak of about 8 million tons by 1970, and involved about
60 regular liner services. For about a decade, between 1959
and 1970, major lake ports also were fairly important ocean
ports. They developed international trading complexes typical
of successful ocean ports. Employment opportunities multiplied
for the longshoreman and for all of the marine service trades.
As transatlantic and transpacific container services matured,
with large and fast ships, rapid port turnaround, and effective
"land bridges" via the new interstate highway system and newly
competitive rail intermodal systems, the Seaway general cargo
trade encountered severe competition. It declined in the early
1970s, as rapidly as it had developed in the early 1960s. In
the middle 1970s only about a dozen direct overseas liner
services are operating into Lake Michigan, and there has been
a parallel decline in port activities, terminal operations
and employment.

With respect to both internal Great Lakes and St. Lawrence
traffic, and direct Great Lakes-overseas ocean traffic, Great
Lakes ports and shipping are losing much of their former
versatility and diversification. The Great Lakes package
freight trade disappeared after World War II except between
Canadian ports, and that is rapidly declining now. A fleet
of versatile ships handling automobiles, steel products, pig
iron, machinery and other high-value traffic, and capable of
entering almost any port in the Lakes system, has largely been
retired. The Great Lakes passenger trade, once flourishing,
is virtually extinct. The Lake Michigan car ferry service,
of major importance since the 1890s, is facing the competition
of the "run through" train and modern highways. All three car
ferry routes face imminent abandonment.

The conclusion is inescapable that the Great Lakes-St.
Lawrence Seaway is now concentrating largely on the mass movement of industrial raw materials (iron ore, taconite, coal
and limestone) all fundamental to the steel industry; along
with grain, a major factor in the mid-continental economy and
in North American food supply to the world. The waterborne
role of petroleum on the Lakes is rapidly declining, even as
world use of this fuel has been increasing.

There is a growing tendency toward centralization of
commerce at relatively few "load centers" on each of the sea-
coasts of the United States and other countries. The technology
of the ship has run far ahead of the technology of the port.
Ports are being required to respond to the need for deeper
channels; to provide intermodal facilities which require large
land areas; and to overcome partial or complete obsolescence
of much of their physical plant. Inflation, high cost of
equipment and accelerating construction costs, require massive
amounts of capital.

Many public ports are creations of local government
entities which are struggling with environmental, social
and human demands upon their resources. Traditional governmental services suffer from the competition of needs or causes
having higher social or political priorities. Thus local and
private bases of financial support for port development may
not be adequate.

It may also be questioned whether existing institutional
structures responsible for Great Lakes public ports can respond
adequately to many new developments: deconcentration of urban
populations, inflation, shifting resources, new technology,
the declining Seaway commerce, environmental challenges, and
new "coastal zone management" concepts which will vitally
affect ports on fresh and salt water.

The United States and the Great Lakes have long depended
upon local initiatives in port development. This philosophy
has produced healthy competition and considerable national
resources in the way of port facilities. However, it also
produces redundancies in port capacity.

This study raises the question as to whether conventional ports, as presently constituted in the Lakes Region, can respond adequately to what is the equivalent of a crisis in terms of shifting traffic, new shipping technologies, inflationary pressures, environmental requirements and a considerable atmosphere of change, largely uncontrollable, from local resources. Local initiatives may inevitably have to yield to regional or state-wide planning concepts, and greater federal participation. The fiscal pressures on the federal budget may require selective application of criteria for port expansion, looking at regional or national total requirements, rather than local initiatives, once encouraged but perhaps no longer economically justified.

Recommendations

A number of general recommendations and suggestions relative to the future of Great Lakes and Great Lakes-St. Lawrence Seaway shipping and ports emerge from the findings of this study:

1. <u>Improvement and Systematic Treatment of Basic Data-</u>

There should be increasing coordination and cooperation among the various reporting agencies in the United States and Canada in the gathering and reporting of statistical information on the Great Lakes-St. Lawrence Seaway System. Further coordination requires that codes used for commodities and ports in the different data sources be directly comparable.

Rapidly changing technology in transportation, both in transport equipment and in the movement of goods, requires that current data be available to assess changing conditions. This also implies that there should be frequent updating and monitoring of projections in order to evaluate noted deviations in commodity flows. In addition, the processing of data should be done as quickly as possible. Rapid dissemination of data is required to respond to changing conditions with formative policies.

2. <u>Promotion of Bulk Cargo Movement by Water for Conservation of Energy-</u>

Because water transportation is relatively energy efficient, use of the Great Lakes-St. Lawrence System should be encouraged as an aspect of fuel conservation. Except where pipelines are available, and in spite of the circuity of many water-routes, transportation, particularly of bulk commodities, produces more ton-miles in proportion to the amount of fuel consumed, than any other mode of transportation.

3. De-emphasis of General Cargo Port and Terminal Development-

Providing container facilities at many Lake ports with the resulting competition among ports for limited container or general cargo traffic will weaken the position of the Great Lakes ports in competition with other load centers.

Prior to any further investment in container facilities by Great Lakes ports, two questions must be answered: (1) will equivalent expenditures directed towards bulk traffic generate greater benefits; and (2) will the System be able to provide outbound general cargo traffic in substantial volumes?

4. Provision of Joint Intermodal Rates-

For both general cargo and bulk commodity movements, joint rates between carriers by water on the one hand and overland carriers on the other will encourage increased use of the water routes. Additionally, removal of regulatory impediments to joint intermodal rates for fossil fuels would promote energy conservation. Included would be unit train rates for coal movements to Great Lakes ports in combination with Lake carriers; or pipeline movements integrated with water transport.

5. Planning for Increased Lakewise Movement of Coal-

It appears inevitable that diminishing supplies of natural gas, and rising costs of petroleum, coupled with environmental resistance to nuclear power plants, will direct American and Canadian energy patterns back to coal as a primary source of energy, both directly and through conversion processes. For the Great Lakes Region this suggests increased volumes of lake-borne tonnages of eastern and midwestern coals, and a major new movement of western low-sulfur coals, moving to eastern markets via unit trains with transshipment at Lake ports of Wisconsin and Minnesota.

With the advent of natural gas and petroleum as basic fuels for the Region in the late 1940s, scores of major coal dock facilities in Lake ports were phased out. Most of these have been converted to other uses, and few remain available or potential. A critical challenge to the Region, to port officials and to urban planners is the imminent need to re-establish substantial shipside facilities for storage and transshipment of both eastern and western coals. The emerging effort at "coastal zone management" at federal, state and local levels, should give major recognition to this approaching reliance upon coal.

6. Continuation of Demonstration Projects on Great Lakes-St. Lawrence Seaway Season Extension-

Extension of the shipping season could improve the competitive position of the System. Test results have shown that under mild weather conditions, the technical navigational

problems of season extension have been solved. Further demonstration projects must investigate the environmental and
human problems created by season extension.

The shipping season for overseas trade must be extended
sufficiently to allow vessels to complete additional round
trips. If extension of that minimum duration cannot be
guaranteed, efforts to extend the overseas trade shipping
season will create no economic advantage.

Future calculations of benefits and costs should be made
under assumptions that recognize that transportation is
undergoing constant change. In addition, future benefit and
cost calculations of regional transportation projects, directed
towards a single mode of transportation, should identify the
costs borne by other regions and modes, as a result of the
project.

7. Investigating the Need For Larger Locks-

A new era of shipbuilding is evident, with ten 1,000-foot
Lake bulk carriers planned, at a cost of about 1/3 of a
billion dollars. Other suitable ships are being "jumboized."
The steel industry and allied industries will for some years
profit from the new shipbuilding era. However, important
related effects must be noted, including a fleet of larger but
fewer ships; a trend distinctly toward a bulk raw material
shipping economy rather than a diversified cargo pattern; greatly
reduced maritime opportunities afloat and ashore; strong trends
toward port centralization, notably at steel production
centers; and finally the overwhelming factor of the new giant
vessels being landlocked in the upper four Great Lakes, and
unable to transit the Welland Canal or the Seaway System.

The locks at Sault Ste. Marie, important in the Great
Lakes economy for more than a century, continue to be of
overwhelming importance. Preliminary proposals are being
made to move toward another generation of even larger locks,
perhaps 1300 feet long, 35-40 feet deep and a width of 130 feet,
potentially capable of serving bulk carriers with capacities
approaching 100,000 tons.

Any investigation of the possibility of larger locks
must, of course, in addition to considering the environmental
impacts, give serious and detailed consideration to the
effects upon competitive and complementary modes of transportation.

8. Development of Specialized Functions Among Ports-

Most ports on the Great Lakes and along the St. Lawrence
Seaway can no longer hope to be general multi-functional or
all-purpose ports. The need must be recognized for various
ports to serve special roles rather than for all ports to
compete with each other for all possible traffic.

9. Coordination Among Port Development Agencies-

Individual Great Lakes ports should cooperate and coordinate activities, but agencies, governmental units and other interested parties must also work cooperatively, coordinating and combining resources in efforts to improve the competitive position of the Great Lakes coast.

At least five major state and federally created agencies deal with Great Lakes issues. Numerous Lake port associations and task forces exist, some representing a few ports in a segment of a Lake. New Great Lakes-identified groups are coming into being, reflecting environmental or coastal zone management initiatives. This proliferation of Lake-interest groups confuses public understanding of legitimate concerns and efforts. Leadership should be asserted in order to centralize these many groups and to channel their diverse efforts effectively.

Coordination among existing regional organizations, especially those responsible for water transportation, should be strengthened and specific responsibilities more clearly defined. States could aid in the revitalization of Great Lakes ports by providing technical expertise as well as serving as a liaison between federal agencies and local ports.

10. Planning for Phase-Out of Some Ports-

Great Lakes ports are undergoing traumatic experiences, with many categories of Lake shipping disappearing; with the sharp decline in the Seaway general cargo trade; and with a considerable trend toward "load centers" at a few major ports, and those primarily related to steel production. It is thus reasonable, in spite of local pride, to plan systematically for a reduction, and in some instances complete elimination, of commercial port activities and facilities at some ports which cannot hope to remain effectively competitive.

With the concentration of commercial shipping traffic at fewer but larger and more specialized ports, the smaller ports may not survive as ports, but some could adapt to new or expanded roles for other than large-scale commercial shipping. There are several possibilities for such smaller ports: (1) recreational boating, (2) sport fishing, and (3) commercial fishing.

11. Re-use of Retired Surplus Waterfront Land-

With the concentration of shipping activity at fewer but more specialized ports, together with the industrial demand for extensive and peripheral sites rather than central and intensive sites, much waterfront land is no longer in demand for use by port activities or by bulk-receiving and bulk-shipping industries.

In many instances, such land, commonly centrally-located
in relation to cities, can most usefully be developed for
other industrial, commercial, or civic functions. Decisions
as to future use must be made in collaboration with local
governments and prospective private or public developers.
In some instances, revenues from the sale or lease of such
lands may accrue to the port agency and can be applied to
development of the port facilities at other sites.

12. Coordination of Port Planning with Regional Planning Agencies-

Both money and urban land are scarce resources, and ports
are by no means the only uses for both. In allocating land
and financial resources, complementary and conflicting demands,
as well as environmental requirements, must be resolved.
Comprehensive metropolitan and regional planning involves
agencies, commonly only advisory, to facilitate coordination
of local governments' planning activities and those of
private interests. In order to assure that port and shipping
activities secure adequate, but not excessive, shares of
capital and land, port agencies must coordinate their planning
with those of other local, regional and state agencies as
well as with prospective public and private developers.
Adequate landward sites and access for port functions and
for port-related industrial and commercial activities must
be assured through such coordination.

13. Increased Consideration of Environmental Impact

The Lakes Region and its ports will continue to be
influenced by environmental considerations, and the costly
burdens which "environment" has imposed on our society and
our economy. A new element, or comparable force, is the new
federal and state thrust in "coastal zone management."
There is emerging a new control system which will require
comprehensive planning, setting of priorities, and probably
a new system of reviews and approvals for all waterfront
and coastal land uses. Here, the ideal to be sought, both
regionally and nationally, is a balance among appropriate
public uses, with recognition that ports, waterfront industry
and utility plants are basic to national survival. It is
hoped that the emotionalism and prejudice that has so often
marked environmental discussions can be at a more temperate
and realistic basis in the emerging "coastal zone management"
movement, which must nevertheless be recognized as a major
new force in the Great Lakes and along the coasts.

14. Maintenance of Stable Labor Conditions

The attitude of cooperation recently displayed in the
relationship between the longshoremen and stevedores should
become the standard. A stable labor environment can serve
to encourage shippers to use the Great Lakes-St. Lawrence
Seaway System. This is especially important because alternative

transportation routes and modes are available for nearly
every movement over the System, and, in the case of the
Seaway, because the route consists of end-to-end links.
If any one link is interrupted, the entire System cannot
function. With a reputation for frequent interruptions,
permanent loss of traffic to competing routes and transportation
modes could result.

Conclusion

This report has presented the picture of a dynamic and
rapidly evolving Great Lakes-St. Lawrence Seaway Transportation
System. It has illustrated that despite the decline or
disappearance of certain types of traffic and the increasing
specialization of bulk transportation, the System and its
hinterlands remain a dominant industrial, urban and agricultural force in North America, capable of playing a substantial role in the economic base of the continent. Problems
of adaptation to the changing technological and economic
conditions are not insolvable. This study points the way
in which some of the problems can be attacked, and ultimately
solved.